THE CLOSING CIRCLE

More Advance Praise for THE CLOSING CIRCLE

"An honest and articulate observer unafraid to embrace life's joys and tragedies, Kent accepts her husband's death from Alzheimer's and a son's death from AIDS in a poignant retrospective that, in its best moments, attains to wisdom."
—Sally Patterson Tubach, author of *Memoirs of a Terrorist,* co-author of
    An Uncommon Friendship: From Opposite Sides of the Holocaust

"Mary Kent, daughter, wife, mother, traveler, political player, and mature writer, offers a memoir of person, family, city, and times that is hard to put down."
—Allan Jacobs, Professor emeritus of city & regional planning, U.C. Berkeley, author of *Making City Planning Work, Looking at Cities, Great Streets*, former director of city planning of San Francisco

"*The Closing Circle* is a brilliant and absorbing blend of the intimate story of one woman's life and the history of her world through her eighty years of the twentieth century."
—Phyllis Sterling Smith, author of *AI Is a Three-Toed Sloth*, a novel

"Mary Tolman Kent's quiet, carefully paced memoir chronicles not only the triumphs and vicissitude of her immediate family and enduring friendships, but also supplies the reader with detailed memories of almost eight decades of Berkeley history. Her perspective is both personal and articulate . . ."
—Dorothy A. Stroup, author of *In the Autumn Wind*

THE CLOSING CIRCLE

A MEMOIR

Mary Tolman Kent

CREATIVE ARTS BOOK COMPANY
Berkeley • California

For information contact:
Creative Arts Book Company
833 Bancroft Way
Berkeley, California 94710
1-800-848-7789
Fax: 1-510-848-4844
www.creativeartsbooks.com

ISBN 0-88739-528-7
Library of Congress Catalog Number 2003113193

Printed in the United States of America

This book is dedicated with love to my sons, Tom and Dave,
in memory of their father and brother.

Acknowledgements

I could never have written this book without the support over the years of many people. I thank the past and present members of my three Writers' Groups with whom I've been meeting regularly for almost thirty years: Betsy Behrens, Karen Branson, Joanna Bressler, Sue Brown, the late Naomi Cavalier, Susan Fadley, Alice Gray, Mary Hanner, Debby Layton, Joan Mastronarde, Ellen McCaskle, the late Mary McLaughlin, Mary Parks, Renata Polt, the late Mollie Poupeney, Phyllis Smith, Jane Stroup, Sally Tubach, Deborah Whitney, and Maxine Zalkin.

I thank my several writing teachers at U.C. Extension — Susan Griffin who taught me in two classes in the early 1970's; also the late Cecelia Bartholomew and Jeffrey Klein. And special thanks to Diana O'Hehir my teacher at a U.C. Santa Cruz summer writers' conference.

I thank Peggy Love, my co-grandmother and great grandmother (our children are married to each other), who first encouraged me to share the manuscript with family members.

And most of all I thank my large extended family — four generations of them — especially my two sons and their wonderful wives, my five grandchildren and their various mates, my sister and brother and numerous, nieces and nephews, great nieces and nephews and four great grandchildren, all of whom have inspired me in so many ways. And I thank the many neighbors and friends who read the manuscript and enthusiastically shared it with others.

Finally, thanks to Donald Ellis, a fellow native Berkeleyite, and all the kind and talented people at Creative Arts who turned this into a book.

Contents

THE CLOSING CIRCLE

In the mid 90s, as my husband, suffering from Alzheimers' Disease, became increasingly dependent on me, I stopped writing. In a way it was a great relief to face this reality, and in their own fashion those few years before he died in 1998 were as rich as the previous fifty-five. At the same time, however, our middle son was succumbing to AIDS. He died in 1999, not quite a year after his father, and a few weeks later, after this long hiatus, *The Closing Circle* began to write itself. I started, with an urgency I hadn't felt for a long time, connecting circles of thought. For three years I followed this nonlinear meander through time, and this work is the result of the journey my memories have taken me on.

Mary Tolman Kent
November 2003

Chapter One

May 1999

When Steve called from the Eureka hospital and said, "It's okay, Mom. After all, it's been ten years," he was saying good-bye. I didn't catch on right away. He told me that he'd just been baptized a Catholic. That should have been a clue, though I would have expected him to become a Zen Buddhist, or maybe a Navajo. "It was real trippy," he said. That was less than a week before he died.

Yes, ten years ago he called from Montana to tell us, Jack and me, that he had tested HIV positive. Now both of them are dead.

We were doing mundane things that day — our Monday schedule — picking up Rebecca from kindergarten and having her for the afternoon. She was five and a half and talked nonstop, and we, her doting grandparents became her pawns. To brace ourselves for her vigor, Jack and I had taken to stopping at Cafe Roma on the way home. Now it had become her routine as much as ours. We had cappuccinos — she ate poppy seed cake and spilled crumbs all over the table and floor. We watched the chess games — serious displays of four or five regulars who played for speed as well as skill. Rebecca, elbows on the table, chin in hands, seemed mesmerized. What would a five-year-old see in this? We watched the other cafe habituees — foreign students, aging hippies, sorority girls, retired professors, aspiring writers — and realized that they were watching us too. We also were habituees.

It's comforting, habit, soothing the sudden ache of remembrance. Steve had called earlier that day, ten years ago. I was making lunch in the kitchen when Jack answered the phone. I heard the tone of his voice — elation — but not the words. Probably, "Hello, how are you?" Then hushed sorrow for someone else's trouble. His sister falling into another depression, just at Christmas time? That would fit. Or it could be Steve with some problem, not just phoning to get our plane schedule to pick us up for our Christmas visit on his Montana ranch. But it had come, the dreaded **THING** that had lurked in the back of our minds for years.

So I was not surprised when Jack came into the kitchen and said, "It's Steve. He tested HIV positive."

I went to the phone. Steve was furious. His response to trouble has always been anger, then sorrow. It was hard to talk. We both were crying. I told him to take care of himself. He said he would, that I'd taught him to do that, and, though in tears, I felt a surge of smug maternal pleasure. I had taught him something and he had remembered it, even if too late. Then he said he was just so *mad*, that he didn't want to miss seeing his nieces and nephews grow up. Well, he didn't. Rebecca, the youngest, is now sixteen. She drives her own car and has blue hair and rings in her nose and ears, something in her tongue too. He saw her last summer.

"It won't be much of a Christmas for you."

"Be quiet. Just take care of yourself."

"Yes, I'm going for a good long ride on Resolute."

"Take care of yourself. We'll be there Tuesday. Have you got the flight number? Write it down. Delta from Salt Lake City, 4:15. Flight Number 1680. Got it? Read it back to me."

"Mom, you're being bossy."

That's more or less the way the conversation went. We said good-bye. I forgot to ask about the weather. Was it snowing? Was it cold? Here in California it was warm and sunny. But now we had to eat lunch and go get Rebecca from school.

When Jack Kennedy was shot in Dallas it was David's thirteenth birthday. I had just bought a cake and dropped in to see Jack's parents, Tom and Belinda, Ganks and Nana to our children, their grandchildren.

2

He had Parkinson's disease. They were watching TV, slow motion reruns of Jackie scrambling across the convertible in her neat little suit and matching pillbox hat — pink, they said; most of us didn't yet have color TV. Ganks said, "Is the President dying too?"

The details of the day Steve phoned from Montana are as clear as those of that November, 22, 1963, or of December 7, 1941, Pearl Harbor Day, when suddenly our beautiful view out the Golden Gate turned scary. Jack and I had been married less than a year.

After Cafe Roma we came back home and I became Rebecca's playmate prop. She seemed to be my therapist and we were doing role playing to help sort things out. We played Follow the Leader. I followed her all about the house and garden, sometimes hopping on one foot, or clapping our hands over our heads, or walking backwards with our eyes shut. She was talking all the time, so for a while I guess I didn't notice the pitiful mewing coming through a vent in the basement wall. We hadn't had cats for years, or dogs. At this point we only had a parrot named Prince Peter Kropotin, after one of Jack's many heroes — Lincoln, Jefferson, William Morris, Lewis Mumford, Gandhi, Martin Luther King, Jr. When our three boys were growing up we had an endless stream of every sort of pet including turtles, goldfish, budgies. Steve even had pet snails for a while. In Montana he had something like seventy animals and birds to feed each day.

Finally a pathetic sound caught our attention. "I bet it's Twinkle Toes," I said to Rebecca. I opened the basement door, and out she came in a rush, the pretty little striped cat with four white paws. She twisted around our legs, and Rebecca squatted down to pat her head, delighted with the new friend. But Twinkle Toes, after rolling over and scratching her back against the warm brick path, leapt away through the hedge.

"Where's she going?" Rebecca wailed.

"She lives down the street. Come, I'll show you."

On the way we had to stop and watch a carpenter mending a wooden wall next door. (Maintenance work goes on forever. Comforting continuum.) But then, bored, Rebecca pulled at my hand. "Come *on!*" she demanded. We found the steps to Twinkle Toes's house and decided to go tell her owners what was up with their cat. Sure enough, she'd been missing for a day and a half, sleeping and peeing and shitting in our basement. Oh, well.

Rebecca saw Calder across the street coming home in his truck. She used to be scared to death of him because every time he saw her he said he was going to throw her in the creek. Now she adored him and had to run back to our house to get a drawing of hers stuck up on our refrigerator door to give him as a gift. She was big on gift-giving and receiving as Christmas approached. There was only one gift I wanted, and that one I could not have.

"I hope you have a magnet on your refrigerator," she said, handing Calder the drawing.

"Well, thank you," he said. "Come over on Christmas and I'll give you a kiss."

Embarrassed, she pulled her sleeve down over her hand and sucked on it.

"I mean a chocolate one wrapped up in silver paper," he said, grinning and going toward his house.

She laughed. "Okay," she called to him.

Now he's dead too. I've known him since our teens, when our families went on extended skiing weekends in the mountains.

"Let's walk around the block," I suggested, taking her hand.

But first we had to play something exhausting called TV tag on Calder's lawn. Lots of running fast and jumping up and down.

"Come on. Let's go," I said, and for once she obeyed me.

In fact all afternoon she'd been sensitive to my mood. Perhaps it was because of several deaths she had been exposed to recently. Her dad's friend, Cassidy, hanged himself that fall. And in the summer her great grandmother on her mother's side died. A little boy she knew in day care drowned in the spring. She hated seeing grown-ups cry. She still does. A year ago when Jack was in the hospital she hid from our bursts of sobs, and sat on the floor in the corridor outside his room in clunky shoes, hanging her head between her knees. Steve was there too, of course. He saw her.

Well, I don't blame her, and I was trying very hard that day when she was five and a half not to cry, for her sake as well as my own. She took my hand and skipped along beside me, stopping to pick flowers, to gather pebbles from driveways. Squatting in a sidewalk strip, she came across a wad of gum, very pink and shiny.

"Oh, I wish I had a piece of nice clean gum *right now*," she wailed, and I thought she might be the one to cry, so I tried to divert her attention from the gum.

"See that funny old woman," I said, indicating an eccentric neighbor who was coming toward us, all bundled up in woolen cap and mittens, even though the afternoon was warm and sunny.

"Why, Mrs. Kent," she said, "how nice to see you. And how is the professor?"

"Fine, just fine," I said inanely. In fact he was brooding at home. One of his old campus friends was failing with Alzheimer's. He himself had the early signs. He didn't know it though, nor did I except in retrospect. And then that morning, Steve's call. I was slowly losing both of them I realize now.

"And who is this?" my neighbor asked, looking down at Rebecca.

I explained, but she didn't listen. Her own ego needs have always been very strong. No one can get along with her over time. Nowadays she seems to have retreated inside her house for good. I haven't seen her for years, though the *New York Times* in its blue plastic cover lies on her front porch every morning as I pass by with my dog Mellow.

But on that day ten years ago she said, "I think I'm going to emigrate, because of what happened in the election." That's when the first George Bush was elected.

"Well, I agree with you there. But there's nowhere, really, to go, is there?"

"Maybe not. I love the Swedes, but Scandinavia's too cold. Switzerland might do. Robert is going to Switzerland, he says."

"Oh, are you and he friends again?" I asked.

They had a falling out when Robert discovered that she caught mice in mousetraps. He offered to lend her his humane mouse-catching cage and to let them go in the canyon, but she refused. They didn't speak to each other for months. Oh, my, I love this neighborhood full of eccentric intellectuals taking care of each other.

"Well, yes, we made up over the election. We're both so unhappy about Bush we could just die," she said as we reached her front door and she went inside.

No more dying, please, I thought, as Rebecca and I walked on. She took my hand and looked up into my face, worried. Now she was taking care of me as I suddenly had an attack of vertigo and had to sit down on the curb. Life's stages were all askew. Youth, age, death flung out of order like anagram letters spilled by mistake, scattered every which-way. Who would take care of whom from now on?

———•———

Why do I feel guilty? I guess because I wasn't able to be the perfect mother, taking care of Steve, though I really did try. He was very ill by the time he came in February. The plan was that he and his little dog, Otis, would stay with me and my dog, Mellow. Maybe he would die in this Berkeley house, #74 Tamalpais Road, the house that Jack and I moved into twenty-five years ago, after the boys left home. Full circle. Well almost.

Steve and his brothers actually grew up next door, #84, in the house that Bill Wurster designed for us. We lived there for twenty-five years also. But my mother lived here, next door to us, years before we did, and even tutored Steve in English and math, for he was much more interested in horses than in high school. She had bought the house, after my father died, from Jack's brother-in-law. He had grown up across the street. His mother was one of my mother's best friend. It was, and still is, that kind of neighborhood, that kind of family, all inter-tangled across several generations, settled into one, winding hillside block. So it was in the context of this network that Steve came to stay with me for those three weeks, just three months ago. I hoped that I could perhaps help him get better, perhaps not, but I wanted very much to try this ultimate experiment in multigenerational living. Sadly, though, we were both too set in our ways. I cannot bear to be wasteful, a trait inherited from my New England parents. My mother used to save scraps of paper, bits of string, rubber bands for future use. I save leftovers and make stews and soups with them. I believe in conservation at every level. Steve, now obsessed with food, but unable to eat it, made me buy and cook far too much, and when I protested he yelled, "You should have a compost heap, raise chickens, grow vegetables!"

We used to have a compost heap and grow vegetables until Jack lost interest. I suppose that was the beginning of Alzheimer's. Remembering that, I was suddenly both grief-stricken and furious, so I yelled back, "I'm seventy-seven years old!" then ran from the room in tears.

"I'm sorry, Mom," he said. We hugged and cried a lot and those three weeks were mostly Hell. Mellow is a sixty pound black Lab who still acts like a puppy a lot of the time. She was longing to play with Steve's small Pomeranian, Otis (named for Otis Redding). But he was too little, his fragile bones in danger of snapping under Mellow's weight. So he hid in the bedclothes with Steve, in my study, my former sanctuary, that Steve took over and transformed. He took down the pictures, moved the furniture, and hung fabrics on the walls. I grabbed all my papers, emptied the drawers, and fled, wounded, up here to Jack's study. Now I love being here, sharing with Jack, whose spirit is all around me.

Judy, Steve's girlfriend from junior and senior high school days in the '60s, who has remained his friend all these thirty some years, had driven me up to Humboldt County in order to bring him here. The idea was that he would come and stay with me, build up his strength in preparation for a medical procedure at Stanford Hospital to insert a shunt into his failing liver. If this were successful he would perhaps have another five years.

I enjoyed that four-hour drive with Judy. We talked like equals, amazed at our individual "takes" on Stephen William Kent. Back in the '60s we were leery of each other — the mother and the girlfriend. She had a face and figure too mature for her age. On prom night she wore a slinky apricot-colored satin dress and her heavy hair was piled on top of her head. It was somehow wrong, but now she's grown up to her looks — dark and handsome. She's a carpenter, and active in her union. Just the other day I ran into her on Shattuck Avenue, each of us on our way to a different solitary movie. We hugged, and cried a little. She said, "Let's have coffee someday soon." Will we?

It seems that our family represented the security she badly needed as a teenager, recently come with her parents and siblings and grandmother to Berkeley from New York. At some point, before Steve knew her, her father landed in jail. All those years I never knew why, and I didn't ask as we drove along the Russian River, through Hopland, Ukiah, Willits on our way to Steve. There was a second husband, a stepsister, a half brother who was retarded, a Jewish grandmother who didn't get along with her Jewish daughter, Judy's mother.

And so Judy found this Steve who was solidly rooted in Berkeley. He was always attracted to people in trouble, minority groups, malcontents. Together Steve and Judy walked all over the hills and down into the town. They hung out on Telegraph Avenue, which seemed to have changed while we weren't looking, from a gathering place for college students in saddle shoes and peggers, with Mom and Pop stores and soda fountains, to the counterculture headquarters of the world. Years later I learned that Steve and Judy had pooled their allowances and rented a party pad room on Telegraph. I didn't ask Judy about this either, as she drove her secondhand Volvo station wagon through Laytonville and on into the redwoods and along the Eel river.

———•———

It must not have been long after Steve and Judy had their pad on Telegraph Avenue that Jack and I put on a twenty-fifth wedding anniversary party for ourselves at the Town and Gown Club just around the corner on Dwight Way. In fact I remember us on our way to the party that January afternoon, walking down Haste Street across from what later became Peoples' Park, all dressed up — me in red chiffon and silver sandals, Jack in gray flannel suit — when I spotted a girl on the steps of the old Berkeley Inn, now gone, a victim of arson. My French teacher at the Anna Head School for Girls, just up the street, used to live there, a dignified pompadoured lady from France whom I adored. Perhaps that's why I was so offended by this girl lounging there on the steps with all her grimy possessions about her. She had a goat on a leash and as we approached I saw her filthy clothes and stringy hair. She was watching us, and my heart began to pound as I pulled Jack along, knowing she was going to beg and that Jack would probably stop and listen to her pleas. He was never threatened by the Telegraph Avenue scene. I was brought up to think kindly of the downtrodden, to give to the poor, and yet I was scared to death of that girl with the goat as she asked for spare change, which of course Jack gave her.

I came across the photo album of that party just the other day. Ever since Jack died I've been rummaging in drawers and closets. I found a folder of watercolors my paternal grandmother Tolman painted a century ago; photos of my mother with her five siblings and parents in China where she grew up, surrounded by coolies and amahs, the women all looking like Gibson girls. I found our children's grammar school drawings — round yellow suns, gingerbread houses, horses and sailboats and cowboys performing heroic feats. I came across our love letters back and forth between Germany and Scripps College. Oh, my, they are so sweet! And then I found the photo album of that party.

It's embarrassing. I look matronly and smug with an unattractive hairdo. *"Come and share our happiness and success, come and meet our lovely children."* It seemed like a marvelous affair at the time. One hundred conscientious citizens, leaders of Berkeley liberalism gathered in that fine Maybeck building, an architectural symbol of an earlier time. Under the dark beams white tables stretched out, laden with crystal, sparkling in the candlelight and firelight, nestling in sprays of holly, for this was the last of the Christmas parties. Black men and women in black and white uniforms poured champagne from napkined bottles and passed tiny canapes, while just outside the door on Dwight Way the whole south campus area seethed. Kennedy had been shot, and Malcolm X. The Free Speech Movement the year before had jolted us as angry, bearded students glared out from the TV screen. Whose children, whose students could they possibly be? Surely not ours.

Hadn't we been listening to Bob Dylan and Joan Baez and the Beatles? I can't remember. I only know that our children were there with us, drinking to our health out of filial respect, in suits and ties and barbered hair, dancing to the combo music, tuned into our tunes, at least for that one evening. They were getting properly high on champagne, not stoned on pot.

The point is, I guess, that our self-confidence was at its apex. But all the time, right then and there, relationships were dissolving, our own children were about to make momentous and sometimes disastrous decisions. Faces of dead people look out from the glossy photographs: Jim Whitney, my brother-in-law and Jack's best friend, smiling his pixie grin as he proposes a toast; Kenneth Hayes, still doing the Charleston at seventy; the distinguished judge with white hair. That boy was later killed in Vietnam, that girl overdosed. At least they never had to know about the assassinations of Martin Luther King and Bobby Kennedy. They didn't have to wake to the drone of helicopters day after day, to smell the stinking tear gas when People's Park almost caused a war in Berkeley. They weren't forced to take sides on elections that split up friendships, marriages, and political and racial coalitions all over town.

<hr />

I have two other sons: Tom, the eldest, and Dave, the youngest. And there was a stillborn son, also named Stephen, born in January 1944, a war baby, conceived in Battle Creek, Michigan, where Jack was going through his second basic training, this time in Military Government. His first, in 1943, was in Bend, Oregon, with the Corps of Engineers, building bridges under water. That base closed down, however, within a year because it was apparently too rigorous. Jack, along with many others, was hospitalized with pneumonia. In Military Government basic training he wore white gloves and directed traffic in downtown Battle Creek.

Tommy was one-and-a-half years old. He and I had moved back to my parents' house in Berkeley when Jack was drafted in late summer of 1943. On $50 a month I couldn't afford to stay on at the wonderful apartment we had been subletting on Russian Hill while Jack worked for the San Francisco city planning department. It was hard for civilians like me to get train tickets, but I was determined to visit him and start another baby. War seems to bring out the domestic, nesting needs of women to do something we can do, since we cannot, apparently, control world events.

———•———

Jack's father pulled some strings and got me a train ticket to Michigan. The trip was eye-opening. Though brought up in Berkeley academia, exposed to the great minds — Oppenheimer and Meiklejohn among them — of my parents' friends who came for tea and meals, though I'd been twice to Europe and had learned French at a boarding school in Switzerland, I had been completely removed, or perhaps protected from, the masses of working-class America.

Oh, there was Ora, of course. But she seemed more like an older sister than household help. She lived in our house and taught me to knit. I wish she'd taught me to cook. She tried once, years later, when I had a home of my own. I wanted to make chicken gumbo the way she did. But she could barely read or write, and the cooking lesson was all a pinch of this, a dash of that. I didn't have the instinct for it that she did. We kept up with her until she died as an old woman. Jack and I and my sister were the only white people at her funeral, a magnificent affair with ushers in white gloves, and the singing of all the soulful songs she used to sing herself when she had "the miseries," when I was a child.

And there was Mrs. Oshida, a quiet Japanese woman who did the family laundry once a week. By the time I was on that train to Michigan, leaving Tommy with my parents at 1530 LaLoma Avenue, Mrs. Oshida had been interned, to the great distress of my civil libertarian parents. I never saw her again, though her trunks were stored in the basement along with many of our possessions during those wartime years.

I was not quite twenty-three. The train was full of soldiers and sailors, and women like me on their way to visit husbands. One who fascinated me was a young mother who seemed like a child playing grown-up with her baby doll. Chewing gum, she brushed her little boy's wispy blond hair and dressed him up in a miniature sailor suit to match the daddy he had never seen and was going to visit now. His name was Butch. He tried her patience as any two-year-old does. She slapped him around a lot. God knows I could sympathize with her. I thought of Tommy and me, facing each other across the highchair tray, as he rejected the perfect little patty of scraped top round and the pureed artichoke heart that I, who hardly knew how to boil water, had made especially for him. I wanted to shake him. Once or twice I did. Once I bit him. I was too ashamed to ever tell Jack.

He met me at the station in Kalamazoo and it was just like all those wartime movies, hugging and kissing and me posing for a picture, sitting on a luggage cart, trying to look like Betty Grable, showing off my legs. Actually it's not a bad picture. I look so absolutely happy, and I was. I took pictures of him too, with his beautiful curly red hair all cut off, in a big overcoat and boots, looking like a real GI. We were so young.

We took a bus to Battle Creek. He had rented a room in an Army wife's house, and we made love like crazy. His fellow trainees were mostly policemen who would go overseas when we won the war and police our occupied enemies — Germany and Japan. I think Jack was there because some recruiting officer thought City Planning would also be useful for the occupying Army.

I'd probably never met any policemen before and found them and their wives as fascinating as I had the girl on the train. We went drinking and dining with them and jitterbugging at the USO. Jack was a natural-born social mixer, pulling me along with him, broadening my exposure to life and culture. He told me what to read and took me to museums, a good teacher even then. Heaven knows why he ever noticed me, four years younger, tagging along after him and his older crowd on Inverness beaches. Perhaps it was because of Erich, my wonderful German Boxer. He'd never been allowed to have a dog. But Steve reminded me, "Dad was attracted to your Achilles heels, your ankles from the back, remember?" He said this almost a year ago at the family gathering in Inverness where we buried Jack's ashes and reminisced about him. Everybody cracked up and I said my Achilles heels were long since shot to Hell.

Years ago, when Jack was still growing vegetables in our Berkeley backyard he said he wanted to be buried there. But the vegetable garden had gone to weeds (although the other day I found a lingering tomato plant and burst into tears). It was Steve who lowered the cedar box with mitered corners that Dave had made into the deep hole that Tom had dug in a clearing on a bluff above Tomales Bay. I hope he would approve of our decision to bury him, instead, next to Jim, his best friend and my sister Deborah's husband.

———•·———

June 1999

Watching Steve lean way down into that hole I knew he was in no condition for physical stress. I fantasized, in fact, that he might fall in head first, and then I thought what a blessing it might be if he could die like that, falling into the hole with his father's ashes. Everyone was standing in a circle, watching. The moment passed, and he would have to struggle on for almost another year.

Oh, he was brave. When he arrived in Inverness that time, I'm afraid I let out a sob. He had become and old, old man, with a scrawny neck and haggard eyes, and when I hugged him his shoulder blades were sharp because there was no muscle left at all, he who had been so physical his entire life, lifting calves, riding horses, building barns, digging trenches, chopping wood, to say nothing of swimming and dancing.

He had a plan. His brothers say he was delusional. Maybe, but he was imaginative and brave. Since he could no longer ride his horses or hike in his hills, he would learn to camp, outfit his truck for comfort so that he could go out to the ocean or up in the mountains and sleep in the truck bed beneath the open skies. He bought an almost new Nissan pickup — partly paid for by me, the rest from his most recent marijuana crop, I suppose — with automatic shift and comfortable adjustable seats. His bloated belly, his cramping legs and hands made comfort and ease while driving a high priority. He had tarps and a mattress and blankets and a barbecue and an icebox and a camp stove, and he brought baskets of food to share that week that he was in Inverness last summer: onions, potatoes, shallots, tomatoes, squashes, carrots, greens, apples, pears that he had grown himself, and frozen chickens and beef and lamb that he had raised himself, and many small jars of spices and herbs, and brown rice and pasta, for he had become obsessed with cooking and food, although I observed that he ate very little. He was tempting his appetite with aromas. I think this must be like the obsession of anorexics. I understand that now, but at the time I wanted to cry.

He had become a gourmet cook! I especially remember his Swedish meatballs wrapped in cabbage leaves and cooked in a tomato sauce, perhaps because it had so many steps and used so many pots and pans that I had to wash. For breakfast he wanted spicy stews or chicken with a couple of poached eggs on top. I prefer cereal or toast and would feel slightly nauseated by the smell of garlic and onions cooking in oil in the morning. I did my best to keep my emotional outbursts in check, my occasional floods of tears and rage confined to the bedroom or the bathroom. But I was so tired.

<hr />

July 1999

Steve always required a great deal of work from us, mental as well as physical. But even though the culture shock was intense when he first moved onto his land in southern Humboldt County, we were younger, we were inspired — albeit bewildered — by his life and projects, both humbled by and proud of the incredible amount of hard work that he himself was doing, encouraging the rest of us to do so also. I washed a million dishes in an outdoor tub. Jack laid bricks and shoveled manure. Tom felled trees. Dave laid foundations for the house.

How well I remember those trips up there a couple of times every year, from about 1974 on. As usual, good Boy Scout that Jack was, he seemed prepared for whatever came along, and just pitched in as needed. Back in the '60s when Steve became a hippie and I agonized over his matted hair and beard and dirty sandaled feet at dinners with Jack's Republican family, Jack would admonish me, "It doesn't matter. That's not important!"

And he was right, of course. What mattered was that he understood about the fragile earth, the cycles of life as native Indians had in bygone days. How did he learn all that stuff? At eight he was already horse crazy. His friend Laura had a horse. His friend Nanette had a saddle and was saving money for a horse. I myself had been horse crazy once and fell in love with a cowboy the summer I was fifteen. (I guess I never told Jack that, since I was also in love with him, though he didn't know it.) So what was my problem?

"Don't be ridiculous! We live in the city and I'm not going to spend my time driving you over the hill to Orinda so you can ride a horse!"

Jack and I were completely absorbed in the excitement of local politics. I was not about to become a taxi driver for my children, although I did sometimes drive a bunch of boys to baseball practice, and I did sometimes do one of the boy's paper routes if he was sick. I did do my stint as president of PTA, and as den mother three horrible times. But these were the duties of an urban mother.

"Grandpa has a horse."

Ah, and so he did. My father, Edward Chace Tolman, eminent professor of psychology, later to become a leader of the fight against the Loyalty Oath, recipient of honorary degrees, with a building named for him on the U.C. Berkeley campus, did indeed own a horse named Cookie, which reminds me of my idyllic childhood.

Chapter Two

*B*erkeley was known in those days as the Athens of the West. In 1918 my parents arrived by train all the way from Boston with my older sister, then just a baby, and moved into an apartment on Virginia Street, only two blocks from where they would settle and raise their three children, only six blocks from where I sit now writing. I was born three years later at Alta Bates Hospital, the first native Californian in my family. My brother arrived three years after that. I look out at trees that are older than I am, at the San Francisco Bay and Mt. Tamalpais beyond, timeless landmarks. I sometimes wonder whether if, in fact like so many Americans, and like my own parents, I had moved away from my childhood place, my childhood would still seem so idyllic in my memory. I don't think so, for it is the continuum that gives me so much comfort, especially now as I grieve. It's true that I grew up apart from my grandparents, aunts and uncles, cousins. That is something different, something very rich that my children and grandchildren, and now great grandchildren, have. We are all Northern Californians, mostly in the San Francisco Bay Area, and though Fletcher may move to Chile with his Chilean wife and twins, the rest, I think, are here to stay. David and his family, in fact, have just migrated back to Berkeley after an eight-year hiatus in Santa Fe. Steve, too, returned, after ten years in Montana, to southern Humboldt County.

So I grew up in this earlier Berkeley where indeed my father did have a horse in a stable two blocks from our house. Wide open country began there and we rode and hiked and picnicked all over the hills that are now occupied by the Lawrence Berkeley Lab, the Cyclotron, the Hall of Science, the Botanical Gardens. LaLoma Avenue, where we lived, and the cross street, Buena Vista, had many spacious gardens and houses, several of them designed by Berkeley's perhaps most famous architect, Bernard Maybeck. LaLoma was then a quiet winding street where we sailed boats in the rain gutters, walked to school right behind our house, had friends to play with across the street, up the street, down the street, around the corner. My father walked to and from the University, and, in the early days, had rats running around in mazes right in his home study. For my entire childhood he was writing **THE BOOK:** *Purposive Behavior of Animals and Men.* I still remember his pads of yellow paper covered with his small irregular scrawl. The couch in his study was covered with piles of books and those yellow sheets of paper. When he came home from the University in the afternoons he would sometimes say, "I'm cross and tired; don't touch me," and retreat to his study, which had double doors and double windows to protect him from the distractions of the family and the street. My mother would take him a cup of tea and go in there to be with him. I never resented this. I seemed to understand that they were older parents — they married when they were thirty, had all three of us in their thirties — and that raising children and nurturing my father's academic career simultaneously wasn't easy. My mother, nee Kathleen Drew, a Radcliffe Phi Beta Kappa and Magna Cum Laude, Class of 1907, taught Greek for a while at The A to Zed School, then English at the Ransom School in Piedmont, but she gave up teaching when my younger brother had so many health problems as a baby and toddler that she felt she had to stay home. Perhaps she regretted this. My sister, who is older and remembers more of that time, believes she did. I don't know.

They were very loving parents, albeit in a somewhat reserved New England mode, especially my mother. My father was more physically demonstrative and all his life I loved to hug his tall slim frame. I think that their marriage was exceptionally rich and solid. Their pet names for each other were "Kak" and "Tombey." I have no idea why. They were intellectuals with many interesting friends who came for tea, which my mother poured out every afternoon from a silver teapot in the gracious living room that ran the entire width of the house. It had floor-to-ceiling mullioned bay windows at each end, a walk-in fireplace, Italianate patterns stenciled on the high ceiling beams, bookcases covering one wall, and a panoramic view to the west. I was married in this room. So was my sister.

We children were always welcome at tea time, but never forced to attend. On weekdays there might be a couple of my mother's women friends. On Sundays graduate students would often be invited, and on these occasions my mother added rum to the tea — but only for the men — which she poured from a blue glass pitcher. I loved listening in on conversations I couldn't possibly understand, but knew were exciting, just from the tone of my father's voice. I, and I presume my sister, engaged in a childish sort of flirtation with some of the younger men. I had quite a crush on Oppenheimer, who strode around the room with a pipe clenched between his teeth, gesticulating, his eyes a piercing blue, though many years later I would come to think of him as a tragic character worthy of Shakespeare. I remember my father's delight when someone presented some new thought. "What a cute idea!" he would exclaim. That was the ultimate praise.

My mother as hostess maintained a stimulating intellectual and social milieu. There were dinner parties to which we children were not invited, before which my father would have to make contact with the bootlegger. Our house, like many in the Berkeley hills, was upside down. That is to say, the top floor, a short flight of stairs above the street entryway, housed the living room, dining room, kitchen, my parents' bedroom and bathroom, my father's study. The children's bedrooms, bathrooms and playroom were on the floor below as the hillside sloped down toward the west. And so the hilarity of these parties we children could hear went on over our heads.

Another full floor, with a laundry and maid's room and bath, was at the very bottom of the house. We called this the basement, but in fact it included an airy, sunny suite for the live-in help, with a view of

San Francisco half a flight of steps above the terrace and garden that rambled down the hill to Hillside School. In the garden below I had a playhouse, and my brother had a chicken house. Perhaps it was intended that my older sister, Deborah, was to be the student, I the domestic, and my younger brother, Teddy, the farmer, though none of us turned out exactly that way.

In those days friendships within the academic community crossed department lines. My parents' friends were mostly, though not exclusively, like themselves, newcomers to the west. Some of the wives formed a Lunch Club — Kathleen Tolman (Edward - Psychology), Kate Loewenberg (Jack - Philosophy), Kate Linforth (Ivan - Classics), Mary Lewis (Gilbert - Chemistry), Mary Adams (George - Philosophy), Ruth Peterson (Torvil - Classics), Ellen Pepper (Stephen - Philosophy and Aesthetics). Nell Calhoun (George - Classics), Margaret Schevill (Rudolph - Spanish). And another part of the continuum of my life in Berkeley is that we daughters of those women have a Lunch Club too, though we have dwindled now, due to death or illness or physical distance from each other, to almost nothing.

There was also the University Section Club of which my mother was a founding member. This is still an organization built around interest groups, open to membership for faculty wives and female faculty and staff, but, in the case of drama, for instance, bridge, and later (in my day) tennis, husbands could be associate members. My parents, along with most of my mother's Lunch Club friends and their husbands plus quite a few others, including the George Stewarts, Edward Strongs, George Potters, Robert Brodes were lifetime members of the Drama Section. As children my sister and brother and I were sometimes allowed to attend their plays when they were held at our house. Then we were enchanted to watch these grownups cavorting about our living room and even kissing each other's husbands or wives. As soon as Jack and I and our then two children moved back to Berkeley and Jack started teaching at the University, we joined the Drama Section; our children watched us, too, kissing each other's husbands and wives. Tennis was the other section that my mother was active in for years. (So was I.) I remember her, looking not unlike Helen Wills, dashing off in her white tennis dress and red leather coat in her Ford coupe with a rumble seat named **"THE CUTIE."** My mother was no flapper, but that was the '20s.

Throughout my entire childhood we had household help; a series of college girls who lived in the basement and worked for room and board; a nanny, Miss Goodman, brought from England when my baby brother was born; an enormous black woman, still referred to in those days as Negro, Sarah Day Sephus whom my brother, by then a jabbering three-year-old, jealously guarded as his very own; and then Ora Lee Thompson, a miniscule and scrappy twenty-something, straight from Louisiana about which she told me stories of growing up in the country with chickens and feather beds and a dirt yard that had to be swept clean every Saturday. She was my friend, my protector, and my disciplinarian all in one. I loved her. I love her still, though she's been dead for about thirty years. Eventually she married Hollis Perkins, a Pullman porter on the Southern Pacific Railway, whom she always referred to as "Dear." She, and sometimes her sisters — Anna and Katie — worked for my parents for years, off and on, and also for Jack and me. It was another time, a leisurely time, and, at least as I remember it, devoid of stress, like an entirely satisfying old motion picture. We ate well, we travelled, we were nurtured in both body and mind.

There was, of course, a lot of talk about IQs in our household, my father being a psychologist, Binet having coined the phrase "Intelligence Quotient" and Terman's Stanford-Binet longitudinal studies of gifted children under-way. Perhaps, being a stubborn child who once caused my father to break his front tooth as he gritted his teeth in exasperation, I was simply not going to compete. At any rate, I either knew or decided early on that I would not be an intellectual like my parents. That seemed to be okay with them. Perhaps Deborah, being the first, and Teddy, being the boy, had a harder time, but my parents never put pressure on me. They took me out of public school after the fourth grade, I think because I had a terrible teacher who accused me of something I didn't do and boxed my ears. I began to play hooky with a friend and lied about it to my parents.

I was then sent to a small experimental school in the neighborhood where David Park, later to become the revered figurative painter of the California School, at that time only nineteen years old, taught both history and art. He was very shy and we pupils took great pleasure in making him blush. The mother of one of my best friends taught science in her basement. Each of the three years that I attended that school we performed a Gilbert and Sullivan operetta in U.C. Regent Farnham Griffith's basement, which had a stage. They were elaborate productions that involved us in making costumes and stage sets and we took them very seriously. The headmistress, Miss Munn, gently warned us that the audience might laugh, but that was all right and we shouldn't worry about it. Of course they roared with laughter, and somehow we came to realize that what we were doing was meant to be funny. And it was. In *The Mikado* I had the female romantic lead role of YumYum. In *Pinafore* and *Iolanthe* I was in the chorus.

I took piano lessons during this time, but that didn't amount to much. I wish it had. My parents, with a heritage of Quakerism and Unitarianism but by then agnostic, wanted, nevertheless, to expose us to religion so that we could make our own choices. How typical of intellectual New Englanders that Catholicism and Christian Science were apparently not offered as options. Nothing really took, but the religious exposure I enjoyed the most was reading the Old Testament with the eminent Jewish law professor, Max Radin, on his roof terrace half a block away where several neighborhood youths and children gathered weekly for a while. "He pisseth against the wall," I suddenly heard Professor Radin expound in a booming voice. It was just about the most exciting, shocking thing I'd ever experienced. I guess I was nine.

Three times during my childhood we went on extended summer visits to New England, where we became reacquainted with many of our Eastern relatives. The first time was to Jaffrey, New Hampshire where we Tolmans rented a rambling house in the woods. My Grandmother Drew, and all the aunts, uncles, and cousins who came and went and alternated with each other most of the summer, rented another rambling house on the edge of Gilmore Pond. My grandmother sat in a rocking chair on the wide verandah most of the day, holding court as the titular head of this family, all in black, a velvet choker around her neck and snowy white hair pulled up to a bun on top. She can't have been much older than I am now. Perhaps she was in mourning for her husband, who had died when I was three, but I never saw her in any other attire until she died when I was eleven.

These were mostly my mother's family, and she was one of six children, all born and brought up in China where my grandfather had worked for the Chinese Customs Service. His family had lived in the colonial manner of comfort — amahs, rickshaws, and enormous houses in Peking, Foochow, and Shanghai until he retired and returned to his home base of New England. Two of my mother's sisters never had children, but still there were plenty of cousins.

Another summer, sometime in the '20s, my grandmother rented a compound on Martha's Vineyard, where we resumed our cousinly love and flirtations and communal living, along with swimming and croquet. My father's brother, Richard, and his new wife, Ruth, visited. We went to Salem and Concord and Plymouth. All of the place names still give me a thrilling sense of my connection to pilgrims and puritans and Quakers and seafaring men.

The final New England visit of my childhood was in 1933, stopping off on our way to a year's sabbatical in Europe. We had a few days with my father's nieces and their families in New Bedford and his sister in West Newton. And then I was billeted at my mother's oldest sister Aunt Dora's house in Cambridge, where her husband, well known educator and critic, Irving Babbitt, was dying, and I was made to have an audience with him, to receive instructions from THE GREAT MAN. "Learn Latin and Greek," he told me as I quivered in fear at the foot of his bed, becoming aware of the reality of death so very close to me. By the time we had crossed the ocean on "The American Trader," and reached the four-story Kensington house of my mother's next-to-oldest sister, Elsa, in London, Uncle Irving was dead. Aunt Elsa had "married Empire" and was more British than the British. All voices were hushed, as we ate cucumber sandwiches with our tea. Death was kept private and quiet in those days, or at least in my New England family, and tea was served, regardless of what was happening in the outside world.

Some of these relatives occasionally came to visit us in Berkeley, staying, usually, at Cloyne Court, a residential hotel on Ridge Road, now a student coop, where David lived during his brief attendance at the University. (All of our sons dropped out of college, despite, or perhaps because of their father and grandfather and two great-uncles being university professors.) Deborah tells about a visit from our Grandmother Tolman when we were very young, before Teddy was born. My parents went off to meet her at the train station at the foot of University Avenue, leaving us in the care of the current college girl. Deborah had a fearful fantasy about this grandmother, and she scared both herself and me almost to death, saying that our grandmother was a witch and we'd better lock ourselves in the bathroom, which we did, so that's how the poor old lady was greeted by these granddaughters she had crossed the continent to see. I don't even know when that grandmother died. Though it was she for whom I was named, Mary Chace Tolman, I don't remember her at all. I do have a wonderful collection of letters between her and my father from those halcyon days of my parents' first years in Berkeley. And there is a framed black and white photo of her as an old woman sitting at her easel.

I do remember my mother's sisters Dora, Elsa, and Lucy, who came to visit many times and lived long lives. Much later they got to know all three of our sons quite well at various times, in many places — Berkeley, Inverness, New Hampshire, Martha's Vineyard, Boston, London, The Hague. As a child, I remember dinners with them at Cloyne Court and at the Men's Faculty Club on the campus and at the old "Black Sheep" on Telegraph Avenue, situated just about where Sproul Hall stands now. At that time, before the University gobbled up the wild hills behind our house and extended its tentacles into the town, Sather Gate was the entrance to the University. What is now Sproul Plaza was a busy block of shops — the Black Sheep Restaurant and the Sather Gate Bookstore and Vaughn's clothing store and the Varsity coffee shop where my father spent countless hours conferring with students and colleagues, just up the street from the old Campus movie theatre, where in the '20s I saw my first movie — *City Lights* — and Jules Creamery where, when I was in high school, I would drink countless lemon Cokes, and Roos Brothers clothing store, which also had a beauty parlor where I, at age fourteen, received my first disastrous permanent wave. The disaster was that I thought I shouldn't disturb the perfection by brushing or combing my hair. My mother, who'd reluctantly allowed me to have this permanent wave, knew less than I did about how to take care of it. Well, after several weeks of such neglect, of course it became a rat's nest. I had to have it all cut off and start again.

My prepubescent years were filled with extracurricular activities. The outdoor neighborhood games were hopscotch, jacks, jump rope, Kick the Can, Sardines. There were also endless Monopoly games across the street at Patty Donald's house. (Her father was chief physician at the University's Cowell Hospital; her brother was later one of my first boyfriends, though of course "boyfriend" then didn't mean what it does today.) Sewing instructions were given to the girls by my mother's good friend, Mrs. Pepper, who lived up the street. Saturdays my best friends, Sally and Edith, and I went to matinees at the United Artist Theatre downtown. Our favorite movie stars were Janet Gaynor and Norma Shearer. We also liked to ride on the Euclid Avenue streetcar, across the trestle over Cordonices creek, where the park and the Rose Garden are today, on to the end of the line at the Reservoir, bouncing on the wicker seats and buying Juicy Fruit gum from the vending machines. And finally there was tennis on a funky court on what is now Greenwood Common, then known as The Knoll and serving as the playground for Miss Munn's School. Several of us girls formed the The Greenwood Tennis Club and even had uniforms — white dresses with dark blue and red diamond-shaped plackets inset at the waist. Pretty cute. Looking at the photo now I see that my hair was short like a boy's. That was because of the explosion.

Those three years that I attended Miss Munn's School were almost entirely happy. But two major events — the onset of The Great Depression and the explosion — must have seriously upset the near-perfection of my parents' lives. My recollections of The Depression are confined to a man at the kitchen door asking for food, which our little maid, Ora, gave him without question, feeding him a plate of our leftovers at the kitchen table, and a few overheard conversations between my parents that leave me still with the sense of my father's guilt about money, something that I, perhaps unfortunately, inherited from him along with some of that money. Though professors suffered less than the general populace from the Depression, my father was aware that he was better off than many of his colleagues. His father, a New England manufacturer, had become a financial success, of which my father and his brother and sister were beneficiaries. The Depression had little effect on our lives; in fact when I was twelve and thirteen, 1933-34, we spent the year in Europe.

The other event, the explosion, took place December 3, 1930, and was a neighborhood disaster. I still agonize with my parents and all the other parents of those thirty children, myself and Deborah among them, one of them killed, the oldest child and only son of our friends the Peppers, along with one of the firemen. I was knocked unconscious, so don't remember my own pain. But just imagine coming home on the ferry boat from Christmas shopping in San Francisco, as I believe our parents were, and learning that a house blew up on the next block, that your two daughters were somewhere in a hospital but no one knew which one. Fortunately Teddy was confined to my parents' bed with a cold and only got to observe it from the window, the lucky kid. I always envied him that. What a sight it must have been. I worry that I sometimes prefer observing life to participating in it, but no one could fault me for envying Teddy's position as the observer then. I should add that my sister remembers things differently, that she was moping around the house in adolescent boredom, and that Mother, fed up, told her to go outside and see what all those sirens were about. Which was the truth? We'll never know, and cannot ask our mother now. She's been dead for thirty-six years.

My memory of the explosion is this. It was about three o'clock in the afternoon, just as Hillside School, which was almost an extension of our back garden, was letting out for the day. I suppose that Miss Munn's, which I attended, and Anna Head's, which Deborah attended, had let out earlier for both she and I remember being at home when we heard the sirens. She was still in her school uniform — middy blouse and dark blue pleated skirt. My friends Sally and Edith and I were inventing a Christmas play. The next thing I remember is being down at the corner of Cedar and LeRoy, along with a whole bunch of school children, where the house that had been on fire seemed to not be on fire anymore. There were fire trucks and hoses and firemen all very busy and friendly who let us — thirty or so — swarm around. I poked my head in the basement window. Suddenly someone yelled, "Gas!" That's the last thing I remember until I woke up hours later in a hospital bed with my mother and father's faces hanging above me.

The gas that caused the explosion had been leaking from old pipes left over from the Berkeley Fire of 1923, the one that had destroyed my family's first house on LaLoma Avenue. I was only two years old when that fire occurred, and we were on my father's sabbatical leave at the time. I have no memory of it. And yet my childhood was filled with its lore. Every autumn when the hot north winds blew, my mother would tell us to pack a bag of our most treasured possessions in case we had to flee. And that reminds me of another pleasure of growing up on Nut Hill as our neighborhood was known, either because of the nutty people who lived there or because of the diet of nuts and fruit that some of the bohemian residents were said to survive on. That pleasure was playing in the abandoned foundations from the fire of 1923 that dotted vacant lots with free-standing chimneys and flights of concrete steps that led to nowhere.

In the explosion I received first degree burns over much of my body and face, which resulted in a beautiful new baby skin devoid of all my old freckles. My hair was burned off and I got three large third degree burns on my back. I don't remember the pain of changing the dressings, only that I winced and dreaded it when sheets of porous celluloid-like material had to be peeled away and new ones applied.

Deborah had a much worse time of it. She received third degree burns on her hands and around her waist, where there had been a gap between her middy and skirt. She had been conscious, in pain and fear, wandering, crying until someone took her to Cowell Hospital.

That's where I was too. Some of the children were at Alta Bates, others at Herrick. Poor Deborah remembers that when our parents finally appeared she was so happy, but almost immediately they said, "Oh, now we must go find Mary."

But in some ways that was the best Christmas we'd ever had, Deborah and I, although that was probably the first time in our lives that we missed Christmas dinner at the George Adamses. From the very first year that my parents were in California they had dinner with them, and it became our family tradition. The Adamses were a musical family, along with their many other talents. George Senior, an intellectual giant, had been a leader of the faculty revolt of 1920, one of those periodic assertions of their academic rights and freedoms. He also played the cello. Cornelia played the piano. I can't remember what instruments George Jr. and John played. Perhaps one of them played the flute. George Jr. later would have a distinguished career as professor of philosophy at Cornell. John became an eminent neurosurgeon at U.C. Medical School. Cornelia taught piano, married a Swedish sea captain, and was responsible for activating the Junior Lunch Club when we daughters were married with children of our own.

On those Christmases in the '20s and '30s, we sang carols, ate wonderful, traditional Christmas food that Mary Adams, who seemed rather impractical and eccentric, nevertheless created in the kitchen without any assistance. Then we played charades. Almost everybody among my parents' friends had costume boxes filled with scarves, hats, purses, cast-off uniforms from bygone wars. Perhaps it was a New England tradition. Jack and I had one too for years. Dressing up and acting silly was what we did. The Gilbert Lewises and Stephen Peppers and Ivan Linforths would often be at these Christmas dinners too. Even after Jack and I were married, we had a few Christmases there at their spacious shingled house on Santa Barbara Road. But though the year of the explosion we couldn't go to the Adamses, my sister and I had more attention and gifts than ever before or since.

Our family's Christmas gift tradition was a little peculiar, I realize now. Since most of these gifts came from Eastern relatives they were wrapped in brown paper tied with string. I don't know why my parents didn't unwrap them so that the festive Christmas paper and ribbons were on display. I suspect it had to do with their New England Puritanism that cropped up in funny ways. Their own gifts to us three children were devoid of frivolous wrappings. Although we had a tree, our gifts were not under it, but sorted and arranged on small tables, one for each member of the family, rather like at a department store sale. I still get a thrill at the sight of packages done up in brown paper.

Deborah and I were home from the hospital by Christmas that year, but still bedridden, so we each had a Christmas tree in our respective rooms. I wonder now why we weren't in the same room. Perhaps we didn't want to be. We weren't that fond of each other, after all. She thought I was a pest and I thought she was mean, even though I longed to be included in her crowd, and used to kick at her bedroom door to be let in. "Duck, duck, go to your pond," she would call through the door, a taunt that wounded me deeply.

———•———

And then there was Inverness and that's where Jack came into the picture, though we wouldn't actually be aware of each other until 1933. At least I was aware of him, immediately, intensely, that first summer after coming back from a year abroad. I was just Deborah's little sister to him.

But first my parents discovered Bolinas, before I was born, searching, I believe, for a special place by the sea, such as they had known together in Maine and on Cape Cod, where my father loved to sail. There are pictures of my father in Bolinas carrying Deborah, dark-eyed like our mother, in a homemade wooden chair strapped to his back. Just think, there were no baby backpacks then. It wasn't until our David came along that we found that wonderful new contraption from Australia — a canvas sling to carry babies in. What did we do with Tom and Steve? How did we get to Shell Beach, for instance, carrying them half a mile through the woods along that treacherous path with roots of oaks and bays to trip over? I know we did. There are pictures in our albums to prove it.

29

There are more Bolinas photographs, with me in them now, a fat blond child in a striped, one-piece wool bathing suit with short cap sleeves. Some of my early memories are of Bolinas. I remember a store with bright-colored beach balls and buckets and shovels for digging in the sand. I remember the boarding house right above the beach where we stayed. But there wasn't any real sailing in Bolinas for my father. So then come the first Inverness pictures — my parents on a beach — Chicken Ranch, Shell, Heart's Desire, or Indian — with their friends the Lewises, the Peppers, and the Gibsons, in silly poses. The women wore white tennis dresses, cloche hats, loose sweaters, tennis shoes. The men wore knickers and caps and neckties. It was a house party, my mother told me, at the Lewises, who had moved to Inverness where their children were being schooled at home. That was considered quite eccentric by my parents, but the great genius, G. N. Lewis, intended that his children's education should be directed by him. I bet it was his wife, though, who had to carry out the plan, for I believe he spent his weekdays and nights living at the Faculty Club in Berkeley. He was a pompous, egotistical, albeit brilliant, man whom we children took delight in finding at fault. I remember once when we were on a joint family outing to one of the ocean beaches and Gilbert insisted on driving through a boggy patch of ranch road. He got stuck in the mud and had to be pulled out by his more cautious professorial colleagues, much to the mirth of everyone, except, perhaps, for his poor long-suffering wife.

And of course later Jack got to know him very well, at least on one level, as young suitor to Gilbert's beautiful and voluptuous daughter, Margery, one of my sister Deborah's best friends. Deborah, Teddy, and I were then at boarding school, "La Pelouse," near Bez-Les-Bains in the French-speaking part of Switzerland, somewhat homesick and anxious, at least I was, about what seemed to be scary, violent incidents in Austria, caused by a man named Hitler. Although the following quote from a letter I wrote to my parents does not convey this anxiety, my memory of it is very strong. "You must be having fun in your little apartment. When I grow up and get married I am going to come to Vienna and have a little flat just like you only I am going to do the work myself instead of having a maid." I never did get to Vienna.

30

My parents were living there that year (1932-33), my father conferring with, though not being analyzed by, Freud. (He told me once that he'd never be brave enough for *that*, although my sister tells me that many years later he did "work with" the Jungian psychoanalyst, Joe Henderson.) At school we were encouraged by the headmistress, Mlle. Hemmerlin, to listen to the news on her radio in the Salon. It would help us with our understanding of French. I could not have known that this was, indeed, one of the preliminaries to World War II, nor could I therefore have been anxious about the fates of my five male cousins and my brother. He was only nine years old, and safely there at school with us. Nevertheless, I had a strong premonition of evil. And they all did go into that war. One was killed. But that was more than a decade later, and a decade is forever when you're twelve going on thirteen.

Deborah got a letter from Margery. Perhaps we were sitting up in a cherry tree gorging ourselves on fresh fruit when she showed it to me. Perhaps we were sneaking into the village to buy chocolate to hide in our closet. I don't know what, but something clandestine, no doubt, because we were forbidden to be alone together or to speak English. I worried about poor little Teddy, off in another building — La Grande Maison, where the younger children lived (only one other boy, named Claude) and were also forbidden to speak English. Deborah and I were housed in Le Chalet with American Joan and Helen, English Suzanne, and the glamorous French Marianne and Janine, also Tati. These are the ones I remember. We all ate meals in La Grande Maison, and that was about the only time we saw Teddy. It's curious that I was so concerned about him, for earlier I had taken him for granted, only relating to him as he suited my needs as a prop for my games — my baby when I was playing house, my pupil when I was playing school, my patient when I was playing nurse. And I would use him again as a prop when I practiced ballroom dancing and pushed him around the living room with my mother's phonograph blaring out the latest "Hit-of the Week."

"I met the cutest redheaded boy named Jack... ." That's all I remember of Margery's letter.

By then we Tolmans had already begun to spend most summers in

Inverness. My father rented an awkward broad-beamed sailboat with a centerboard named "The Brownie." We never owned a house there, so had the fun of living in several over those summers, in different parts of town.

There was usually a guest cabin in which my father labored on **THE BOOK.**

My mother, the intellectual, had to cope with more domestic life than was her wont. Ora came once or twice, but she hated Inverness. In the beginning there was no electricity or telephone. She had to cook on a kerosene stove. There were mice. She killed them with a hammer. There were skunks and raccoons prowling around in the night. It was odd that these things bothered her, for she'd been brought up in the country. I think the real trouble was that she was lonely for her church and her sisters; she was the only black person for miles around; she was afraid of the water.

So my mother, who was accustomed to full-time live-in help, had to get along with Elizabeth, the local fisherman's sister, to clean once in a while, and the Chinese laundry on the shore next to the butcher shop where our clothes were washed in a machine in the kitchen where the Hum family toothbrushes hung above the sink. Vegetables were delivered by Pete Giubbini. Milk was purchased at McConnel's Dairy. Garbage was dumped by my father (and everyone else in town) at a specified part of the Bay shore, reached by walking out on a rickety pier. You could see rats running around in that dump under a huge oak tree. It's near where Barnaby's Restaurant is now.

While Jack's Auntie Margaret, or his mother, was cooking competently on a wood stove, I imagine, right there in the charming little house that his grandfather, his father, and he created, my poor mother hardly knew how to cook at all. But she did insist that we have tea every afternoon at four, and brought a little sterno stove, walking about a mile from where she and Daddy parked the car at Chicken Ranch Beach, up the hill, over the stile, across the field of cows that belonged to the dairy and now is the development of Seahaven (where Deborah and Jim built their house, where Jack and Jim are buried) over another stile, then finally on through the woods to Shell Beach, where she brewed the tea. Or perhaps she left the sterno in the bathhouse. I remember those dressing rooms where we hung our bathing suits and towels and stored our inner tubes, open to the sky except for wire netting to keep out skunks and raccoons and falling branches of the alder trees, built in the marshy woods behind Shell Beach. At the beginning of summer we got our keys from Amy Eastman, Jack's good friend's mother. That was because Bill's father, Latham, managed the huge Shafter Estate including all the dairy ranches out to Point Reyes and most of the beaches along Tomales Bay.

(Bill, an only child, grew up in Inverness with his parents at #10 Inverness Way, now a B&B charging $125 a night. About twenty years ago our daughter-in-law worked there, making the breakfasts. Bill went to the one-room Inverness School up on the Mesa. Decades later two of our grandsons went there also, though by then it had three rooms.)

The Tomales Bay State Park and the Point Reyes National Seashore came much later of, course, when Jack and I were all grown up, responsible citizen activists who helped to make it happen.

A typical summer day for us children, after the age of ten or so, would include pickup tennis games in the mornings on the one and only court in town. This belonged to The Inverness Tennis Club, which had been created by the pure energy of Amy Eastman because she had big tennis ambitions for her son, Bill, which, as it turned out, were justified. He played team tennis all his life and was the star of our club for many years. (He also was in our wedding, though at one point he admonished me to stay away from Jack. I guess I threatened his friendship with him.)

At the tennis court one just went and sat on a bench, getting a tan, yakking with the other kids, until she or he was included in a game. Then we might go pick up the mail, hang around the Post Office, gather from this friend or that where everyone was going that day and evening, for practically no one had a phone. Usually it was to Shell Beach in the afternoon, to which we walked, about four miles from home. We walked everywhere in those days. Even adolescents with driver's licenses didn't often have the use of the one and only family car. But on weekends a motor launch, "The Keemah," left Brock's Wharf near the center of town every hour or so and headed for Shell Beach. It cost ten cents. Brock Schreiber was a taciturn seaman who owned the wharf, in addition to several houses and boats that he rented out and kept shipshape. In fact he was in charge of most of the boats on Tomales Bay during the Depression, for the elegant white Inverness Yacht Club had closed after the Stock Market crash of 1929 and was boarded up for many years.

Another Motor Launch, "The Queen," bigger and more seaworthy than "The Keemah," also skippered by Brock, took parties of fifteen or twenty down to Honeymoon Beach near the mouth of the long skinny Tomales Bay for crabbing parties. He had constructed rough picnic tables and benches there near a stand of eucalyptus trees at which we sat and gorged ourselves on the crab Brock caught in nets, then boiled and served with French bread. I probably only went on one or two of those parties during my childhood, but they were part of the Inverness lore. There are photographs of men in boaters and shirtsleeves, women with cinched-in waists and big straw hats. Those expeditions became the prototype of our own tradition of crabbing trips as our children were growing up. "The Queen" finally languished on Children's Beach, gradually disintegrating so that by the time we took our children there to wallow in the mud flats along with the jelly fish, we used The Queen as backrest and climbing apparatus for our toddlers.

I tried to find her the other day, poking in the clots of seaweed and driftwood the way Jack used to do, looking for treasures to add to the overabundance of shells and feathers and weather-polished whorls of wood on our mantle and window sills and shelves, but she too is gone.

It's so strange to think that we were experiencing the same things and yet didn't even know each other then. Later we figured it out — that the grownups from Berkeley and San Francisco were really very provincial, each group suspicious of the other, each group feeling superior to the other, and they simply didn't mix. Jack told me how he and all those Gould and Stanton cousins went to the beaches and played

"Simon Says" and "I Doubt It" in the evenings, just as I did. Did his family rent a bathhouse too? When did he first meet Bill? Did he remember the Haunted House? Did he go there at night and scare himself to death, bumping into things in the dark, screaming? Did he remember the Boy Scout Camp in Second Valley? Did he join in their campfire sing-alongs? "Every little breeze seems to whisper Louise....." and "Anchors aweigh, my boys....." And Fourth of July foot races. God, I was competitive! I remember once — I was probably ten — getting so excited and worked up over the race that I threw up behind the gas station. Later, when I knew who Jack was, I watched him at the starting line — that disarming smile and wild red hair, in blue jeans and an old white dress shirt with the sleeves rolled up.

Today is the 7th of July, and our son, Tom, our firstborn, just finished his thirty-year stint emceeing the foot races. We have many photos of him standing tall on the back of a flatbed truck. Sometimes there's a toddler on his shoulders, or hanging onto his hand, or a boy sitting between Tom's boots, dangling his sneakers over the side of the truck. In straw hats, baseball caps, or bareheaded, Tom jokes into the mike, political jokes, subtle friendly barbs at the participants out there racing, most of whom he's known all his life. He is fifty-six years old. He and Dave are both grandfathers now and join the other grandparents strolling down to Vladimir's for a beer. Of course Tom doesn't drink, hasn't had a drop of liquor since after the flood of 1982.

Chapter Three

*L*iquor. Yes, it's been an ever-present force in the lives of our generation and our children's. Jack and I grew up during the Prohibition. My childhood memories include the knowledge that my father, as I mentioned earlier, sometimes got in touch with a bootlegger. I believe there was actually very little liquor — occasional rum in the tea, a bottle of wine at a dinner party — but I caught on that it was illicit, therefore exciting. I don't believe my mother or father ever said a word about it to me as a child. I guess I simply absorbed these impressions from their grown-up conversations. My father was a compulsive coffee drinker and smoker. Even my more repressed mother occasionally smoked, though almost as a pose, holding the cigarette between stiff fingers, not inhaling. But I never saw them drunk, or even high. There was a strong puritanical streak in my parents' ethical code, their New England backgrounds steeped in Unitarianism and Quakerism. One of my great grandmothers, having been an abolitionist with an underground railway station in her house, then a suffragette became a member of the Women's Temperance Union, believing, as other activists of her generation did, that liquor was a curse that destroyed families and subjugated women. I can't remember when I first had a drink. On dates in high school? No. My first real date was a tall dark lad named Ed Barry who had a yellow Plymouth coupe. We did other dangerous things like skidding in his car on the streetcar tracks, whizzing around the corner of Hearst and Oxford Streets on our way to a Cal basketball game at Harmon gym. Charles Evans, Phil Ferrier, Donny Mackay, John and Fred Cushing, Jay Miller, Jim Schevill, Fred Dyer-Bennett. I don't remember drinking with any of them, though I started smoking at fourteen. In high school Shirley Okell, a year older than me, who lived in wealthy Piedmont and had her own car, drove me around during lunch hour while we smoked.

Jack's freshman class in the Beta house at Cal were known, for a while, as the "cookie-pushers," for they refused to drink themselves silly at fraternity beer busts. One of his best friends and roommate, though, became a heavy drinker, and Jack occasionally had to put him to bed, blind drunk, I learned much later. I don't remember drinking with him during the summer of our courtship in 1938. But soon after he left Inverness that time on his way to his year's exchange fellowship in Germany, he and Tom Hogan and Ed Umphred were in a serious automobile accident caused by drinking. Jack was driving the car when it crashed into a telephone pole on Upper Market Street near Twin Peaks in San Francisco. And during his year in Germany he drank lots and lots of beer.

Old-Fashioneds were always served before family dinners at Jack's parents' house. His father made quite a ritual of the preparation and then the offering on a silver tray. Those are the first drinks I came to expect and look forward to. I'm sure that I had an occasional drink during my two years at Scripps, but I honestly do not remember. By the time of our engagement party in the fall of 1940 cocktail parties were a normal part of social life, and a frequent way of celebrating an engagement. Ours was no exception. When we got married six months later our wedding presents of course included the ubiquitous martini shakers, the silver coasters and wine coolers and ice buckets. But we hardly ever used them. I remember occasionally buying a bottle of sherry, almost as an afterthought, if we were having a couple over for dinner. It wasn't until 1945 in Washington DC, when we were the parents of two-and-a-half year old Tommy, and Jack a second lieutenant in the old un-air-conditioned Munitions Building on Pennsylvania Avenue, that we became nightly drinkers. Blame it on the high humidity and heat, the tension of war, or the recent stillborn loss of our second son, but at the end of Jack's work day he would strip off his uniform (I would already be barefoot and down to my slip because of the heat) and we would turn on the radio to hear the horrible news and drink rum and coke with lots of ice.

———•———

August 1999

In January 1945, a few days after Jack had been home on Christmas and New Year's leave from Officers' Training School in San Antonio — yes, it was predictable that he would become an officer — the baby so joyfully conceived in Battle Creek the previous spring, was born. Apparently it had been dead inside me for days or weeks. My labor, though on schedule, was abnormal. I was nauseated and faint due to internal hemorrhaging. "Premature separation of the placenta" was the medical term that I heard in my fog of pain and depression. A Cesarean section was performed, and afterwards I lay like a stone next to a woman whose healthy infant was brought to nurse every four hours. I heard that infant bleat. "La, la, la." I heard the mother coo, the relatives admire. For ten days I lay there, unmoving, in Alta Bates Hospital where I had been born.

After the loss of the baby who would have been Stephen, had he lived, I returned to my parents' home. (*And then the Stephen we had several years later, the one who lived so intensely and had such an impact on the lives of everyone who knew him, who died this past spring not quite a year after Jack did, would he have been born at all?*) I returned to my parents' home on LaLoma Avenue where I had spent my idyllic childhood, where Tommy and I had been living the past year-and-a-half while the war went on and on, and Jack had still not gone overseas but had been sent from training camp to training camp and was now about to become a second lieutenant in military government and be posted in Washington DC with the Provost Marshall General's Office. Ted had been drafted and was somewhere in Burma, and Deborah's husband, Jim, was a Navy doctor in the Pacific, and all five of my male cousins were in some sort of service, at least two of them fliers overseas, one who had to parachute to safety over France where he was hidden by partisans for a while, and another with an ambulance corps, as I recall, somewhere in Africa.

Now our luck, too, seemed to have left us, with the loss of the baby. I was back in my parents' bed in the upside-down house with the master bedroom on the top floor in the southwest corner from which the view of San Francisco and the Golden Gate was spectacular, from which Teddy, sick, had watched the explosion, where each of us children were nursed when ill because it was more convenient for Mother to care for us there on the same floor as the kitchen and living room and dining room and study instead of running down stairs with trays to our bedrooms on the floor below. Deborah had attacks of acidosis, Teddy had asthma, and I had many colds and earaches, and Mother, before the days of Kleenex, tore up old rags for throw-away handkerchiefs.

I seemed to be a helpless child again, back in that bed. I lay still like a stone and saw my two-year-old Tommy develop a puzzled expression as he watched his supine mother. And then, because I'd hardly moved since my Cesarean two weeks before, I developed a blood clot in my groin, so back to the hospital I went for surgery again, abandoning my anxious hyperactive two-year-old again. This time, instead of the cooing mother of a newborn baby, my roommate was a trashy, loud-mouthed girl who'd had her appendix removed, but that didn't keep her sailor boyfriend from climbing right into her hospital bed during visiting hours. Thank God, in those days visiting hours were strictly observed and did not go on and on throughout the day and night. I had no tolerance for such carefree pleasure.

My depression worsened. Did I write Jack all this? We couldn't easily telephone each other. Mail was slow and inadequate as I remember. I felt completely cut off from him, worrying alone about Tommy whose deep-set hazel eyes gazed at me sadly those days I was home, and I worried, too, about my overburdened parents, who were taking care of him and dealing with their own anxieties about the war. They were terribly concerned about Ted, and being pacifists by inclination were naturally conflicted as German Jewish scholars began to arrive in

Berkeley, apparently refugees from Hitler's policies, although, of course, we didn't know about the ultimate horrors of the camps until the war was over.

Some of my parents' friends were America Firsters, others may well have been communists. Still others, including some relatives, were superpatriots, especially Aunt Elsa, who had returned from London when the blitz began, lived in Cambridge with Aunt Lucy, where they both did war relief work for Britain and China. I remember some correspondence from Aunt Elsa to Mother, reprimanding her for faint-heartedness, vis-a-vis concern for Ted. It was supposed to be an honor to send one's son off to war. Aunt Elsa had no children and I found her cruelty unbelievable. I also remember the thoughtless remark Jack's mother made to his Aunt Ruth after Donald was killed: "Well, you sent him to military school. What did you expect?"

It's hard to believe, now, how badly friendships and family ties were strained and sometimes broken. Mother salved her conscience about the Jews and innocent soldiers by becoming active in the Red Cross. She always claimed to be a manual moron, but she learned to knit socks and scarves for the soldiers. And finally Daddy obtained a top-secret job with the OSS, something to do with psychological testing for potential spies. He periodically went to some hideaway near Washington. (*What would he have thought of OSS's successor, the CIA?*) His older brother, the physicist, my Uncle Dick, was working in Washington then, also secretly, for General Groves and The Manhattan Project, as it turned out.

At last Tommy and I were to join Jack in Washington, to live together as a family again, although the future was uncertain: the war continued; I'd been notified that my blood type was RH Negative, a new discovery that must have accounted for the recent stillbirth of our baby, and that would make subsequent pregnancies risky; and I was still frail with a postoperative gimpy leg that had to be wrapped in an Ace Bandage from crotch to ankle. That long cross-country train trip, however, proved to be therapeutic. I had a leash and harness — very like the one I now have for Mellow — because Tommy had never learned to walk, only to run. (Now my infirmity, as I'm pulled by my dog, is arthritic knees, detritus of age.) People in wartime care for each other. My father, the pacifist, who was fired for that reason from Northwestern before I was born, once wrote a book titled Drives Toward War, which touches on some of the psychological aspects of war. Our fellow passengers on that train were eager to help me with Tommy.

The last time I'd been on a train was the Battle Creek trip when the baby just lost had been conceived. I quickly deleted the memory of that happiness that ended in despair and scrolled backwards to other train trips — on our way to MIT, for instance, where Jack was going to attend graduate school in City Planning and I was going to have our first baby — Tommy, this same Tommy — and then when we came home again, also by train, to show him off a few months later. Even today I still have to laugh at how I panicked, suddenly, at the new responsibility of motherhood — I would never again be able to go out to lunch, do anything at all, on the spur of the moment, I realized as I looked down at the perfectly beautiful baby that somehow was ours. All during my pregnancy I had worried that I could never love a baby as much as I loved my dog Erich, but of course I was wrong. We adored this baby. Thank goodness, at the last minute, we decided **not** to name him Gleb, a good Russian Revolutionary name, as we had planned, for how could we break the line of Thomas Kents? Jack's grandfather was Thomas Edwin, his father Thomas John, he Thomas John, Jr., and our Tommy, Thomas Edward after his two grandfathers. Now his eldest son is the fifth, Thomas Grayson, twenty-five years old this month.)

So much a part of my growing up was going East on the train to visit our relatives in New England, five nights, four days of heavenly clickety-clack, mesmerized by the ribbon of tracks retreating westward behind the observation car as speckles of soot settled onto my clothes (a favorite yellow pique dress I particularly remember), of meals — white tablecloth, a rose in a bud vase, a solicitous black waiter hanging over me as though I were grown-up — and the wonderful sleeping arrangements behind green baize curtains, looking out at the little towns in the night, sometimes staring right into a face that watched the train fly by, like Walker Evans photographs.

And from fantasies of earlier train trips I moved on to memories of our blissful, leisurely courtship, Jack's and mine, carried on after that first rush of recognition in the summer of '38 when we went on a hike over the Inverness Ridge, "rabbiting" as he called it which meant cross-country regardless of trails, down to Drakes Bay and got lost for a while, but ended up in front of the fire at his family's cabin, lying on the floor, touching hands, the wooing carried on by correspondence back and forth between Freiburg, Germany and Scripps College in Claremont, California for a year.

The time frame and backdrop of our courtship was, of course, the war. In the spring of 1938, as we each graduated, I from high school at the Anna Head School for Girls and he from the University of California at Berkeley, Hitler had recently annexed Austria to the Third Reich and the Vatican had recognized Franco as leader of Spain. In that summer when he finally noticed me, the Japanese were bombing Canton. He left for Germany, a most inappropriate place to go at that time, but a year's exchange fellowship had been arranged by his fraternity. It gave him a convenient respite in which to figure out what to do, since he had determined at the time of his graduation that he would never practice a day of architecture in his life. He had become a social radical, and architects, like his father whose firm he was probably supposed to enter, only built houses for the rich, or so he thought in his youthful rebellion. Much later he felt that he'd treated his father, whom he loved and respected, unkindly, but I'm sure he was just as understanding of the necessity of sons breaking away from their fathers as Jack was, so superbly, with his own three sons. I often told him that. His father, I'm sure, was immensely proud of him, even though he chose a different route, and I hope Jack finally knew it in his heart.

He had begun to read Lewis Mumford, and was so impressed by his "Culture of Cities," that before he went to Germany he arranged to meet with Mumford and asked him to be his informal advisor as to what he should read, what and whom he should see in Europe. Such youthful nerve! Jack never lost that nerve, a kind of creative optimism where anything was possible, even the way in which he died, at home with all of us, as though it were another wonderful family party.

43

Our love letters from 1938 and 1939 record the heightening of anxiety as German troops marched into Sudetenland, as Kristellnacht occurred, as the Germans marched into Bohemia, then Prague, then Danzig, and on and on. We seemed to reach toward each other in those letters, Jack, so close to these ominous events, for comfort perhaps, and I for guidance as I at last began to open my mind. That year I wrote a paper on "Jesus and Socrates." I studied painting with Millard Sheets. I read French and English literature. I went out with a variety of young men from football players at Pomona to brainy students at Cal Tech. I skied, I smoked, I swam and entered into dormitory life, but the backdrop of my life was the war and Jack to whom I wrote all those letters, the ones I found, with his to me, after he died.

May 9, 1939 — In response to a recent trip he'd taken to Switzerland, I reminisced about my own memories of that country when I was in boarding school. "It seemed almost unreal, for the blue of the lake was too intense, and the green of the mountains too green, the flowers too many, and the mountains jutting out of the calm, cool valleys much too bold. It is a fairyland in the middle of the bickering European countries around it."

May 24, 1939 — "I hate to end these letters, for, although they are stumbling and vague, they are my favorite occupation; they are a record of my hopes and aspirations; they are everything just because I write them for you. . . . I wish I could hide in your coat from happiness." There are several references to this coat, also to a "green valley," something we must have seen on that famous hike in Inverness.

The letters read like a Jane Austen novel, as the language of endearment gradually grew — Dear, Dearest, Darling, Darlingest and we used pet names more often. He called me *Duck*, I called him *Rum-Dum*. And then he came home and the passion intensified, until one day in the summer of 1940 my father asked me, "Is Jack Kent tampering with your affections?" This, too, sounded like a Jane Austen novel and I think I burst out laughing. This language from my father's mouth was totally uncharacteristic. Was he joking? Perhaps it was the only way he could broach a subject so intimate. But it worked. I told Jack what he'd said. We laughed hilariously for a while, then looked at each other. Were we...? Should we... ? Well, what next? Apparently we couldn't go on forever necking furiously in wooded glens, on remote beaches and grassy hillsides. Jack's budding career as a city planner might take him anywhere, even back to graduate school. Talk of drafting young unmarried men into the military was getting louder too.

He came for dinner with a box of candy. He and my father played out the game with great wit, even to sending me and Mother out of the living room after dinner while Jack formally asked for my hand. I have a photo of that evening, or one at about that time — a profile of him that shows off his adorable nose, his mischievous smile curved around his pipe, sitting back comfortably in my father's favorite chair by the fire, his long legs crossed — and his grin was probably for my father, whose own grin I can also imagine, though his would have been wrapped around a cigarette instead of a pipe.

Jack was like my father in many ways. Of course. That's what girls are apt to do, go out and subconsciously look for a replica of that first man in their lives. Sometimes it's the other way around. A boy looks for a replica of his mother. Oh, I wish we could talk and laugh together, about those other girls before me, Margery especially. Why, yes, she *is* like Jack's mother — full-breasted, flirtatious, exuberant. She has even aged in the same way Jack's mother, Belinda, did, joking her way through difficult aspects of aging, still cinching in her waist, wearing stockings and heels, keeping up her morale by keeping up appearances. Margery has guts; I can see that because she's of my generation. And this makes me see that Jack's mother, too, had guts. They both tug at my heart, though I go about the business of living and aging quite differently.

Margery rejected Jack, so I caught him on the rebound. Well, not really. He swore off romance for awhile, after a bout with mononucleosis that was probably brought on by the shock of being spurned, then he enjoyed being a serious student at Cal in the School of Architecture and one of the rebels of course, who questioned the Beaux Arts tradition, active at Stiles Hall (the campus YMCA where even communists were allowed to speak!), captain of the first Cal championship water polo team that almost made it to the Olympic Games, member of the Student Judicial Committee, Rhodes Scholar candidate, and when he had recovered completely from Margery, there I was, as I'd been all along, with, according to Steve, my sexy Achilles heels. Lucky, lucky me.

———•———

We are always living in history of course, but in wartime the contrast between the mundane — ironing Jack's summer khaki uniforms, pulling my whining child to the store, standing in lines with ration books — and the momentous — seeing people crying on the streets after Roosevelt died — was intense, especially in Washington DC (Years later we read a wonderful book aloud: *History: A Novel,* by an Italian woman, Elsa Moranti, about ordinary life in times of war. The title says it all.)

Tommy and I finally arrived to join Jack there in March, just about the time that the British invasion of a Japanese base cut Burma in two. My brother Ted was in Burma, we thought, but weren't sure. The Russians took Danzig then too, and crossed from Hungary into Austria.

Housing was tight. We had to stay, at first, with my Uncle Dick and Aunt Ruth, who were part of the wave of scientists and intellectuals who came to Washington to work in connection with the war, some of it secret, just as my father had. Uncle Dick, a physicist, disappeared periodically, then returned with silver and turquoise jewelry for Aunt Ruth. That should have been a clue. Jack and I and Tommy slept in a commodious family room, directly beneath the dining room, in their rented house in the Northwest section of town, where, in the evenings, we heard Aunt Ruth scrubbing the hardwood floor under the dining room table and just over our heads. Tommy had apparently made a mess with his supper. He still wet his bed. Oh, dear. Their life was gracious and orderly. They had no children, only a succession of wire-haired terriers.

My father had always made psychological jokes about himself in relation to his brilliant older brother. And Aunt Ruth was brilliant too, a psychologist, urbane, attractive. My father took care of his inferiority complex with jokes. In time I understood that he adored them both, but I'd never been at ease with them. When Uncle Dick was teaching at Cal Tech and I was a student at Scripps, they invited me for occasional weekends, arranged blind dates for me with brainy Cal Tech students, provided tickets to the Pasadena Playhouse, had both Frank and Robert Oppenheimer for dinner. Again I was struck dumb with awe as I'd been at those tea parties at my parents' house on LaLoma Avenue during my childhood. And again my awe translated into a streak of stubborn anti-intellectualism. Jack knew all about that for I pulled the same thing on him.

In Washington we were on a list for an apartment at McLean Gardens on Massachusetts Avenue, but we couldn't stand the tension at Uncle Dick and Aunt Ruth's, so in the interim we rented two rooms (including kitchen privileges) in the Bethesda house of a one-armed taxi driver and his very domestic wife, who never took off her apron. Why in the world would a man with one arm decide to drive a taxi? We never could ask him, of course, but somehow they were a refreshing contrast to my worldly relatives. It was nice in that house, set in pretty woods full of fresh spring green leaves and dogwood coming out. At last we were alone together, like a family again. At night we sat on the bed after we put Tommy to sleep in his room and played chess on that cute little miniature chess set we had for traveling. The men were less than an inch high and were stored in a small drawer fitted right into the six inch by six inch board. I wonder what happened to it. Tommy crayoned on the brand new flowery wallpaper by his bed. I can't remember how we made reparations for that.

We didn't have a car and wouldn't for several months, so Tommy and I were stuck out there and Jack had a long bus ride to work, but by April we were in our own apartment. McClean Gardens was a rather new, imposing red brick colonial arrangement of several four-storied apartment buildings grouped around large lawns. There was a sandbox and jungle gym and swings for the kids. It looked like a college campus and felt like an Army Base, but with furniture sent from home by the Army — the Aalto chair, the mattress and box springs that doubled as a couch, the record player and radio and Tommy's crib, the Gladding McBean pottery ware and pots and pans — it soon felt familiar and nice. We didn't have much. All the fancy wedding present china, silver, crystal was stored in barrels in my parents' basement, along with Mrs. Oshida's trunks. But we were so glad at last to have a home of our own again. We bought a card table and four folding chairs. I made curtains out of bed sheets and nurtured several potato plants that became quite lush, even trailing along the window sills by the end of the year that we lived there. The apartment was small but adequate. Tommy had the one bedroom and we slept in the living room. It was cheery with clean white walls and cross ventilation, which at least gave the illusion of relief from the humid heat of the summer to come.

But before that there was spring. We went to see the cherry blossoms in bloom around the Washington Basin, the Jefferson and Lincoln Monuments, for they were among Jack's heroes. (About fourteen years later we did this same pilgrimage with Steve and Dave; thirty year later with Tom's son Fletcher. By then there was another Memorial erected on the Mall commemorating the Vietnam Veterans. Now there's one for Roosevelt too. About time! I don't suppose I'll ever go to Washington again.) We walked in the woods behind our apartment full of dogwood in flower. We walked in Rock Creek Park. Washington is a beautiful city, at least it was then, especially in springtime. That's when Roosevelt died, in April. We were in a taxi and the driver told us, and looking out the window we saw people standing on the street corners, sobbing. I was sobbing too. He'd been president since I was eleven years old.

In San Francisco the United Nations Conference was held that April also, and perhaps there was a similar feeling there of being at the center of history. In Europe, Vienna was liberated, and the concentration camp at Bergen-Belsen. On my twenty-fourth birthday, April 17, we heard that U.S. troops had liberated Buchenwald, and the horrible facts of these camps began to be known at the very same time that Jack and I seemed to be falling in love all over again. April 20 Nuremberg fell to the Allies, April 28 Mussolini was executed, April 30 U.S. troops liberated Dachau, April 30 Hitler shot himself, May 2 all the one million German troops in Italy and Austria surrendered. On June 5, a whole year after D-Day, the war in Europe was finally over.

Washington summers are awful — hot and humid with no relief. We both developed sinus trouble. The sleepless headachy nights, the noisy parties given by the Swedish diplomat who lived below us contributing to our insomnia, the cockroaches that scuttled under the kitchen sink were the negatives. And Jack's job was pretty boring, sitting at a desk in uniform and necktie in that un-air-conditioned Munitions Building, answering complaints and fears of citizens who lived near prisoner of war camps in the Southern states. I don't know what Jack knew about any of that, but he was a nice guy, probably reassuring. I was amazed that we had German and Italian prisoners brought to America.

My job as a housewife was boring too. The heat, the uncertainty and anxiety of wartime made even the simplest tasks seem difficult. My job as a mother, I felt strongly, was to keep my boy child from playing with guns. Ha! Impossible! All the boys in the communal playground had toy guns. Tommy's best friend was a little guy named Scotty. He had a GI haircut, chewed gum, and acted tough just like his sergeant dad. Tommy and Scotty played war all summer while the real war dragged on. But there were also intense, if unlikely, friendships growing out of mutual anxiety — other mothers with young children, people from parts of the country (Ada, Oklahoma, and Cleveland, Ohio) we never would have known except for the war. And there were quite a few old friends and acquaintances from home who were working, both as civilians and in the military, in Washington. Gordon Griffith, who had grown up right around the corner from me in Berkeley, was there working for the Board of Economic Warfare. His English wife, Mary, worked for the British Embassy. A few years earlier, just after the war broke out in Europe and Jack was temporarily stranded, they had let him spend a few nights on the living room floor of their student flat in Oxford. They were probably communists, as were plenty of young idealists at that time (as Jack himself might have been except, he claimed, nobody ever asked him to join), the very ones who less than a decade later would be targeted by Senator McCarthy.

On July 16, my Uncle Dick was away again on one of his secret missions. We later learned, of course, that that was the day that the first atomic bomb tests took place in the New Mexico desert. Again he brought Aunt Ruth some beautiful silver and turquoise jewelry. On August 6 the bomb was dropped on Hiroshima, August 8 on Nagasaki, and on August 14 the Japanese surrendered. The war had ended at last, but now the interminable and arguably more difficult job of mending everything began. Nothing, after the bomb, could ever be the same, although it took a while for that to sink in.

More real to us was that we were to be separated again — Jack and I, Jack and Tommy — just when other families in the service were being reunited. In September he was sent to Berlin as part of the reconstruction effort. In fact, I believe Gordon Griffith and Bruce Wayburn had something to do with getting him that opportunity. Once more there were heartbreaking letters from him about the destruction of Germany and the despair of her people. We decided that I should stay in Washington, since there was the slight possibility that Tommy and I might join him in Berlin. I got a job — my first and last real paid job in my whole life — with the National Planning Association. I liked it a lot. Tommy went to a day care for children of working parents, quite a new idea in those days. But he, of course, picked up germs, and I had to juggle baby sitters and sometimes take time off. My letters to Jack of that time are full of his coughs and earaches and trips to Walter Reed Hospital. There are also references to adoption, since we still thought we couldn't safely have any more babies of our own. Then, one day I received a letter from Alta Bates Hospital in Berkeley, saying that the blood test they had given me back in January had been in error. I was not RH negative after all!

Chapter Four

And that was the beginning of Steve, the idea of him. Jack was still in Germany, I worked throughout that snowy winter. But then, Jack came back in April and we were finally on our way home in our black Dodge convertible. Tommy was a wonderful traveler, occupying his own private space behind the seat where we'd set up a bed of pillows and blankets for him. He thought that each tourist home or motel along the way was where we were going to settle but then, stoically got into the car again for another day of travel, and welcomed the next overnight stop with revived enthusiasm. A traveling child of war, in his three and a half years he had already lived in five different homes, some of them twice. (He would be seven years old before we spent two consecutive Christmases in the same house. That was on Scenic Avenue, our tenth home, Tommy's eighth, Stevie's second. This doesn't count Inverness, where we went every summer. Maybe that's why today, at fifty-six, Tom's such a homebody.) I remember him sitting in a vast desert somewhere near Santa Fe, his head bent over his Tootsie-Toy cars that he was arranging in an intricate pattern of roads in the sand. I remember another desert on that trip and the surreal vision of unending acres of crippled airplanes, the detritus of war. But we were heading home that April of 1946. Only a little over one year later, on June 16, 1947, Stephen William Kent was born by cesarean section at Children's Hospital in San Francisco.

He, more than Tom before him or David after him, seemed to

51

arrive in this world with his personality completely formed. He yelled and his little face was furious and red, his hair as black and shiny as the Miwok arrowheads we sometimes find in Inverness. Even then his eyebrows were distinctive, a premonition of the thick black eyebrows that so distinguished him as a man. There's a picture of my grandfather Drew with those same eyebrows. The black hair of his infancy soon turned to the reddish-brown it remained throughout his childhood, sometimes bleaching out to almost blond in summer, and then becoming thick and curly in his early twenties, perfect for the hirsute '60s. In the end it was iron gray.

Nowadays when there's a family party, Steve's and Jack's absence jars, suddenly, all over again each time, as though a couple of outrageous guests have failed to show. It causes awkwardness in all of our behaviors, especially in Tom and Dave in relation to Steve. Sons expect their fathers to die, but brothers? And his position in the middle gave him the power of the go-between as well as a convenient joint adversary for them. (I know this well, also being a middle child, and remember both protecting my little brother from our older sister and our parents, but also using him as a scapegoat if need be.) In dying at only fifty-one, Steve left them not only feeling vulnerable to death themselves, but also, or so it seems to me as I observe them, shy as they relate to each other without him there in the middle. His power and influence over people was immense and in death has taken on almost mythic significance.

His being gay only added to the mystique, and made him a challenger. What were we all to make of this difficult fact? Even the word, "gay" was stolen by his generation of homosexuals, changing forever a lovely word, it seemed to me. *Roget's Thesaurus* lists *lively, vivacious, blithe, convivial, festive* as synonyms. Ah, but now I see in my father's *American College Dictionary* the fourth meaning given is *dissipated; licentious.* Once again he seemed to be in on some knowledge that he got from somewhere other than at home or school. In the days of his childhood, homosexuality was considered a problem that could be cured.

At Children's Community Center, the co-op nursery school Steve attended, we, as a family, were plunged into our first involvement with a whole community of families and teachers with pretty radical theories about child development, also politics in general, a curious mix of over-permissiveness and doctrinaire Marxism. Jack and I stumbled around somewhere in the middle of these extremes, being both stricter parents and more moderate in political theory than some. This was the early fifties, a time when many in our generation began to be politically active, and Children's Community Center was our training ground in how to participate and cooperate and reach consensus, thanks to Steve who had a difficult habit of biting other children, especially the girls. An emergency meeting was called to discuss him. A child psychologist who observed his play patterns — opting to play with dolls instead of trucks — declared that his older macho brother was the cause of his behavior. He did not wish to compete with Tom. So we put aside our suspicions and anxieties, and turned our energies to neighborhood precinct work for Helen Gahagan Douglas, who was being victimized by McCarthy and Nixon.

Steve always intrigued and charmed his teachers though they couldn't teach him to read. He was a favorite with all the neighborhood parents, and at dinner time I had a long list of phone numbers handy. We didn't have TV. It was against our principles, although of course we relented eventually. We were the last parents on the block to get a set, so Steve was either at the Lawrences, the Damis, the Worswicks, the Hayeses, the Choys, the Schevills, the LaRues, or the Bratenahls. Early on he had more girlfriends than either of his brothers, so of course he was not homosexual.

His grandparents never knew. Three of them had died before he came out of the closet when he was twenty-one. But before that he had a brief, sweet marriage to Annemarie, whom he'd met at Friends World Institute, the Quaker College he attended in New York and Europe. Jack's mother, Nana, flew with us to the wedding, a wonderful hippie affair on a Long Island Beach. Annemarie wore a miniskirt and Steve, a leather vest. They both were barefoot, but the heels of Nana's high-heeled shoes sank into the sand, I remember. Nana was in her eighties by then, and quite delusional and disconnected from reality.

Annemarie's family was Catholic. Her mother was dying of cancer. That's probably why they had to get married, because of her dying mother. Yet that marriage was so touching. They lived for a while in a tent on our Inverness property, then moved into the cabin, that love nest where all three of the boys had affairs and marriages, and now the next generation is doing the same. Both of them worked as dishwashers at Manka's Lodge, and would sometimes bring us treats of rich cheese cake or strudel. They grew vegetables and pot — Jack and I thought those were tomato plants — and raised chickens and rabbits and goats, and owned several hound dogs. Our quiet green valley by the bubbling creek became an automotive junkyard full of noise and mess and sweat as Eastmans, Shoemakers, Whitneys, and Kents took apart and reconstructed a variety of vehicles. Steve and Annemarie had beautiful young bodies and swam in the nude, for this was the '60s.

But the marriage only lasted about a year and a half, though I know they loved each other on some level. Steve told me so over the years. He had other women from time to time. There was, of course, Judy, and that Ute from Sweden who hauled river stones from the Eel and created garden paths. I could have told her not to try to domesticate him. There was Ruby with the bright red hair and a two-year-old child. I suppose he was bisexual, but just as one drop of Negro blood makes one black, bisexual means homosexual in our society. I asked him once what the difference was between sex with men and women. "Women want damn commitment," he said. And it's true, he could never have stood commitment, to one woman or one man. Annemarie went to nursing school after he abandoned her, met a doctor with children, and married him. She never had children of her own, though she had a miscarriage when Steve and she were married. Of my four ex-daughters-in-law, she is the one I felt saddest to lose. She lives in Massachusetts and wrote me a sweet but rather distant note after Steve died.

I sometimes think that my father, Steve's grandpa, might have been bisexual, without ever admitting it to himself. He, too, had a strong older brother to compete with. One of his parlor tricks was a scarf dance a la Isadora Duncan. (He was a wonderful dancer. I adored being waltzed around the living room by him when I was young.) Once he warned Jack not to make too much of his artistic accomplishments or tendencies in a job application; he might be considered effeminate. My parents often slept in separate beds, even separate rooms, he on a sleeping porch off their bedroom, the excuse being his allergies to dust. And yet, as I have already mentioned, theirs was an exceptionally good marriage.

Steve, picking up on family lore, as he was wont to do, speculated that Nana's father, Thomas Stanton, might have been gay. He was a railway man, and was divorced by Nana's mother, the beautiful Louise, presumably because when little Belinda (Nana) was old enough to go to school they could no longer roam around, living on a caboose. He was seventeen years older than his wife, forty-eight years old when Nana was born.

"We don't have divorces in our family!" Nana protested decades later as all five of her grandchildren, one after the other, got divorced. Her denial, I think now, was rather touching. How else can one survive the violence and sadness that abounds in the world, the disappointments of life?

Jack only met that grandfather once in his life. He remembered a large man in formal dark clothes coming to the door at San Benito Way in San Francisco when he was a boy. Thomas Stanton ended his days not far from where Steve ended his in Humboldt County, in a little railroad town where he was known to love all the children, who called him "uncle Tom," so the obituary said.

The evening before Steve's scheduled birth by cesarean, Jack and Tommy, who was only five, and I went to Chinatown for an early dinner before I was due to check in at the hospital at 8:00, and Tommy to go stay with my sister Deborah in Berkeley. I don't remember how we thought of this zany kickoff to the events of Steve's birth. Everything was ready for him — the bassinet and crib and diapers and Carters baby shirts and wrapping blankets, just the necessary minimum. Nobody had dared to give a baby shower after what happened last time. We were very excited and tried not to be anxious, but of course we were, Jack and I, each separately, after the loss of that first

Stephen. I must ask Tom if he remembers any of this, if he remembers the dinner in Chinatown.

All went wonderfully well. I told Steve the story dozens of times, because when he learned that his had been a cesarean birth, he was mad and felt cheated. But honestly, it was such a thrill! There was no pain or discomfort at all, only what felt like a pin deftly tracing the line of incision, and there he was, yelling at me. Before Tommy was born I was knocked out with twilight sleep and knew nothing of his birth. I would not have believed I'd been through that long labor except for the fact that my elbows were black and blue. (Now, of course, I feel cheated, as I hear the tales of childbirth from the younger generation of women who have had home births with midwives and husbands and even siblings of the newborn in attendance.) Jack was the one who lived that birth. My God, it was his first baby too, and we couldn't quite make up our minds when to go to the hospital. Were these really contractions? I began washing socks and underwear. We'd both learned how to cook, sort of, but Jack hadn't a clue about laundry in those days. Finally we took a taxi to Boston Lying In Hospital and pretty soon I was put out. There was a terrible fire in a night club, The Coconut Grove, that night, and ambulances kept wailing through the night. Jack learned later that dozens of people had been trapped in the fire as he waited for Tommy to be born.

We lived in a little stucco house on Fifteenth Avenue in San Francisco when Steve was born, near the Zoo and the sand dunes and ocean beach, only a few blocks from where Jack had grown up in St. Francis Wood, but this was on the opposite side of West Portal, the shopping street, and not such a classy neighborhood, only a few blocks from where he zipped through Cub Scouts and Boy Scouts at the Forest Hills Club House. He got merit badges as fast as he could — birds, ferns, knots — until he got to be an Eagle Scout, then quit.

The houses were, like ours, mostly one-story above a garage, painted brick-red concrete steps leading up to the small stoop and front door, with a little patch of lawn in front and a tiny backyard. All the rooms — living room, dining room, kitchen, bathroom, two bedrooms — were small, but there were plenty of windows and light. The large bay window in the living room faced west and the wooded grounds of a Christian Science Home across the street, and to the south, just outside our front door was a vacant lot that in the spring and summer was full of colorful, fragrant wild mustard. The street was quiet, even though we were right around the corner from busy West Portal. It was like a village.

We felt lucky, having moved from the Hunters Point Housing Project, which, though fascinating and stimulating because of the sociological and racial mix, and the dramatic view of the city and Bay so different from the ones we were used to, was cramped and noisy and stressful with the nauseating stink that wafted up the hill from the tannery works below. We hoped that our neighbors at Hunters Point, mostly black or blue-collar whites who'd come west to work in the shipyards during the war, kind and friendly folk who gave Tommy a puppy, and tolerated him at the nursery school where he was one of three white children, would not see the article announcing Jack's promotion from acting director to director of planning for the city of San Francisco with a salary that was embarrassingly ample. *"KENT TO HEAD PLANNING COMMISSION...Kent is 29 and the youngest city planning director in the country and one of the youngest men to head any of the city departments... ."* But one set of neighbors did. They stuck the article under our door with a note attached. *"Congratulations and a Happy and Prosperous New Year, Eddie and Sadie Lother."* They came from Oklahoma and were the ones who'd given Tommy the puppy.

In the Fifteenth Avenue house there was, of course, a fireplace, which, as everyone in the family knows, was one of Jack's great pleasures, and he'd been without one in Washington and at Hunters Point. I can still see him squatting on the hearth, making fires, or lounging in a big armchair in front of the fire, or sitting on the footstool, a driftwood poker shiny with age in his hands, poking the fire, or just gazing into it. In the summers he collected wood on ocean beaches for pokers, for construction projects, or just for beauty. He built bonfires on beaches to cook on, to sing around, while the children were building dams against the rising tide, dropping their hot dogs in the sand, or falling asleep in somebody's lap.

Our first apartment, when Jack was twenty-three, working for the National Resources Planning Board in the main Berkeley Post Office for $150 a month, and I was nineteen, in the middle of my junior year at Cal, had three fireplaces, one in each of the three rooms that wrapped around a central chimney. What a way to begin married life. I could barely cook, but it didn't seem to matter as long as Jack could have his fires. The apartment was at 2665 Shasta Road in Berkeley, only a block from where I sit writing this fifty-eight years later, and had recently been vacated by Robert Oppenheimer. Yes, there he was again, playing Spanish Civil War songs on his phonograph when we went to look at the apartment; he was also about to get married.

Before that, on our honeymoon, after roaming around the Mendocino Coast, looking at romantic ghost towns and graveyards in the rain, we ended up at Jack's family's Inverness cottage, where it had all begun with our first hand-holding three-and-a-half years earlier. This was in January and the kitchen roof leaked onto the old wood stove. My first cooking attempts were disastrous, but again, it hadn't seemed to matter. Jack had his fireplace, the one that he and Ganks had built during the Depression. We cooked steaks with sprigs of bay leaves over the flames. We slept in the big double bed there right next to it. I've noticed in honeymoon pictures how dreamy and glazed-over the faces are, stupid with love. There are pictures like that of my parents on the beach at Annisquam on Gloucester Bay in Massachusetts. There are pictures like that of Jack and me on Ten Mile Beach at Point Reyes.

As for cooking, here is a quote from a letter Jack wrote to my parents — they were in Tucson on sabbatical leave — soon after we were married. "Mary's cooking is having outstanding successes and difficulties. Boiled onions, cauliflower, artichokes, potatoes and Brown Betty have been notably conquered; and the salads are, of course, excellent." My mother, who became a very good leftover cook on the maid's day off, had taught me how to make cream sauce, which I translated into creamed chipped beef over toast. Another of my supper dishes was poached egg on top of canned corned beef hash.

At the house on Fifteenth Avenue Steve slept in a pink crib (I suppose we wanted or expected a girl) in a little dressing room, with a window, off our bedroom. Tommy threw blocks and broken crayons out of his bedroom window onto our neighbor's lawn. I can't remember her name, but she made a fuss. I guess he was bored. But pretty soon he went to kindergarten at Commodore Sloat School, where Jack had gone and had his first successes in the less competitive world of those days. He was cheerleader. He also had his first (and last) fist fight, got a bloody nose, lost the fight and was further humiliated when he went home and his mother burst out laughing when she saw him. I'm still mad at her, when I think about that.

We lived in that nice little house for about a year and a half in 1947-48. I remember feeding Steve his bottle in the middle of the night, lying on the living room sofa we had recently purchased from The City of Paris Department Store on Union Square downtown, reading *The New Yorker,* and thinking what a lovely life — this baby, this story, the rest of the world asleep, at peace in this postwar era. Those nights, feeding him, were divine. Jack's career was zooming. He was smoking cigars and putting on weight from all those martini lunches. We bought an Aalto dining room table and coffee table and began collecting phonograph records. Brahms, Beethoven, Louis Armstrong, Burl Ives. We were learning to entertain. Tommy's puppy, Micky, one of a long succession of dogs and cats, was run over up on West Portal. The next dog was a black cocker spaniel named George.

But everything changed again when Jack was invited to create a new Department of City Planning at the University. He leapt at the chance. *The San Francisco Chronicle* wrote, "T. J. Kent, Jr., who quit his $10,000-year job as city planner yesterday to become a $6,000 department head at the University of California, received glowing recommendations from many San Francisco officials. 'Only since Kent came to the planning commission had that body gone anywhere…we're losing a very good man…Kent has had an outstanding record for the past 10 years.'" Etc., etc. In the fall of 1948 we moved to a big house on Scenic Avenue in Berkeley. That's where we lived when Dave was born and that's where we had the first two consecutive Christmases in one house.

September 1999

I talked to Tom on the phone today and he said, "It's been six months." I had not remembered, but perhaps that explains the odd way I felt when I awoke this morning, empty, weak. I went back to bed after feeding Mellow and slept a couple of hours. It's the autumnal equinox. I remember the awe I felt last March at the time of the vernal equinox as I watched the radiant sunset, even though I did not yet know that Steve had died.

This evening I came up here to Jack's study where I was six months ago. The sun was an enormous orange ball, parts of it disappearing behind banks of fog that drifted and moved so that sometimes it seemed to be rising instead of setting behind the fog and the pink-edged clouds, and then because I'd stared at it too long the sun turned blue. One can imagine believing in the sort of God depicted by William Blake, rays of light extending from His outstretched hand. Is this how Steve thought of Him? Later, in the middle of the night, there was a thunder and lightning storm, another sound and light show in memory of Steve and Jack. Mellow and I climbed up here. I opened the door to the deck and huddled together we watched the jagged needles of light that lit up the sky. Thunder rolled and roared and it was awesome. Today I have a headache and feel sad.

I look back on the '50s and '60s with amazement that we could do it all — build a house, raise boys, immerse ourselves in politics and academia. Well, we were young. In 1950 I was twenty-nine, Jack was thirty-three. Some of his graduate students were older than we were, so we socialized easily with them. Davie was one year old and still in diapers. *The Year of the Oath,* as George Stewart so aptly named his book, when the U.C. Regents forced teachers at Cal — all the way from teaching assistants to full professors — to sign a "special oath" proclaiming they were not, nor ever had been, communists, literally came to an end, though its ramifications were endless. Jack reluctantly signed, my father did not, but both of them were deeply involved in the fight against it. My father, in fact, became somewhat of a national hero, though he always insisted he didn't want to be thought of as such, and even advised young vulnerable professors, like Jack, to sign and keep their jobs, that he was nearing retirement anyway and could afford to be dismissed, which he was.

Hero or not, he was the one who first stood up in the Academic Senate meeting and said he wouldn't sign, giving courage to others to follow his lead. Yale gave him an honorary degree, praising him for his contributions to the science of psychology, but also as "a valiant defender of the freedom of the human mind." The University of Chicago hired him, though he did come back to Cal in the end when the fight had been won and received yet another honorary degree. (David, then ten, sat in agonized boredom in the Greek Theater, his head in his hands, reluctantly bearing witness to this important event.) I don't think my mother, who was on the Board of the ACLU, who almost always voted for Eugene Debs or Norman Thomas, ever recovered from the stress of losing friends in the now divided University community and of having her convictions severely challenged. This year is the fiftieth anniversary of The Year of the Oath. There was a two-day symposium reassessing and commemorating the event at which both Jack and Daddy were honored along with the others. Many old friends and memories, and I was proud and weepy. Someone from the Bancroft Library is coming on Monday to interview me about my recollections.

Also in 1950 the Korean War broke out and Deborah's husband Jim had to serve for a time as a Naval reservist. Senator McCarthy began his witch hunt. But we built that house and raised those boys and many dogs and cats. Jack launched the Department of City and Regional Planning at Cal, and I learned to be a pretty good faculty

61

wife, inviting all his students, year after year, for suppers of spaghetti, salad, garlic bread, red wine. I wonder what we had for dessert. At the same time Jack was first a Berkeley City Planning Commissioner, then an elected City Councilman.

What a time it was for Berkeley and for us, with the final swing from a conservative Republican business-dominated town to a liberal Democratic one. These were the Stevenson years, and with those same nursery school liberals whom we'd met when Steve was biting little girls, we formed a club called The Grassrooters, one of many Democratic clubs that cropped up at that time all over California. In Berkeley there were The Boatrockers, The Young Democrats (both more radical that we), The East Bay Democratic Club, The New Era Club, The Women's Democratic Forum, and probably others.

Damn. If it weren't for Alzheimer's, Jack would undoubtedly have remembered them all and helped me out with the details here, even from the grave, I bet. But never mind. This is not meant to be an accurate account of anything except for my feelings as I recapture the excitement we shared with each other and all those other activists. I am suddenly quite sure that Jack would like what I'm doing here, though he and I have always approached our writing projects so differently. I find myself circling ideas, then connecting the circles. Jack always made an outline.

There was also The 18th Assembly District Precinct Organization (ADPO), the official party coordinating group, and The Berkeley Caucus, made up of representatives of the clubs, which became the umbrella for all this grassroots energy and quite an important political force, endorsing candidates for local offices in both City Council and School Board as well as State Assembly and U.S. Congress. Jim, who had become a successful and much loved Jungian psychiatrist, ran for City Council once and for State Assembly once. I think he was too intellectual to get elected, like Adlai for whom of course we all worked in '52 and '56, though Steve, aged five, declared, *"I like Ike!"* The rascal.

Jack used to brag about me being in charge of all the precincts in Northeast Berkeley, which wasn't quite true, but I thank him anyway.

I also managed three campaigns in those years — Alex Sheriffs for School Board, Winton McKibben for State Assembly, and Joe Grodin for City Council. None of them won, but two of them later became judges. Yes, we had to be young to put out all that energy, going to meetings, walking precincts, talking endlessly on the phone, and going to California Democratic Council meetings in Fresno, Stockton, and Sacramento.

The only time I ever had a traffic accident was during this time with too much on my mind, I guess. Driving west on Addison Street on my way to a printer's with a mocked-up political brochure to work with him on, and going over in my head the agenda for a campaign meeting to be held in our living room later in the day, I drove right through the stop sign at Sixth Street, out into the arterial traffic, suddenly seeing the horrified face of the poor woman who was about to crash into me. I had a few cuts from broken glass, but I wasn't really hurt, except for my pride. The car was totaled, and I had to call Jack to come and get me from the Emergency at Herrick Hospital. I was so embarrassed. Some of my over commitment to politics rubbed off on the family. I remember David, before he was old enough for school, in his highchair, throwing food and tantrums while I was on the telephone. I remember a few of Tom's report cards from Hillside School that reflected a certain amount of domestic stress and confusion. But on the whole I think we managed pretty well, and at least I was not a bored housewife.

I remember the morning routine. We had only one bathroom in those early years on Tamalpais Road. So I would use it first, being sure to put on some makeup because Jack said his mother used to look like a dried apricot in the mornings. Then, in my bathrobe, I'd go downstairs and start making breakfast, which was hearty — eggs and toast and cereal and orange juice — because I believed, and still do, that breakfast is essential for efficient mental endeavor. It's been proven scientifically, but parents these days don't seem to pay any attention to that, though they listen to psychics and read horoscopes. I bet our Alice Waters, guru of food, agrees with me.

Next it was Jack's turn in the bathroom, for shaving, and then the boys, who had to be urged to hurry along so they wouldn't be late for school. Jack sat at the round dining table, bathrobe over his clean white shirt and tie, reading the paper. (I was reminiscing with Tom about this the other day, wondering if his hair was still red in those days, but he never remembered Jack with red hair, only that on those mornings at that breakfast table it was all slicked down with water.) I dished up the food, and finally shoved them out the door. At first it was just Jack and Tom. Jack loved walking to school with him, then on down to the campus, but tactfully let him run on ahead when they neared the playground to spare him the embarrassment of having a parent. By '52 Steve joined them and by the fall of '55, after we'd returned from our sabbatical year abroad, all four of them took off, joining other professors, other children who in those days all went to Hillside School just a few blocks away.

Did we all kiss before they left? Jack was a wonderful kisser, but people didn't do it as much in those days. Now my two remaining sons, my daughters-in-law, my grown grandchildren kiss as casually as saying hello. Sex got awfully casual, too, in the '60s and '70s, until AIDS came along. Now I'm too old to know just what goes on.

The pleasantest time of my day then began — a quiet reading of the paper, doing the crossword puzzle in that house next door that I still love but do not covet anymore, though our anger and pain at the time of Dave and Chandra's divorce twenty-one years ago was fierce for a while. Tom's two divorces and Steve's one had not hit us so hard. Those marriages were all kind of crazy '60s aberrations, but Dave and Chandra had been in love since junior high school. They'd been married eight years. Four years earlier we'd come back from our third sabbatical, most of it on the island of Corsica, inspired by the extended families, peasant gardens, and our new ecological and environmental fervor. They were ready to buy a house. Why not ours — an early inheritance arrangement? We had already helped Tom and Steve buy land. We would move to this smaller house, which I had inherited from my mother, before we were too old to adjust to change. Our own parents' agings and deaths occurring during the past two decades had made us sensitive to our own needs, and our children's, in this retirement period of our lives. Undoubtedly we were too eager in our enthusiasm for sharing a garden, sharing our lives. It's sad that it didn't work, similar to the sadness of my failure to ease Steve's dying days last winter. But I'm glad we made the effort, and I still prefer the expanded family communal living mode to the retirement community solution that Deborah has chosen. Well, we shall see.

That house next door had several generous vistas of trees and sky and rooftops across the canyon, and a sunny brick patio facing east. The bricks had been carried up from the street by our children and their neighborhood friends for a penny a brick. For a while, when Steve and Dave were still very young, there was a sand plot in the middle of the brick patio. There are photographs of preschool neighborhood children — Violiches, Hayeses, Schevills, Bratenahls, Damis, LaRues, Worswicks, Lawrences — hunched over sand castles, toy trucks, and miniature roads. There are pictures of some of these same children, naked in a plastic wading pool on a small lawn we created later, with the steep wooded Berkeley hills soaring up behind us to the top of Grizzly Peak. At least seven of these children, now in their 40s and 50s, are living here in the houses they grew up in and are raising their children, some of them fourth generation on the street.

So it was there, next door, at the kitchen table or on the brick patio that after my four guys had gone off to work and school that I quietly read the paper all those years ago, before the political phone calls began.

But it wasn't all politics. Jack and Jim played golf at the Richmond Golf Club every Wednesday for years and years. They also had lunch about once a week at the White Horse Inn way down Telegraph near Jim's office so they could have drinks. I can't remember when they changed that law. All through my childhood and adolescence and early adulthood no liquor could be served within a mile of the campus. That's why, incidentally, that the Claremont Hotel was gerrymandered into Oakland, though it's almost surrounded by Berkeley, and why Spenger's down on Fourth Street was such a success. The White Horse Inn is a gay bar now, I understand. I wonder if Steve ever went there?

Jack and Jim were a wonderful pair, complementing each other in so many ways. Jim was fiercely competitive in sports and games. Jack was not. I used to get so mad when we were playing mixed doubles in tennis. I wanted to win, but Jack was just clowning around, having fun, making jokes with our opponents. He always did love his adversaries, in politics too, as long as they were honest. Some of his professional colleagues who differed with him intellectually were devious and that made him furious. But he really loved those conservatives in Berkeley government: John De Bonis and Arthur Beckley and Lee Brekenridge Thomas. He understood and respected Arthur Beckley as the leader of the opposition, the person to negotiate with. And as for De Bonis, well, he challenged Jack's imagination to shake things up a little. Jack suggested that instead of just pledging allegiance and saluting the flag each week before the Council meetings began, that it would be more meaningful if members took turns reading something, probably quotes from Jefferson or Lincoln, his favorite reading matter at the time. "You mean we have to do homework?" poor John lamented. To make him feel better Jack invited him for dinner and he just couldn't figure us out. I'll never forget his expression as he stood in our living room, looking us all over, as Jack offered him a drink. The boys, intrigued that the enemy had come to dinner, were charming. We were perfectly nice respectable people after all, maybe not communists after all.

When we played **THE GAME** (a form of charades) at Christmas or Thanksgiving with all the Kents and Whitneys, Jack was more interested in the costumes and the acting and gesticulating with his wonderfully expressive hands, drawing pictures in the air, than in winning. Oh, those hands. There's a photo on the wall above me of him with nine students standing on a high point in Tilden Park, looking west, his right hand stretched out, the fingers slightly curled, enclosing his vision of a greenbelt that would encircle the nine counties of the Bay Area. Yes, it was the Big Picture, the Grand Concept that interested him more than in helping his team to guess what he was doing, which was the point of **THE GAME**. Not Jim, though. He knew all the signs and shortcuts and used them to win! He used to play all four hands of bridge by himself, and loved doing his income tax, then pushing against the deadline, which was March 15 in those days, driving down to the main Berkeley post office just before midnight. He watched sports on TV *ad infinitum*, driving Deborah crazy. The Whitneys had TV long before we did so that Jim could watch baseball, football, tennis, and then the McCarthy hearings.

It was pure chance that Deborah and I got married within six months of each other back in 1941 to two men who became best, best friends. Or maybe not. They each had a lot in common with our father. Jim was a psychiatrist, Daddy a psychologist, albeit one was a Jungian, the other a Freudian, which only added to the family jokes and fun. Jack and he were both professors at Cal, all three of them were political liberals with deep commitments to the freedom of the mind and decency to their fellow human beings. All three of them had mischievous senses of humor and wicked, lovable grins. All three of them were leaders and teachers in their individual ways. I was surprised at first, then deeply sad, that Jack never played golf again after Jim died of an embolism when he was only forty-nine. The game had not meant much to him, I then realized, the friendship everything. There was no point in golf anymore.

No, it wasn't all politics and golf and teaching and PTA. There was tennis, swimming, hiking, baseball, football. We never used our carport for cars because it was an active basketball court. The Tamalpais Sports Club had a big green wooden box on our path full of balls and mitts and bats, etc. There was a padlock and all the kids had keys. Our boys played instruments too — Tom the trombone, Steve the violin, and Dave the trumpet — in the Hillside School and Garfield Junior High orchestras. We attended all their concerts of course, hoping, once more, that music would become a permanent endeavor and pleasure in all of our lives. I had taken piano lessons as a child. Jack played the ukulele (or was it the banjo?) in a St. Francis Wood neighborhood band in San Francisco where he grew up. They played at tea dances for his older sister Janis' friends. Once Jack bought me an upright piano and I took lessons again through U.C. Extension. Janis and I took Jazz piano for a while. I think Jack wanted me to be a performer, or at least an entertainer for family and friends. I wanted to do music on my own terms, just as I want to write about what comes from within rather than acceding to someone else's wishes, or the currently popular genre. With music I became self-conscious, practicing loudly right in the middle of the family, so I gave it up, stupid, stubborn me!

Encouraging the creative process is so tricky, especially by family members. I always wanted Jack to take up painting again in his last years, thinking it would give him so much pleasure as it had earlier. The loss of interest was probably another symptom of his disease.

My mother loved music in an intellectual way. My father was tone-deaf but was a great dancer. My brother played the drums. Off and on, over the years, Jack and I went to the symphony both in San Francisco and in Berkeley. We had records of both classical music and jazz that we enjoyed, but it was as a background to life rather than an integral part of it. Singing with family and friends around a fire on the beach with two or three people with really good voices, with one or two guitars, flutes, or recorders was the greatest musical pleasure we had, and no one seems to do that anymore.

We tried to like opera, but that was a total failure. I prefer drama to be drama, music to be music. In Bologna we went to the opera, "La Forza del Destino," by Verdi, I think, sure that in Italy we would finally get it. God, it was a terrible gloomy thing and we walked out after the first act. So it was inevitable, I suppose, that our children's musical efforts didn't amount to much. Many of their generation played guitars and sang folk music. They all went to rock concerts. Steve even ruined his hearing. He and I were both pretty deaf at the time of his death, adding to our misunderstanding of each other. Dave's son, Marlowe, though, is the marvelous exception. He is a real drummer who plays gigs with bands and communicates through music and rhythm, even to me. But as for our three sons, it was in the visual arts, both as spectators and practitioners, that they have found creative pleasure, I think.

Jack was a wonderful father in that regard, encouraging them in an easy way. There were always supplies on hand. He painted with them, either at a table in the living room or out in the West Marin countryside. He used to say, "Stop!" to Tom as his imaginative painting unfolded before our eyes. Was it for fear that he'd spoil them by doing too much? We still have many of those paintings around — sailboats rushing through empty space, live oak trees in unfinished landscapes — with lots of white background. Both our Inverness and Berkeley houses are filled with the boys' paintings, mostly done before they were grown, and now there are paintings, etchings, sculptures and photographs by our grown grandchildren.

Tom recently started a class in harmonica blues, but dropped it. We bought him a harmonica in London for his twelfth birthday and he taught himself to play *"The Happy Wanderer"* very nicely.

Chapter
Five

*S*o that was our busy life. Also smack in the middle of the '50s, before Jack ran for the city council, but after he had launched the Department of City and Regional Planning and served on the City Planning Commission, he received a Fulbright Fellowship to London coinciding with a sabbatical year. Whoever invented sabbaticals understood that even the most fulfilling and useful life and work must be interrupted from time to time — every seven years in the world of academe — for the purpose of renewal of the spirit and reassessment of the big picture. And so we gleefully left the Berkeley political scene in the middle of McCarthy and Nixon slime, traveling on a Dutch freighter, The *Duivendyk,* from the Port of Oakland for a solid month at sea, cut loose from all that.

We sailed out through the Golden Gate at sunset, then down the coast, past Los Angeles, San Diego, along Baja California, up the Gulf of California to Guaymas, where we took on huge slabs of beef to go to Yugoslavia, south past the twinkling lights of Acapulco. Approaching the Panama Canal our vast lonely sea narrowed down and other ships appeared — looming — from home ports of Japan and India and Holland, like ours, and crowded quite close. We took our turns going through the locks, then gliding past the jungle that we could almost touch from either port or starboard, while intermittent downpours of tropical rain soaked us with blessed relief from the heat. Then the sea widened again, the other ships disappeared from sight, and all alone once more our *Duivendyk* sailed across the Atlantic to Antwerp.

A young blond steward named Nicco took care of our children. The food was divine, big Dutch breakfasts of cold meats and cheese and a variety of breads and hard-boiled eggs, and sometimes Indonesian meals because the Dutch had colonized that part of the world. We swam in a canvas pool set up on the deck. (This was before freight containers like railroad cars covered the decks of freighters.) We played shuffleboard and Scrabble, drank Dutch gin (ten cents a shot) before dinner, and slept, and slept, and slept. Jack wrote in the photograph book of that trip, "35 calm, sunny, peaceful days. The Dutch win our hearts. Mommy won the shuffleboard contest, all women's swimming races, the Scrabble tournament, and didn't have to cook, feed the boys, or make the beds!!" I did have to do the family laundry in a bathtub, but that was literally my only household chore.

In Antwerp, while we waited to board our English Channel ship, we went to the zoo, the first of many that, along with beaches and museums, would become our antidote to the occasional boredom of restless boys during the following year. By the evening of that late August day, having crossed the Channel, taken a train to London, finally an upright black London taxi with our two trunks loaded on top took us from Victoria Station to our soon to be beloved Milton Court Hotel, where my aunts from New England always stayed, on Cromwell Road at Queen Anne's Gate. Ah, those lovely British place names. At the Milton Court, where we stayed a week while we found a flat, we were pampered by Francis, the doorman, who allowed the boys to operate the old-fashioned elevator (a cage that ascended and descended slowly), by a bevy of pretty Irish maids, and by elderly English gentry, who welcomed us into the "telly" room to watch wonderful BBC. We didn't yet own TV at home, so this was quite a thrill, and English television — like their transportation, health care system, theater, parks and museums — was first class. We were immediate Anglophiles (despite the tapioca pudding that made Tom gag) and we would return to the Milton Court many times over the years.

Within a week we had found a wonderful apartment, the top two floors (called a maisonette in London), of a four-story house in West Kensington. On the lower floor was the living room and two bedrooms, one of which we chose for ours, lashing the twin beds together to make a double, the other a single which the boys rotated into once a month, the other two sharing the upstairs bedroom. The bathroom was on the upper floor, but in those young days, with sturdy bladders, it didn't seem to be a problem. Upstairs also was a tiny kitchen and dining room. The living room is where Jack wrote his book, *The Urban General Plan.*

The boys wore grey flannel shorts and jackets and ties and kneesocks, even David who was in what the English call "Infant Class." When he turned five in November, we had a birthday party. The guests were schoolmates, several of them from Czechoslovakian refugee families who lived in basement apartments. (Sometimes we bought homemade sausage from the parents of these children.) We rigged up a spider web of ribbons that wound up and down the stairs in our five rooms with a party favor at the end of each child's ribbon. We had a marzipan cake from Harrods, ice cream, cambric tea, but one child, almost in tears, asked in a good cockney accent, "But where's the trifle?" I'd never heard of a trifle, but eventually learned that the strange confection is the traditional party dessert in England.

Both Dave and Steve, went to St. Barnabas and St.Phillips, a County Council-Church School on Earls Court Road about four blocks from our maisonette at 136 Lexham Gardens, and Steve became enamored with the Anglican Church (the music, the ritual, the candles, the stained glass windows) that the school children attended every Thursday. Someone at school, feeling, I suppose, that this poor little American boy had been deprived, gave him a Bible, and he made me read it to him aloud before bed. Jack didn't live to see him get religion again, just before he died. I had read a lot of the Bible in my Humanities Courses at Scripps College. For me it's mythic like Faulkner's Absalom, Absalom, which our oldest grandson, Grayson, read aloud with me this past summer. It was his idea. How could one so young — twenty-five — know that I was desperately missing reading aloud with Jack? Perhaps grandparenting, like marriage, goes two ways, both caring for and needing from. And our instincts led us to choose something legendary.

I credit the no-nonsense but loving attention Dave got at that school,where he sat on the teacher's lap like a baby but was whacked on his chubby thigh if he failed to pay attention and take his lessons seriously, for his easier time than his brothers in school later on. Steve, as usual, charmed his teachers and just barely got by academically. Tom's adjustment was the most complicated. He turned twelve in November, an awkward age. He hadn't started to grow to the six feet he would eventually become, and he put on weight. In the English school system, twelve is when the decision to try for college prepara- tory grammar school or continue in the less demanding County- Council school, similar to a public junior high school in America, must be made. We knew he probably couldn't pass the exam for Grammar School and decided not to put him through that pressure for just one year. Perhaps it was a mistake. Perhaps we should have sent him to a private school. At any rate, the school he went to, St. John's Secondary Modern on Clarendon Road, was some distance from our neighborhood, near Nottinghill Gate. He had to walk up Earls Court Road to Kensington High Street, where he took a bus to the other side of Holland Park. I don't recall his complaining. He coped as best he could.

His teacher, a retired Army man, ran his classroom like a drill ser- geant. He had a stash of tennis balls he threw at the students he caught goofing off. Poor Tom, he had trouble with his cockney schoolmates too. Of course America had won the war! *"Oy, Kenty, you're off your head; it's the limeys did it."* So he had fistfights defending his country, and injuries resulting from climbing around in bombed out heaps of rubble the boys played in at recess time. But as I've said, The National Health Service was excellent and free, even for visiting Americans. They just stitched him up and sent him home. Photos of him at that time don't show him as unhappy, posing with his new bicycle, grin- ning in front of the statue of Peter Pan in Kensington Gardens with David sitting on his shoulders and Steve holding his hand, sailing model boats in the Round Pond, feeding ducks on the Thames. In one there's a bandage over his eyebrow, the only evidence of his troubles.

Regarding health and adventure, Dave and Jack both had pneumonia, and again the National Health people were wonderful. Dave went to the hospital where he was coddled and loved and given tea at a little round table with the other ailing children. The atmosphere was that of an English home nursery with a nice nanny in charge. For Jack we had an excellent doctor who came and saw him at home. Those health experiences were so civilized compared to the way we do it in America. (But that was before Margaret Thatcher got her hands on things.) And Dave had another adventure. I wrote a story about it once, called, "Davie's American Mum." I can't find it, but here is the gist of it.

Soon after school began in the fall, maybe a week or two, I felt so liberated without any children at home, for this was David's first school — it had been eleven years since I'd had a morning to myself — that I decided to go shopping downtown. We didn't have a car (that came later when we drove to Austria for Christmas), but public transportation like public health in London was absolutely first-class. I could have gone on the underground from the Earls Court Road Station, but I decided on the bus instead because I would be able to sit on the upper deck and see the wonderful sights and skylines of London. So off I went, leaving Jack writing his book in the bay window of our pretty little living room, a small coal fire burning, three floors up from the street. I headed up Earls Court Road to Kensington High Street, where I boarded the bus. The freedom was so heady and the city so vibrant and beautiful and everything an urban place should be, as Jack had taught me well, with magnificent buildings, relieved periodically by equally magnificent parks with enormous old trees and lawns and ponds and ladies walking dogs, and nannies pushing prams, and preschool boys kicking soccer balls that I almost cried with happiness, sitting there on the top of the big red London bus. I don't think I bought anything, just roamed along the gracious curve of Regent Street past Liberty House and Jaeger, then had lunch at Selfridges, admiring how civilized the British were. Even their sense of superiority over Americans was polite. Instead of assuming we were Americans because of our accents, they always said first, "Oh, you must be Canadian," which would have been a far less embarrassing nationality, considering what Nixon and McCarthy were up to at home.

Oh, but the boys! David got out of his Infant Class at two. I'd better get back there to meet him at the gate. There was a crossing guard, but so far I'd gone to walk home with him every day. This was before the birthday party; he wasn't quite five. I hopped on a bus and looked at my watch. Heavens, he'd be let out of school in ten minutes. Suddenly the traffic seemed to crawl. Finally, finally we got to Earls Court Road. It was twenty minutes past two. I ran into the school yard, but no one was there, so I ran all the four city blocks down to Lexham Gardens. Our #136 was about four houses from the corner, and there sat David, on the steps, crying softly into his hands. He'd found his way home, he knew that Daddy was upstairs writing his book. The door was locked, of course, and there were several doorbells. He didn't know how to get inside the house, so he just sat down and cried. David is almost fifty now and doesn't remember this, I'm very happy to report.

What a year that was — watching the young Queen Elizabeth ride by in her coach on her way to open Parliament; walking in Holland Park, Kensington Gardens, Hyde Park; going to the zoo; shopping at Harrods and Liberty House; visiting the Natural History Museum and the Tate Gallery; seeing Shakespeare at the Old Vic and Stratford; going to Austria for Christmas; and taking trips around England to Brighton, Hastings, Oxford and Cambridge looking at castles and country Estates along the way; meeting some wonderful people — Mrs. McLaughlin, the Scotch woman who baby sat for us and was able to knit an entire boy's sweater in an evening; Mrs. Hingely, the social worker who showed us the seamier side of London's East End; the Johnson-Marshalls who had seven children; the Wicksteeds from Cambridge who we met in Austria. (Their daughter, Jill, was the second girl that I know of whom Tom took an interest. The first was Roxanne at Hillside School.) Tom had a week with them sailing and camping — sailamping they called it — during Easter vacation. And finally the Grand Tour of Europe in the spring and summer of '55. Steve wrote, on the occasion of Jack's eightieth birthday almost three years ago now, "Thank you, Dad, for taking us to Europe twice (we went again in the early '60s, soon after Tom had flunked himself out of Cal.) It was paradise, that and the summers in Inverness."

And I thank him too, from the bottom of my heart, for he was the one who planned it all and made it happen. (Of course he was a professional planner.) And he devised the system of alternating periods of recreation — going to zoos; and loafing on beaches (Biarritz in Southern France, Lloret de Mar on the Spanish Costa Brava, Cannes on the French Riviera, Lake Lucerne in Switzerland) — with serious sightseeing — (art galleries, museums, cathedrals, monuments, historical sites, and battle fields.)

We began our tour in the spring, when we took the boys out of school and crossed the English Channel to Holland and The Hague. Bicycles assaulted us as we drove in our Morris Minor from the ship into town. We were quite intimidated. And early on Jack established his authority over squabbling boys, stopping on a narrow dike and ordering them out of the car, whereupon he gave each one a swift kick in the seat of the pants while I stood by, aware that motorists and bicyclists were gaping at this unusual scene. At home he used to threaten them with his bedroom slipper, but only occasionally followed through. I was more apt to whine or cry or yell. Once I threw a coffee cup at all four of them when the testosterone level seemed more than I could bear. Again I'd almost broken my butt because, again, the toilet seat was left up!

In The Hague we visited with my Aunts Elsa and Lucy, the "black aunts," as we used to call them. That was because they and their older sister, Dora, and their younger sister, my mother, Kathleen, were all very dark-eyed, dark-complexioned, which, incidentally, both my sister and my brother inherited. It remains somewhat of a mystery, but we think it might have had to do with the Spanish Armada when Spanish sailors consorted with English maidens centuries ago. I did not get those exotic looks but share a fair-skinned, bland complexion with my father.

77

When we met them in The Hague Aunt Elsa and Aunt Lucy were on one of their frequent trips abroad. I see from the photograph Jack took of the aunts, the boys, and me that they wore hats and gloves, a formality that my mother would also have honored had she been there. I admired and respected my mother, especially because she never, never gave me advice unless I asked for it, but it got back to me once through a friend — probably one of the Junior Lunch Club bunch — that Mother had said to her mother, "I do wish the girls (Deborah and me) would not wear jeans downtown." I wonder why I'm rambling on about this. It has to do, I suppose, with a kind of civility that has long since vanished from society.

October 1999

(I'm currently reading a novel by the excellent Canadian writer, Robertson Davies, in which the protagonist's story is told to a Jungian psychiatrist in Zurich. It strikes me that I am talking to Jack and Steve, in the same way. They are very quiet, as good psychiatrists should be, and I ramble on. The sad difference is that they can't talk back, tell me to shut up, say I've got it all wrong, nor can they give their own versions of our lives together.)

Dave caught a cold in The Hague, and by the time we got to Normandy, spending nights and having wonderful meals along the way in Arras, Beauvais, Rouen, he had a raging earache. We went to a doctor in Caen, who gave him one of the miracle drugs and sent us off to Biarritz, prescribing warm weather, advising us that many ear, nose, throat specialists practiced there and that Dave probably needed to have his tonsils and adenoids removed. Yes, probably. We'd been through this before with both Tom and Steve. (Fortunately the worry and pain and extreme inconvenience of health problems — Jack's years of migraine headaches and sleeplessness; my frequent and severe colds that left me coughing for weeks; the childhood diseases; stitches, concussions, poison oak, impetigo, and constipation — recede in memory.) So we headed south, but not before reliving D-Day at

Omaha Beach and relearning the history of the Norman conquest of England from the twelfth Century Bayeux Tapestry and sipping some Calvados, the incredible apple brandy of the area. (I read in the *New Yorker* that Alice Waters, when she was eating her way through France as a girl and getting turned on to her mission regarding food and drink, had that wonderful "apple juice" every day after a charcuterie lunch in some farmer's field, then fell asleep by the side of the road. No wonder, she figured out years later!)

Biarritz in an unseasonably warm May couldn't have been nicer. The hordes of tourists had not yet arrived. We found a small hotel, Le Nadaillac, perched on a bluff above the Bay of Biscay, and watched the sunset in the west again, which reminded us of home. Lolling in bed with breakfast of brioche and cafe-au-lait in that room with a view was a special pleasure for me. One Sunday a little French girl's Communion party and feast was held at the hotel, and we were invited to join the party. Steve hung around that party, probably grinning at the girl, and got us the invitation. I can just see that seven-year-old smile of his that was so disarming, his front teeth large with a gap between them, his ears sticking out. He looked like Charlie McCarthy, Prince Charles and Mickey Rooney, only he was cuter. The food at that party was the sort that Julia Child would describe on TV almost a decade later — a whole boned fish, eggs en gelee, timbales, pates, crepes and platters of tomatoes with basil, sliced meats, fresh raspberries piled in cut glass bowls served with creme Chantilly, and on and on. Divine. And so were the beaches and the swimming. After a chilly English winter it was absolute heaven. And a pleasant medical surprise — the specialists did not want to take out David's tonsils after all. In America they would have been yanked out as a matter of course. Oh no, the tonsils and adenoids were there for a purpose, the doctor insisted, as a protective shield against deeper infection. He added that Dave would soon outgrow the susceptibility to infection, and he did.

Before leaving Biarritz we drove south to San Sebastian on the Spanish border and gazed at that long beach that forms the southern edge of the Bay of Biscay, where Steve, with his wife-to-be, Annemarie, and his cousin Nick would camp many years later for a couple of weeks, having purloined a van from Friends World Institute shortly before he dropped out of school for good.

And then, for the rest of the summer we continued our journey, picnicking every day that we were on the road. We had bought an English picnic case at Harrods, outfitted neatly with cups and plates and silverware and containers for food. The English can be seen throughout Europe with cases like this, incongruously having their tea right on the edge of the road, a national tourist trait as definite as the German one of talking loudly and filling the spaces around them with ego. Jack and I, though, wanted to please and not seem ostentatious, since we knew that was the impression many Europeans had of Americans. I do not speak for the boys. Once Tom waved a small American flag at the customs officials as we crossed the border from Austria into Germany. Steve hid on the floor in embarrassment for he always wanted to blend into the culture of whatever country we visit-ed, picking up a few words and the accent of the language right away, adapting his clothes to that of the natives — sombrero in Spain, biki-ni in France. Dave was just Mr. Amenable. In Italy the chambermaids called him "Bambino" and tucked him into cribs, even though he was five years old. But that was okay with him.

For our picnics, first as we crossed Southern France, spending a night in Toulouse, climbing around the walled city of Carcasonne, we sought more secluded spots than the English. Our search for a town and a charcuterie or market place in which to buy our cheeses, pates, baguettes, fresh tomatoes, peaches, cherries, and wine usually began around eleven in the morning. We began to discuss and argue about the merits or disadvantages of this town or that. It was a game, really, whetting our appetites for both the food and the atmosphere. River banks; fields with wildflowers; shady woods; hilly outcroppings or Roman ruins with long-range vistas; sometimes a small town park with benches, linden trees whose feathery white blossoms blew across the hard-packed earth, and undoubtedly a boule game being played by old men.

A pension on the beach at Lloret de Mar was our next vacation spot for a couple of weeks, with a trip to Barcelona and a bullfight thrown in. Steve and I hid our faces in our hands a lot. But then he stood up and yelled, "Ole!" And I remember the time he was swimming in the strangely tideless Mediterranean when the wind came up. I was on the beach, becoming anxious because the usually serene waters were suddenly turbulent. Steve's smiling face was like a beach ball bouncing on the waves. "Stevie, come in," I called, running toward the water. "I can't," he called back, still smiling. Just then our nice host at the pension, Alfredo, appeared from somewhere, strode out and carried him back to shore. Was he scared? Was he ever scared of anything?

The next beach was at Cannes, crowded like Coney Island as I imagine it, with the French on summer vacation, a fascinating spectacle, all those practically naked bodies crammed together. The chatter of French flirtation, the smell of tanning oils and sweat was overwhelming. Our years of beach enjoyment had been of such a different kind — serene, with expanses of sand and sea and sky, only the sound of gulls or waves breaking on the shore. So we moved on, driving along the Riviera toward Italy on that amazing stretch of road, a winding narrow ribbon high above the sea, where countless romantic or adventure movies have been shot. And soon after crossing into Italy where the sand turns black we found a small arcaded city — I don't remember the name. It might have been Lucca. At any rate, it's where we had our first wonderful pasta in a small family hotel — white table cloths, carafes of Chianti, the musical sound of Italian after the staccato of French, "Oh, Bambino," the waitress cooed at David, patting his hair and feeding him a mouthful of linguini. He loved both the pasta and the attention. He grinned; the waitress tenderly wiped his chin with a napkin. And that night was one of the times he slept in a crib.

"It's so sweet and tender," Jack raved each time we had pasta in the following weeks, and oddly enough it was, a subtle sweetness underlying the taste of tomatoes and parmesan, or pesto sauce, or mushrooms or clams in cream, or any of the endless variety of toppings.

Now the serious sight-seeing began as we toured through Italy, eating sweet and tender pasta twice a day. We did all the tourist things. Tom held up the Tower of Pisa. Italy was hot, and in Rome we took up the Italian obsession with water and fountains, throwing coins in the Trevi and trailing our hands in the fountains of most of the Piazzas of Rome. But somewhat nostalgic for London, we had many cups of tea at Babbington's English Tea house near the foot of the Spanish Steps where, if I recall correctly, there is a plaque honoring John Keats, who died in Rome when he was only twenty-six. And didn't Jack tell me that the Spanish Steps were actually French? We did the Vatican, where I, at age thirteen, had had to hurry off to a nearby shop with my father (why my father and not my mother?) to buy my first pair of long stockings. In those days thirteen-year-olds were still considered children. I had bobbed hair and wore little girl dresses just above the knees. But bare arms and legs, even those of a child, were not permitted in the Vatican. My memory of that visit is dim. I was too busy trying to keep my rolled stockings from falling down around my ankles to take much notice of Michelangelo's frescoes. But this time, 1955, we all were in awe at the scale and exquisite detail of those biblical figures.

We went to Saint Peters, climbed up inside the dome and gaped at the splendor, both inside and out of that bewildering, to us agnostics, overwhelming expression of faith. And I wonder if Steve carried that impression with him throughout life, and that's why when his end came he embraced it. Jack, had gone from Freiburg to St. Peter's in 1939 with his friend from home, John Bryan, who was a Catholic, who had come all the way from San Francisco for the momentous event of the coronation of the new Pope Pius XII — Pacelli, the one who later collaborated with Hitler.

We went to the ruins of ancient Rome by then occupied by feral cats — Palatine hill with its baths, and the Colosseum where the boys developed their game of Sneaking to perfection. Sneaking had started in England. Tramping around in Hampstead Heath, Hyde Park, Brighton, Kew Gardens, Bodiam Castle, Jack and I would realize, all of a sudden, that the boys had disappeared. We'd panic, naturally enough, and start darting about, while they, we eventually discovered, were watching us from their hiding places behind rose bushes, oaks, castle turrets, or outcroppings of rocks. Once we caught on — of course we didn't let them know that we knew — our travels took on still another dimension of delight. It was generation against generation, three American kids abroad with their two parents. And in the Roman Colosseum the boys became gladiator slaves performing feats of sneaking and hiding surpassing everything to date. Jack and I must have told each other stories from our previous trips to Rome, as we must have done all over England and Europe, compared and shared our earlier trips without each other or the boys.

We drove to Siena for a day and a night. We drove to Florence. Jack did all the driving then. I was much too timid in the midst of the crazy Italian drivers and horrendous traffic. Besides, I was in charge of the laundry, sometimes under very bizarre conditions. On the freighter for a month I washed all of our clothes in a bathtub by hand, even handkerchiefs which I flattened wet against mirrors. In London I took the bag of our dirty clothes slung over my shoulder to a commercial laundry a couple of blocks down Earls Court Road, then picked it up, wet, later in the day. Jack helped me carry it home though, heavy now because wet, where I hung as much as would fit on an ingenious clothes rack that lowered on pulleys over the bathtub, and draped the rest all over the bathroom on chairs, hooks, curtain rods, whatever. Sometimes, in Spain, Italy, France I took the laundry to a maid's house in some back alley and picked it up a few days later, beautifully folded and ironed, but mostly I washed all of our socks and underwear and shirts every night in a bathroom sink and hung it wherever I could. I'm looking at the photographs to see what kind of clothes we wore. It seems to have been before the days of drip-dry. And we look pretty nice, I must say. I always wore dresses in those days. We both were thin. No wonder, all that running around, doing laundry by hand and driving in Italian traffic.

(Jack always did do most of the driving. And for quite a while in the '70s and '80s he took up baking bread, and gardening, inspired by Steve, who by then had become an accomplished subsistence farmer. Jack did the laundry too, after he retired, taking it down to the laundromat at Shattuck and Vine, hanging out at coffee houses, reading the paper and chatting with other old men. That was a nice time for him, those years. Gradually, though, he gave up those activities, even the garden. In the end, I did the laundry again because he began to bring home the wrong clothes, sometimes, or leave a load in a dryer by mistake. In the end I did all the driving too.)

In Florence it was the Uffizi Gallery; statues of gorgeous naked men; embroidered blouses and tooled leather purses and cloisonné jewelry on the Ponte Vecchio; and driving through olive groves and vineyards to Fiesoli high above the city; palaces, gardens, churches, bridges, paintings, sculpture, fountains. Then it was on to Venice, via Ravenna, Ferrara, and Padua, still eating pasta, still having everyone admire David, our bambino.

I have the classic tourist family photograph of pigeons flocking around us in Piazza San Marco, and of course it's Steve, who actually holds a pigeon in his hands. We stayed in a balconied pensione on the island of Guidecca, a pleasant gondola or water bus ride from San Marco and from which we had a wonderful view of the city. It continued to be very hot and the boys were longing to swim in the lagoon as the natives did, but we were sure it must be polluted. Professor Albert Elkus of the music department at Cal and his wife were staying at the pensione, and as Americans abroad are wont to do, we became immediate close friends, though they were almost a generation older than we. But he was one of the nonsigners of the Loyalty Oath and those people belonged in a special category of our admiration. I'm sorry we didn't keep up the closeness after we all returned to Berkeley. But together in Venice, from the great stone balcony that ran across the front of the building, the Elkuses and we leaned on heavy red fabric hung on the balustrade and watched the most flamboyant fireworks I have ever seen. It was one of those chance travel experiences that turn out to be memorable — like in Arahova near Delphi in Greece when we happened upon the celebration of St. George's Day. That was when the Greeks finally defeated the Turks centuries ago and they celebrate every year as we do the 4th of July. Men in ballooning white skirts and red vests race to the top of a nearby mountain, and then these same men dance in the square. Baby lambs roast on backyard spits. Solemn processions enter the church. It was in the post-retirement second honeymoon time of our lives that we saw that.

In Venice the occasion for the fireworks was the end of the plague in the fourteenth century. We stood on that balcony overlooking the Grand Canal and along the edge of which Italian celebrants ate their picnic suppers and drank their Chianti at long wooden tables at the edge of the water and watched, as did we, the hours long ballet of light that filled the night sky.

Tom did a painting of Piazza San Marco. We had given him a set of oils for Christmas in Austria where he painted a vivid alpine scene — white snow, green conifers, brilliant orange-red sunset — that hangs in our front hall. The painting of Venice was on a wall of our Inverness house for years, but finally it disintegrated last summer. We should have framed it. Never mind, it's indelibly fixed in my mind's eye, another one of his with much white space around the several domes of the cathedral and the campanile (after which, I believe, ours on the Berkeley campus is modeled) because Jack had so often told him to stop before he spoiled it. Venice must be one of the most painted cities in the world. My favorites are the Turners we saw in the Tate Gallery in London, which capture the watery quality of light that is the essence of Venice for me. But Tom's painting expressed the solidity of stone and marble with strong colors, an equally compelling image. He continued to paint through Europe without the self-consciousness one might have expected from a twelve-year-old. In the Luxembourg Gardens one day we left him painting, having rented an extra chair for a few francs on which to put all his stuff, and went off to a puppet show with Steve and Dave. When we returned a small gathering of observers hovered around him, admiring the young artist's work — a painting of a small statue in the park, the model for America's Statue of Liberty. I made the mistake, later that day, of suggesting that when we got back home he might like to take some painting lessons. "You're trying to make me into a Little Lord Fauntleroy!" he protested.

After Venice it was time for another period of pure recreation, so we went to Switzerland via the Simplon Tunnel, where we drove our Morris Minor onto a flatbed train car. The train then whizzed us through the Alps. Tom pretended adolescent nonchalance, reading a book in the back seat, even though it was too dark for him to see the page. We spent a night in William Tell's birthplace in the Canton of Uri. In the restaurant where we ate dinner, a dignified matron came in with her dog, a dachshund, who sat politely at her feet as she dined. To us this seemed the height of civilization. We had never owned a dog who could have behaved so well. I was engulfed again with that old American inferiority complex.

Lake Lucerne became our next spa and we spent several heavenly days in a little inn on the water. It reminded me of Echo Lake. Lots of pictures of Steve in the water, grinning. There was a funicular nearby that took us up to the top of the mountain on which a luxury hotel perched and where hikers strode in knickers and carried handsomely carved walking sticks. Again, it seemed tidy and civilized, as though the Swiss were determined to control those awesome Alps.

And then we went to Freiburg, Germany, to visit the Weibel family. Jack had boarded with them in 1938-39, in their living quarters above the family bookstore. It had been such a pretty town before the war. I have a watercolor Jack did of the tile roofs and the cathedral with green steeples and turrets. They must have been copper. Here's his own assessment of the painting written across the bottom: "Rotten Realism and in places beginnings of good pattern — not 3 dimensional however! which it should be. Colors are haphazard. I don't know what I'm trying to do. Freiburg, Sept. 22, 1938." To me it is bold and colorful. I love it. Jack was twenty-one years old. On the other side of the paper is a pencil sketch of his room in the Weibel house — a single bed, the bedstead of solid wood with a rolled edge; a rolltop desk; a chair; pretty round antique table; a rug with one of his slippers on the floor; and a cloth hanging down around the bare overhead light bulb, something he had probably improvised. There's also a list of books I presume are those that Lewis Mumford had recommended he read: *Culture of Cities, History of Western Europe, Making of the Modern Mind, Science and the Modern World, University of Chicago Syllabus, Short History of the World, Liberty Liberty in the Modern State, History of Socialism, Theory and Practice of Socialism,* then another list with various stars and asterisks indicating something to Jack but not to me — "12th

Cent. Medieval World, Humanism and the Renaissance, the Reformation, SCIENCE Galileo, etc., Newton, Deism, Romantic Reaction, Evolution MARX realization of . . . . (?)" Under the drawing of the room he wrote, "JK's room at the Weibel home — Frau Weibel was a wonderful person — Lithuanian."

The sight of his slipper makes me cry. Also the reminder of Mumford, for years earlier he had been the mentor and lover of Catherine Bauer Wurster. Both of them were important influences in Jack's life and work, as, later, was Catherine's husband, Bill Wurster. Jack was so impressed with Catherine's social conscience and grasp of public housing matters, which was her specialty, that he in fact persuaded me (as part of his educational plan for me) to take her course on housing. This was before we were married, before Catherine and Bill were married, before the war. Catherine swept into California and the University from the east, taking us all by storm with her charm, friendliness, and vigor, at about the same time — 1939, 1940 — that Jack and the other young Turks of that day in the Bay Area were creating an environmental research group, Telesis. They put on a show, "Space for Living" at the San Francisco Museum of Art that received acclaim from, among other national figures in the field, Lewis Mumford, Rexford Tugwell, Walter Gropius, and Catherine Bauer.

Bill, a good deal older than she and still a bachelor, was a native Californian, and had created an indigenous architectural style that we both admired. That's why, some years later, we chose him to design our house at 84 Tamalpais Road. The courtship and marriage of these two creative people were great events, as was their moving into a lovely John Galen Howard house around the corner from us where, over the years they entertained generously and beautifully. They served a wicked rum punch. Catherine did not allow stiletto heels to be worn inside because of the damage they did to floors. Good for her. I admired her feminist spirit. She rolled her stockings just below the knees, refused to follow the dictates of the fashion industry, yet was one of the sexiest ladies I ever knew. She had a loud exuberant laugh and didn't believe in cutting flowers, so decorated her dining room table with shells or polished rocks. She smoked (as did we all) and took her flask of whiskey on airplane trips. I liked her.

Bill was appointed as the first dean of the College of Environmental Design for which Jack had drafted the legislation with the support and participation of Bill and the rest of the faculty. And so it came as a shock when years later, as he retired, Catherine went against the faculty committee's recommendation that Jack succeed him as dean.

From old files I am reminded of her rather surprising doubts about Jack's leadership style, as expressed in a letter to U.C. President Clark Kerr "...*gradual* and *non-flamboyant*, with a bias toward *local self-determination* ...too conservative for a cosmic reformer like me." (italics mine) Well, yes! That was his great strength as a leader and teacher. But in the '60s Easterners were flooding into California and the University with grandiose ideas about planning on a global scale, ignoring or ignorant of the vibrant activist local scene. And so an Easterner was appointed Dean. He only stayed a few years and then returned to the East.

I don't know how much Jack wanted to be Dean, maybe not at all — after all it could be considered just another boring administrative job — but he should have been asked. He was the obvious candidate, the one recommended by his colleagues. I'm baffled still, though I should know, having grown up in the University community, that all is not serene in academia. My father's Psychology Department was always full of intrigue and disagreement. The Loyalty Oath fight had been too. But I do see, at last, after reading the biography of Catherine, why Jack stopped going to meetings at the Faculty Club of the group that called itself, "The Little Thinkers." I think he felt he had been somewhat betrayed by both Clark Kerr and Catherine, who were members of that group, although Jack had been a founding member. I suddenly remember again the migraine headaches and sleepless nights. Oh, my dear Jack.

At the time of the Loyalty Oath, more than a decade earlier, Clark Kerr had been a stalwart supporter of the nonsigners. Then, in the '60s, he had become architect of the "multi-University," against which student activists, including Mario Savio, would soon rebel.

Catherine's actions will always remain a mystery, as will the exact cause of her death while hiking alone on the western slopes of Mt. Tamalpais one November afternoon in 1964. Jack joined the many students and colleagues in the search for her after Bill, by then suffering from Parkinson's Disease, sent out the word from their Stinson Beach weekend house that Catherine was missing. For all of her brilliance and charm and hundreds of admirers, in the end she was alone. No one will ever know why she lay there, dead on the mountainside. Did she stumble, even though she'd hiked there often? Perhaps it was suicide. She had developed a glandular disorder. Perhaps the drugs she had to take had affected her sanity. For surely, she wouldn't leave Bill, helpless and alone, trapped within himself as his speech became increasingly impaired.

We had kept up with the Weibels by letter after the war ended. Although Herr Weibel was a Nazi, he wasn't around much while Jack was living there. Was he off on sinister Nazi activities? "Kristellnacht," happened that fall. Jack had no sympathy for Herr Weibel, but was very fond of the Frau (the fact that she was Lithuanian seemed to have exonerated her from guilt in his eyes) and he loved the children — Zeppi, Monica, Hilda. Another girl, Anne, was born after he left. He took Frau Weibel on an all-day outing to Switzerland once to show her the world outside Nazi Germany.

Two of the women from my writers' group, who are Jewish, were very disturbed when I read them this part about sending the Weibels hand-me-down clothing after the war — my old fur coat, for instance — not because they were secondhand, but because we sent German Nazis anything at all. I tried to explain that these were gifts to kind people who were in great suffering and need, that Frau Weibel had been a domestic anchor for Jack that year when he was so far away from home, so very young. It had nothing to do with Nazi persecution of Jews. God knows we had no sympathy with that. One of Jack's best friends from college days was Charlie Rosenblatt, a Jewish communist. My father sponsored many Jewish scientist refugees to America. But I think I understand, intellectually at least, the outrage these two dear friends must feel. Perhaps it's presumptuous of me to compare it to my attitude toward our former President, the first George Bush; he was the head of the CIA which assisted in perpetrating untold horrors in Central and South America in the name of democracy. I can never forgive him or our country for that. Now I have this granddaughter-in-law, lovely Kristina from Chile. I am having to learn all over again, that nothing is quite as black and white and simple as I would like to believe. Because she and I do not have a common experience, or a common generation as a context in which to communicate there are misunderstandings. Kristina considers herself a liberal. She was only just born, in Guatemala not Chile, the year that Pinochet's coup overthrew the democratically elected Allende government. She was only four when her family moved to Chile. But still, the subject of Pinochet's crimes had best not be discussed at her family's dinner table, I gather.

The Weibels sent toys for our children. I remember a set of little painted wooden houses, churches, stores. Dave loved those. He was always making "set-ups," as we called them, in the sandbox with roads and tunnels and cars and trucks, and now he had a small German village to work with.

When we arrived in Freiburg in the summer of 1955, we, especially Jack who had known the city, were shocked at the destruction. It had been bombed by the Allies near the end of the war, and the pretty town square of his painting was in ruins, the church badly damaged, the "Bier Stuben," where he hung out with his friends and discussed philosophy, was gone. The Weibels' house and bookstore were gone. They now lived in an ugly housing project on the outskirts of the city. The Frau arranged for friends in the complex to put up Tom and Steve in one apartment; Jack, Dave and me in another. Only Anne still lived at home, and Monica was recovering from TB in a Catholic sanitarium where we visited her briefly. She was charming and so glad to see us. She had been a twelve-year-old when Jack lived with them, and I bet she had a big crush on him. We took the pompous Herr and the sweet Frau out to dinner at a country restaurant in the Black Forest and left the following morning.

This pilgrimage seemed to be very important to Jack, and now I see that he was coping with this horrid little Nazi the way he always did with his adversaries — kill them with kindness — or to put it in the language of Christianity — love your enemies, turn the other cheek. Sometimes it was too difficult to do that. Then he would just walk away, as he did from The Little Thinkers when he felt betrayed by Catherine. "Betrayed" is my word. He never criticized her personally for her actions, nor would he have used such a derogatory term. In his oral history, done for the Bancroft Library, the interviewer, Malca Chall, asked, "Did you take an early retirement in 1974 for any special reason?" He answered, "Yes…I think in a way I was a sort of a casualty of the upheavals of the sixties. The faculty here went through a major change from the early sixties to the early seventies. From my point of view, we were forced to expand too rapidly and in too many directions by people who thought they were doing good things for us, Clark Kerr and others. I was in the minority. I didn't think we should expand so rapidly, nor did I think we should have taken on social policy planning, which we did. So for a period of time there was great, understandable, normal, departmental stress … we more than doubled our faculty, more than tripled our student body, and destroyed for a time any single coherent view of what city planning was supposed to do, what I have referred to as the conservative view of scope and role … I think I may very well have decided that, if I could do it, I would retire early because of that. But I didn't want to leave the department or leave the campus. I took a half-time appointment for three years before retirement to see if I could live that way. My wife agreed completely."

However, this was the time, in the '60s, that Jack sought therapy. His father had died in '63, our sons were rebelling, he didn't like what was happening in his department. He was depressed. Our psychiatrist brother-in-law, Jim, sent him to Dr. Berg, but after a very few sessions, he dismissed Jack, saying that there was nothing pathological about his depression, and that he was handling it very well. He refused to take Jack's money. What a nice man.

On to Paris, approaching it from the south, via the Cathedral of Chartres, which we viewed with awe off in the distance, beyond acres

91

of golden wheat fields. We stayed in Paris about a week, I think, in a small hotel near the Luxembourg Gardens and the restaurant, "Doucet," on Rue d'Assas, where we ate twice a day. The menu was handwritten in pretty, back-slanted, purple-inked French. "Pommes a l'huile," "Oeuf Mayonnaise," "Filets d'Anchois," "Escalpe de Veau," etc., etc. Divine food, simple setting, and care-giving service. Between trips to Versaille, the Louvre and l'Orangerie, and sailing toy boats in the Luxembourg Gardens, we sold the car and tried to reduce our load of trinkets and souvenirs bought on impulse. Now we would go to London for one final stay at the Milton Court Hotel, say farewells to Francis, the doorman, the Irish maids, and friends in London and Cambridge. As we climbed into the taxi outside our hotel on Rue d'Assas a maid came running out with Steve's sombrero, which, being very cumbersome, we had hoped to leave behind on a closet shelf. No such luck. Steve grabbed it and put it on.

A week or so later, after London, we boarded our ship in Southampton, not a freighter, this time, but a big Cunard ocean liner. We were on the home stretch, and eager for New York. There we planned to visit with my cousins, Allen and Bill, and their families on Long Island, introducing ten second cousins to each other. But Steve got seasick, then developed a mysterious limp and pain in his hip. He was put in the infirmary. There was a possibility of polio. All during my own childhood the fear of polio had lurked, like the fear of fire. We were cautioned about public swimming pools, about getting over-tired, about being in large crowds. And more recently we knew two adult friends in Berkeley who had been stricken and crippled. This was 1955 and Dr. Salk had just the year before begun to test his new vaccine on children. But polio was still as scary as AIDS would become decades later. And of course that's what finally got Steve.

I remember watching, with Steve and Jack, the amazing New York skyline from the infirmary cabin porthole. Jack and I were sick with worry. With the doctor's insistence and help, though, we snuck Steve through customs, not without some feeling of guilt, but parents will do almost anything where their children are concerned. Because of the polio question they might have quarantined Steve, and then what? We got to our hotel, The Little Hotel, on 55th Street I think, and called Ganks' old friend, Dr. Ed Chamberlain, who was teaching at Temple University Medical School, and asked his advice. Before the day was out Steve was in bed at the University of Columbia Medical School hospital, but not before witnessing in the emergency room a black man who'd been stabbed in the stomach reeling past him. His roommate was a boy who had bone cancer and was going to lose his leg. Jack told me all this when he finally got back to the hotel. We did see all the cousins and several of them visited Steve in the hospital, where he was getting every sort of test. In the end, as polio, cancer, rheumatic fever, rheumatoid arthritis were each ruled out, he was diagnosed as having tino-sinuvitis, an inflammation (in his case in the hip joint), a residual infection following a cold or such.

Whew, what a relief. We had only one other health threat as scary while the boys were growing up when David was diagnosed as having cerebral palsy. He was a lovely, smiling baby, slow to sit or stand or walk, and when at almost two he did eventually walk we noticed that he had a little limp. Tests were done, eliminating, one by one, all sorts of possible causes, and finally concluding that there must have been some brain damage at birth; the messages from brain to left leg and foot were not getting through. We wouldn't know for some time how great the damage was. We would just have to wait. In the meantime, while we were watching anxiously to see if Dave would learn to talk or read, it was important that the muscles of his left leg not atrophy. He had a night cast to keep his foot at right angles to his ankle. He did exercises that consisted of hanging a bag of canned goods to his ankle and lifting his foot, up and down, up and down twenty-five times or so twice a day to strengthen his leg muscles. Everything turned out fine. In nursery school he learned to hammer, and he has never stopped. He is now a master craftsman and designer, six foot three, good looking, proficient in math and money and business. As for his left leg and foot, subconsciously, I guess, he was determined not to be handicapped; the brain apparently compensated for the damage by helping other muscles take over for the unresponsive ones. He played baseball in Little League, and his disability, such as it is — a small snapping motion at the back of the knee joint when he walks — kept him from being drafted in the '60s.

Not one of them had to go to Vietnam, thank God. Tom actually wanted to join the Navy, having flunked out of Cal and being at loose ends, but he had dislocated his shoulder so many times playing basketball and water skiing that they wouldn't take him. And Steve, of course, was the outrageous one, deciding as he sat in his jockey shorts in a hospital waiting room between one part of his medical examination and another with his entire medical record in his lap, that he didn't have to put up with that crap. He stood up, put on his clothes, walked out of the hospital and threw his file down a storm drain. He got away with it too. We didn't know anything about this until years later, only that we received a few postcards from the Selective Service Board asking us if we knew the whereabouts of a certain Stephen William Kent. We didn't. We were out of touch with him off and on in those days in the '60s, sometimes for months.

When he had tino-sinuvitis back in 1955 he wasn't supposed to walk, so on the train ride home Jack carried him everywhere piggyback — through the Pullman sleepers, the club car, coaches where people lolled in stupor from sitting up all night until we all finally reached the dining car. In Chicago where we had to change trains and go by taxi from LaSalle Street Station to Union Station — or was it the other way around? — Jack carried Steve. He loved it, hanging around Jack's neck. And when Jack was dying, a year and a half ago, Steve said to me, "What a sweet man." Perhaps he was leaping back across all the years of friction between them, in the '60s, when he thought and said to Jack that his life and work seemed stupid, irrelevant, and in the '70s when Steve began to live his own kind of life, learning how to farm and raise animals, to that earlier time when Jack carried him. Jack never resented Steve as he crashed through his rebellious years. In fact, he was proud of him for living according to his revolutionary views, even a little envious perhaps, for Jack had not been quite as uncompromising in his own youth. He wanted to be a pacifist, but wasn't sure enough of himself. But yes, he was a sweet man. He was also good at taking out splinters, lancing boils, cutting hair.

94

Finally, after four days and five nights we roared into the Berkeley Station at the foot of University Avenue, where there was a huge delegation of friends and relatives, and even Tom's dog Laddy, who had been boarded all year with some of these same friends and relatives. Tom was one happy boy and he sat right down on the platform and hugged and hugged his best friend. And Steve still wore his sombrero.

Chapter Six

I remember my mother, every time we came home — from the east, from Europe, from a trip to the mountains or the desert or the Dude Ranch in Wyoming — crying out, as she gazed through our living room window at the panoramic view, "There's no place in the world lovelier than this!" But when Jack and I and the boys came home in '55 we noticed changes. Automobiles were no longer mostly gray or tan or black, with a few bright paint jobs like the yellow of my first boyfriend's Plymouth coupe, the Whitney's red Pontiac convertible, or our blue Ford convertible when Steve was a baby. Those bright colors were for the privileged, foolish young.

We didn't take care of that Ford. Stupid. Neither one of knew beans about mechanics. We never thought of having the oil checked. In the summer of '49 when I was pregnant with Dave, I drove regularly, top down, no seat belt, from Inverness into the redwoods, then over White's Hill, through those lovely small towns that when I was a child were still distinct and separated by fields with cows and orchards — Fairfax, San Anselmo, Ross, Sausalito — though by '49 the open spaces were steadily filling in with housing to accommodate the ceaseless immigration to this promised land — across the Golden Gate Bridge in my blue convertible with my hair blowing, like a pregnant movie star, to San Francisco, where Dr. DeCarl, my obstetrician, probed my birth canal, as I winced and tried to think of other things.

After we trashed the blue convertible we bought a sensible four-door grey sedan, and that was the car we came home to in '55. But when we looked down any busy street it seemed to be a vibrant sea of yellow, red, green and baby blue; white, magenta, and orange; with only an occasional black or tan or gray. And it wasn't long before we too wanted color again. We turned in the sedan for the first new car we'd ever owned, a lime-green Ford station wagon, big enough to drive a bunch of cub scouts or Little Leaguers here and there and on our first and last real camping effort — a Sierra Club trip with the Whitneys to Kings Canyon.

There were ten of us in the station wagon and we hauled a trailer with all our gear behind over the Sonora Pass. More crazy car abuse. The whole two weeks were sort of crazy — 150 campers sleeping all over Reds Meadow the night before we started our climb up to the base camp. In the middle of the night I heard a plaintive far-off cry, "Daaady, Daaady," somebody's child — oh, no, YES, it was David, then aged seven or so. I leapt out of my sleeping bag and ran barefoot across the meadow, dodging the mass of sleeping bodies as best I could, to my baby. He'd been looking for the bathroom and gotten lost. From then on we put Dave between Steve and their cousin Nick, who were supposed to keep him from sleepwalking. The nights were freezing. Jack and I put on all our clothes in layers and even so Jack announced every morning, "Well, another sleepless night." Tom, whose need to question authority continued unabated, got in trouble with the responsible Sierra Club kitchen staff over some detail of carrying out his volunteer help, a preview of his troubles at Thacher School, which he would enter that Fall. The kitchen staff were his contemporaries. Nevertheless they represented authority. Galen Rowell, to become a noted mountain climber and photographer of the Himalayas as well as West Marin where Tom now lives, and whose work he undoubtedly admires, was one of them. They threw Tom into the icy creek, one more learning experience for him, of which he seemed to need many. (Now Tom tells me it had to do with somebody ripping his very favorite Pendleton shirt, something he obviously feels passionate about more than forty years later.)

Another thing we noticed for the first time in '55 was smog. We used to feel so superior to Los Angeles in this regard, as in many others. No longer could we indulge ourselves in that form of provincialism. Once in a great while now in 1999, when the North wind blows or after a rain storm, the sky is the way it always used to be when I was growing up in Berkeley. — blue, clean sparkling. When the fog came in it was like soft white cotton instead of the yellowish, murky quilt of oppression that we have become used to. David, being the youngest, not quite six, and therefore with the most sensitive lungs, complained that his chest hurt when he ran, or when we were burning leaves. On Scenic Avenue when we first moved to Berkeley in 1948, before Dave was born, the street trees were huge deciduous maples and sycamores that in the fall shed their leaves of gold and bronze and red, waxy and shiny at first, then curling, drying, fading all over the lawn. I used to love raking them into a pile in the gutter, then tending the fire as they burned.

The smell of burning leaves as I was growing up in the '20s and '30s was synonymous with new clothes and notebooks for the start of school, and with football games. The house on LaLoma Avenue was only five blocks north of Memorial Stadium, close enough to hear the roaring crowds. All the neighborhoods surrounding the campus on football game days had smiling pedestrian rooters sauntering past, the women dressed in tweed suits or sweaters and skirts. They wore stockings and had chrysanthemum corsages. The men wore slacks and sweaters and neckties. The corsages have disappeared. Now Styrofoam coolers identify the football fans who still walk through our neighborhoods with their dreamy smiles, and the dress code is determined by L.L. Bean.

Actually I've never been a good spectator of sports, except when my own family or close friends are among the players. Then I become such a fan I hardly recognize myself, yelling and cheering, "Yea, Tom, yea, Grayson!" And then it's not football, but baseball or tennis or soccer or lacrosse or swimming or sailing. I wish I had known Jack when he was playing water polo in college. Oh, I would have gone to all those games and cheered for him. But football bored me in those days and repels me now, though I still feel a pang of nostalgia on those autumn Saturdays for chrysanthemum corsages and the smell of burning leaves.

So then, in '55, just back from fifteen months away, there was smog and not only the smell of burning leaves but also of the burning garbage in the dump that was gradually filling the Bay. And Jack and I were back into the political world. We got our first TV and began watching the Huntley-Brinkley news show.

(Other favorites were "Amos and Andy," and "The Honeymooners," with Jackie Gleason and Audrey Meadows. I also remember sitting up late with Tom, watching the movie, "Outward Bound," with Tallulah Bankhead, forced to endure the ads, so trapped by the movie were we.)

The book Jack had been working on all year was put on hold. With a full teaching load and resuming the chairmanship of his department, he was again on the Planning Commission. Berkeley's first Master Plan, of which he had been a principal author, was adopted by the City Council.

The Bay Area Air Pollution Control District was formed by the State Legislature. The Alameda-Contra Costa Transit District was formed. In '56 we all worked for Stevenson, and in 57 Jack was persuaded to run for City Council.

The campaign cost $3,000. His one brochure was in black and white, and his issues were:

> SMOG - "The city dump is obviously adding to the smog problem. Sensible methods of waste disposal are known and other cities have stopped burning. Why does Berkeley always lag behind?"
> TRAFFIC . . . .
> TRANSIT . . . .
> TAXES . . . .
> "Our tax base must be broadened and the University must pay its fair share in order to ease the tax burden of the homeowner. As we homeowners, with proper care, prevent our property from deteriorating, we must

improve our city if we are to avoid decay and urban blight." (That one appealed to neat and tidy Republicans.)

RECREATION ....

The brochure was considered very original in its graphics and made quite a splash. Now it seems quaint and sweet to me, and in the family photo we all look so young. I was thirty-six; Jack was forty, vigorous enough to walk the precincts, something the entrenched Republicans had never bothered to do, and by then we were experienced campaigners. It made a great hit when, standing on someone's doorstep, I introduced myself as the candidate's wife. And I don't deny that I got an adrenaline kick, a vicarious sense of power and boost to my ego. The boys were involved too, organized along with all the other neighborhood kids, by the campaign treasurer, our dear friend and neighbor, Calder Hayes, to wear paper hats decorated with bumper stickers: KENT FOR COUNCIL, and to carry sandwich boards: PLAY FAIR WITH BERKELEY: ELECT T.J. (JACK) KENT TO THE BERKELEY CITY COUNCIL: OUTSTANDING EXPERIENCE, VIGOR, PROVEN LEADERSHIP — blah, blah — down Solano Avenue which in those days was the heart of Republicanism. An elderly woman waiting for a bus remarked, "Some people will do *anything* for a vote!" Using children, I presume is what she meant. Tom ran ahead of us on election night, up the steps of the City Hall; then, as we were climbing the stairs inside, he yelled from above, "Dad's ahead of everyone!" It was true. He won overwhelmingly and at the top of the ticket.

Until the '60s the Council continued to be dominated by Republicans. The rhetoric was that local politics were nonpartisan. But the practice was the Republicans resigned before the end of a term, so that he or she could be replaced with another Republican by appointment instead of having to deal with an open election. The system perpetuated a conservative Chamber of Commerce Council for years. Everything was for business, very little for public amenities such as parks, playgrounds, street trees. In the early '50s there were, until Jack was elected in '57, only two Democrats out of nine seats. His election brought it up to three. So when he ran for a second term four years later the effort was to bring two more Democrats along with him in a slate. It worked. Wm. T. (Zack) Brown of the Coop Credit Union, Wilmont (Bill) Sweeney, "the black Irishman," as he referred to himself, who later became a Judge, and Jack, were all elected in '61. For the first time ever there was a Democratic majority and a black council member. (All three are now dead.)

That campaign was so much fun, mostly because of Sweeney. We went to black churches where he would introduce Jack and Zack and instruct the parishioners to vote for these two white guys as well as for him. And we didn't dare sneak out after the political part, so we spent some uplifting Sunday mornings listening to gospel singers. We went to black nightclubs and danced and drank with Sweeney and his swinging friends. Zack's wife, Joy, and I felt dowdy but exhilarated. It was like going to a foreign country — the Plaka in Athens, Soho in London, Montmartre in Paris. And yet it was right here in Berkeley, all that black humor and soul. We had already gotten to know some of the important black activists — D.G. Gibson, Byron Rumford, Tom Berkley, Del Williams, Frances Albrier, Vivian Osborne Marsh, to name a few. During the war in the '40s when Jack was in the Army and Tommy and I were living with my parents, my father had worked with D.G. and Rumford to set up the Berkeley Interracial Committee. In fact my father was the first President and I was Secretary. And sometime during the '50s we discovered a soul food restaurant on San Pablo Avenue, Albertine's, where at informal political strategy lunches we ate greens and chitlins and gumbo — the kind of food that Ora used to talk about and sometimes fix for us — with both black and white party workers. It was a grand old time.

In 1961-62, along with serving his second term as councilman, meeting every Tuesday night for something like $10 a week, Jack took his second sabbatical in residence to work on his book. Tom, who'd been an Alpha Delt at Cal for two years, but had refused to be initiated because he wouldn't put up with the system of hazing, then flunked out of college altogether. Were we angry, upset, surprised? I think we knew it was coming, based on his previous behavior. Apparently we don't remember pain. Otherwise why would women go on bearing children, why would men go on making war?

In the summer of '62 near the end of Jack's sabbatical, we had one more wonderful family excursion, going by train from Berkeley, leaving once again from the familiar old Southern Pacific railroad station at the foot of University Avenue. It's been replaced by a trendy restaurant, which makes me sad. In Seattle we had to change trains. There was a tremendous scramble by all of us, carrying luggage, leaping across a series of train tracks and jumping onto the train to Vancouver. But Tom, though he'd flunked out of college, was now a big strong man, six feet tall. He shared with Jack the major responsibility of getting us on that train.

We crossed Canada, playing many card games along the way, stopping over at Banff and Lake Louise and Montreal, where, perhaps mesmerized by the cadence of French, or the charm of the honeymoon suite to which Jack and I were assigned by accident — we certainly weren't honeymooners with those three large sons — I washed all my brand new underwear from Hink's Department Store on Shattuck in Berkeley, and left it hanging in the bathroom.

Then on to Europe (without much underwear) via the ocean liner, Empress of Britain, to Scotland, another wonderful ocean crossing by sea with all the amenities — shuffleboard, sing-alongs in the lounge, dancing. That's when I discovered what a wonderful dancer Steve had become. Our first night in Scotland was spent in a small inn on the shores of Loch Ness. We looked for the monster, climbed part way up Ben Lomond which was covered with purple gorse, and the next day traversed the country — me driving, on the left (wrong!) side of the road, because Jack had let his license lapse and Tom was not yet twenty-one. Outside Edinburgh we stayed for a week at Prestonfield House where peacocks roamed the grounds, sculpted angels adorned the ceilings, and the stone stairs were worn down and slightly hollowed from centuries of use. Scottish food was surprisingly good, better than English. It was summer and sliced fresh sweet tomatoes accompanied breakfast, lunch and dinner. We had drinks before dinner in a cozy bar all lined with leather. We played golf, the only time I've ever played in my life, and surely the way the game was meant to be played, on open fields where sheep grazed and kept the greensward cropped. The boys, of course, got into it, wearing Scotch caps, and swiveling their hips.

We reconnected with our friends the Johnson-Marshalls, the ones with seven children, who had now moved from London to Edinburgh. They took us on a memorable excursion including a train ride to the coast, then a boat ride out to an island, Inchcolm, in the Firth of Forth, where we picnicked and explored an ancient abbey and sang in an octagonal room whose acoustics made us sound quite heavenly.

Another outing was to Lochearnhead, by way of two stark castles, Stirling and Doune, driving cautiously all the way because of flocks of sheep that meandered along the road. (By then Jack had obtained a temporary license and did the driving.) The occasion was "The Balquhidder, Lochearnhead Strathyre Highland Games," where enormous Scots in kilts tossed the caber (sort of like a telephone pole) and raced up a mountainside. There was exuberant music played by "The Pipes and Drums of the 7th Battalion Argyll," and judging of sheep dogs. We were adopted by the clan of the Chieftain, Sir Gregor Macgregor, and taken into the clan's tent for shots of Scotch whiskey. And in the bed-and-breakfast, St. Blane's Guest House, where we stayed the night, Jack left his gray flannel slacks in the closet. (Why is it I remember so vividly these items of clothing left by mistake or on purposed in the closets and bathrooms of foreign hotels?)

We went way up north to Inverness to see why those Scots who came to Marin County chose to name the town where they (and we for most of the summers of our lives) settled on Tomales Bay after their hometown. We found that the topography was decidedly similar, although Inverness, Scotland, is a small city instead of a village like ours.

Back in Edinburgh we bought secondhand bikes for the boys, and they took off, southward, staying in youth hostels and having adventures on their own. Dave was only twelve, but we seemed to feel his older brothers would take care of him, and they did. As it turned out, he was the most agile bicycle rider, perhaps because he didn't weigh much, whereas both Steve and Tom had sore butts for days.

Jack and I enjoyed that respite from parenting and headed south. We stopped at Melford near Sir Walter Scott's gigantic home, Abbotsford, then traversed the bleak, impressive borderland from Scotland into Northumberland, England. We spent a few hours in Corbridge, there in the very north of England, getting in touch with Jack's old friend and colleague, Syd Williams' second wife's family by going to the pub where her brother was said to hang out. Just imagine going into a bar somewhere half way across the world and saying, "Do you know Mr. So-and-So?" and the guy you asked this of turns out to be Mr. So-and-So. This was Syd Williams' brother-in-law, and he showed us all over the town, took us home for tea, and introduced us to the entire large family.

We'd been impressed with the police in Inverness, where Tom lost his wallet at a fair, and the police somehow tracked us down when it was found. So we'd worked out an itinerary and a system for keeping in touch with the boys in case of emergency, which was for us to contact the police department in each town we stayed in overnight. It wasn't until we got to York that the police had a message from the boys in Newcastle. They'd had enough bike riding and were taking the train from there to York. They'd ridden about 150 miles. We sold the bikes at auction in York and got a good price for them because apparently the fact that they had belonged to Americans gave them extra value. Why was that, I wonder?

In York we enjoyed the busy, pretty town — its Cathedral, its river, and its street, "The Shambles," named because of the way the upper floors of the buildings jutted out over the lower floors, leaning crazily toward each other in a most haphazard fashion, forming covered sidewalks. This was to protect pedestrians from slops thrown out of the upper windows back in the early days. A few years later we would name our second Inverness house "The Shambles," for it had a similar shambley look.

Now on to London and our old stamping ground, The Milton Court Hotel. Francis, the doorman, was still there after seven years.

The game of sneaking had been replaced by a soccer ball that the boys kicked along in parks and open countryside all over Scotland, England, Denmark, Germany, and France. The continental lap of this trip coincided with an excursion of city planners, meeting up with and traveling with many old friends and colleagues and visiting housing developments, urban centers, greenbelts, and inner city parks. In Paris we went to the opera, to Les Halles, and revisited our favorite restaurant, Doucet, near the Luxembourg Gardens, also still there after seven years. Finally we were on the way home from Orly Airport in Paris to San Francisco. I remember sleeping on Steve's generous shoulder the last part of the fourteen-hour flight. But it grieves me to see in the photos of him on that trip that he has a sad, somewhat wistful expression. At the time we probably chalked it up to surly adolescence. Now I know it was more than that.

In the meantime, two years earlier, my dear father had died in '59, just ten years after the year of the oath began. He was only 72. In the fifteen years or so before his death he and my mother had begun to make some changes, readying themselves for a peaceful retirement and the fulfilling of some old dreams. They bought a ranch in Lake County. We have pictures of Tommy, aged six or seven, sitting on a stout white horse in a field with a view of Mount Konocti in the distance. Daddy had apparently always wanted a ranch. It was part of his dream as he migrated to the west. Years earlier, when I was fourteen, he had befriended the stable boy, Syd Reynolds, where he kept his horse two blocks from our house on LaLoma Avenue. Syd and his brother Spike had just decided to take paying guests at their ranch, Z-Bar-U, in Wyoming, and that summer the whole Tolman family spent a few glorious weeks sleeping in log cabins set in a grove of quaking aspens, eating ranch food like brains and kidneys and sweetbreads. We participated in rodeos and barn dances, rode up into the Wind River Range, and swam in mountain lakes. We were the only "dudes" that first summer, so it was like being a part of a real ranching family. My father loved it; my mother, who'd never ridden a horse in her life, though she played tennis and swam, suffered it bravely.

My brother Ted and I went back the following summer, all by ourselves on the train. We were about eleven and fifteen, and I was supposed to be sort of taking care of him. Once we got to Z-Bar-U, though, we hardly saw each other. I fell in love with a cowboy and learned to roll cigarettes, while Ted pursued his avid interest in horses, and learned to rope and castrate calves.

It was apparently assumed by our parents that Ted was never to be an academic, though he was very smart, and still is. When he finally learned to read, it was the Encyclopedia he pored over. When the war broke out he was just out of high school, eighteen-years-old, but was told by the draft board that he was psychologically immature, to go get a job and come back in six months. He worked for the Railway Express, and after the six months were up he gave our father all the money he had made, thinking he might never come home. I asked him the other day if he'd been scared. He said no, not scared, just practical. He was drafted, and trained at Fort Riley, Kansas, with the last mounted cavalry unit of the United States Army. After that it was tanks instead of horses. Our father, in the meantime, bought Coca Cola stock for Ted, who now has more than 5,000 shares, worth about a half a million. He has spent most of his adult life in Lake County, California, as a rancher, and then for the Forest Service, one of those fearless men who, among other things, are flown all over the State to fight fires. For years he and his second wife, Dorothy, lived in a mobile home on the shores of Clear Lake. He still lives there. After retirement and being widowed a few months earlier than I, building boats and sailing the Lake are his greatest pleasures.

The house my parents built on their Lake County Ranch in the '50s was a block house in the middle of a field and they called it Pasture House. The operation of the ranch, which consisted of sheep, walnuts and pears, was carried out by a tenant rancher. It was a lovely setting, a simple house, and they enjoyed having weekend company. (Sometime later, after both of them had died, I found a log book in which their guests made entries, extolling the beauty of the place and the hospitality of my parents. The last entry was in my mother's shaky hand: "The End.")

They had also bought a piece of land for Ted, "Red Hill Ranch." After the war he had gone to U.C. Davis to study agriculture. On this ranch, too, walnuts and pears were the crops. There were a couple of horses and a beautiful barn. Ted married a woman a few years older than he whom he met at a bar. Her name was Laverne, but she was called Slim. She'd grown up following race track events around the country. Her father was a horse trainer. She had two children, each by a different man. Then she and Ted had Russell.

When Steve was a kid he spent a few weeks over a couple of summers there in Lake County with Ted, Slim, Caroline, Eddie, and little Russell. Later, with still another man, Slim had another child, Tina. Russell, still a child himself, helped raise her, since his mother and step-dad were off tending the bar that they owned. In the meantime Ted Married Dorothy, and when Russell was about thirteen he opted to go and live with them. After high school he went to Davis where he studied psychology and started playing the guitar and writing songs, then on to Business School at UCLA. Today, forty-something, Russell is a musician and a business man. He's traveled and played in Europe often and has married a young German woman artist from Cologne. The country life seems to have no appeal for them, but he remembers looking up to Steve with awe when he was a little kid because Steve was a natural animal guy who could even make their old donkey move! He told me this last June at the Memorial gathering we had for Steve near his place in Humboldt County.

That was sometime in the '50s, when Steve stayed at "Red Hill Ranch." He loved it, of course, actually doing real work on a ranch, and he loved Slim, the way she caught frogs and cooked them, the lower class allure of her. I know my parents, especially my mother, agonized, not so much because of Ted's marrying someone from another world than their own intellectual, academic (and puritanical!) one, but because Slim, it was soon apparent, would not stick around for the long haul.

By then the house on LaLoma Avenue had been sold and my parents had moved to a smaller one high up in the Berkeley hills. It was a nice house with a little garden right off the living room which my father could manage. On LaLoma he could no longer control and enjoy the sprawling garden that rolled down toward Hillside School three floors below the living room. My mother couldn't seem to ignore the unused floors below the one on which they lived. At the time I was impatient. Why couldn't they just let the garden go back to nature, why couldn't they close the doors to the empty rooms? I understand why now. I've been through all that myself. I realize how difficult that decision to move must have been. It's sad that none of the three of us offspring wanted that house anymore. I feel a little pang as I drive by it at least three or four times a week. But we were settled in homes of our own by then.

Those were the years when I felt as though I were the middle part of a sandwich, squeezed between the needs of our aging parents and our growing children. Jack's father had Parkinson's Disease, and his mother was beginning to do strange things, like charging a mink cloche hat she couldn't afford at I. Magnin's for her granddaughter, and hiding money around the house. (Later, after Jack's father had died, and we were moving his mother to a retirement home, Janis and I found over $100 in cash hidden under rugs, behind sofa cushions, in the leaves of books.) And we were so caught up in our own lives roaring along in high gear on many levels, everything from Jack's students in city planning, to politics, to Cub Scouts, to PTA, to yanking Tom out of Berkeley High, and, with my father's encouragement and financial help, sending him off to that fancy prep school, Thacher, in the Ojai Valley where Jim Whitney had gone and both his sons were going. Perhaps it was a mistake. That was one of the hardest things about bringing up children, to make the right decision when we had only one chance.

One of the requirements at Thacher was that each student own and take care of a horse. Tom got a horse named Bourbon that he disliked, but perhaps only because he was determined to be negative about everything at that school, even though his cousin and then best buddy Pete Whitney was going there. All the rest of the Kents and Whitneys loved our extended family excursions at Thanksgiving, when the school welcomed us with sports events and special meals. Steve, of course was longing to go there, because of the horses, but there was no way he could have gotten in academically. He certainly wasn't dumb, but he was probably dyslexic, though nobody seemed to know about that in those days. And like the several dyslexic people I know, on maturing he became an original thinker and developed vociferous and eclectic reading habits: fourteenth century history from Barbara Tuchman, vampires from Anne Rice, cowboys from Cormac McCarthy. And then there was Thomas Cahill's *How The Irish Saved Civilization*, Keri Hulme's *The Bone People*, and the Bible.

At some point we got a phone call from Thacher's Headmaster, Newton Chase, saying that he had just put Tom on the plane home, and that he could only return when he made apologies for his arrogance. We were having some high-level political meeting at our house in a few hours, but Jack drove off to the airport, I fixed supper, brewed a lot of coffee, and held down the fort somehow. Tom did graduate, though he threw his diploma in a trash bin as he walked off the stage. Fortunately this was after my father had died.

November 1999

It's Thanksgiving time again and I'm remembering Thanksgivings on LaLoma when my parents traditionally invited young psychology faculty and graduate students with their wives and children. There was usually a children's table set in the bay window on the west end of the living room, the same bay window in which Jack and I were married. After the midday dinner we all trooped down to the Hillside School playground for a baseball game. It was funny, all those grownup men running around in dress shoes with their shirtsleeves rolled up. Daddy claimed he was no good at athletic games, that he wasn't a very good father to Ted in this regard, and it's true that those Thanksgiving baseball games seemed more of a spoof than the real thing.

I'm remembering Jack's Thanksgiving of 1938, as he told me about it later. He and other expatriates were in Switzerland with Carl Jung and Margaret Schevill. Margaret was Janis' mother-in-law, a friend of my mother's, who built and partially designed two of the houses Jack and I have owned, and an extremely creative, charming, powerful, and also difficult woman, who was in the middle of a divorce and had gone to Zurich to "work" with Jung. Her younger son, Jim, was there also for a while and invited Jack, then in Freiburg, to join a group of Americans for Thanksgiving dinner. Jung asked to hear from the young Americans what Thanksgiving meant, their hopes for the future. As often happened Jack was the chosen spokesman and expressed his usual optimism. Jung countered with the gloomy prediction that rivers of blood would flow all over Europe in the near future. He was right.

There were quite a few Thanksgivings right across the street at 77 Tamalpais Road, another of Margaret's beautiful houses where, by that time each of her grownup sons — first Karl (and Janis), then Jim (and Helen) — lived with their families for many years. Between our three families there were seven children, all cousins or cousins of cousins. Then there were the Thanksgivings at Midland School in the Santa Ynez Valley near Santa Barbara, when our grandsons Grayson and Fletcher were there, again, as at Thacher a generation earlier, with athletic events, lots of food, and a play.

Five years ago Steve, with his longtime Humboldt County friend, Elizabeth, hosted a spectacular community feast at "The Beginnings," a homemade, octagonal community building that expresses the creativity and idealism of the old hippie times. Cooking went on for hours. There was football in the meadow, eating, drinking, and dancing. Then on June 24 last year, after scattering his ashes a mile away under fruit trees he had planted over a couple of decades, reaching into the Chinese urn that held them, in that same octagonal room we remembered Steve, again with his Humboldt friends, sharing memories, songs, food, dancing.

This year, two days ago, I sat next to Tom, now the senior male at this gathering of the clan, eighteen at a table he'd put together for the occasion. It filled his and Deb's living room in that wonderful homemade house that has evolved from a log cabin and trailer and outhouse with no electricity to a spacious hospitable setting with large windows and vistas of Tom's precious trees. The food was magnificent, for not only is this family peculiarly sentimental about tradition, considering the numbers of nonconformists in it, but several of the members thereof are bakers and gourmet cooks as well. A new touch, an idea that Deb instigated a few years ago and is well on its way to becoming one more tradition, is the lighting of candles between the main course and dessert. Each person has a candle at his or her place, which he or she lights while remembering an absent relative, or a special event of significance.

It was a bittersweet Thanksgiving for me, for all of us. The empty spaces Jack and Steve left are overwhelming. They were the main theme of remembrances, and I felt lonely there, the honored matriarch, at the top of the pinnacle, as Tom so lovingly expressed it. As he lit his candle, he remembered the premature deaths by accident, ill health, or suicide of five or six of his contemporaries, "my fellow fuck-ups," as he called them, boys and men most of us had known, and then he honored his own two sons, Grayson, twenty-five and Fletcher, twenty-three, sitting there at the table, for being survivors. I think he meant survivors, along with himself, of his years of alcoholism and risk. He still rides a motorcycle and climbs trees, but he's down to one cup of Peets decaf a day.

I simply marvel at him, as I do at each of my three sons, the way they found their way into doing work that satisfies the soul, in his case being an artist in the trees. It's touching the way, when we go anywhere together, walking or driving, he's looking at trees, intensely aware of their shapes or misshapes or ailments or beauty. With Steve, it was the animals he watched, understanding the configuration of a horse, for instance. With Dave it is buildings, design. He runs his hand across the surfaces of tables and chairs. Thank goodness in our attempts to educate them we didn't manage to stifle that.

In the late '50s my father had surgery for colon cancer, then some months later a heart attack. He died peacefully at home, a few days after returning from the hospital, on the daybed in his study where he lay down for a nap after lunch. So these were, for us, the years of heady success and fun and vitality tempered by the deaths of family members and friends: Edward Chace Tolman (my father), 1959; Kathleen Drew Tolman (my mother), 1963; Thomas John Kent, Sr. (Jack's father), 1963; Catherine Bauer Wurster (colleague, neighbor, adversary), 1964; Alexander Meiklejohn (Tolman neighbor and friend and renowned civil libertarian), 1964; not to mention the assassinations of President Kennedy and Malcolm X, and those of Martin Luther King, Jr., and Bobby Kennedy still to come near the end of the decade. Worst of all, because he was only forty-nine years old, was the death of my sister Deborah's husband and Jack's best friend, James Goodrich Whitney, of an embolism on May 16, 1966. For awhile it seemed as though Jack had put aside his own career and become a professional speaker at memorial gatherings.

The Whitneys had been as deeply involved in politics as we. Jim ran for both State Assembly and City Council, and though he lost those elections, was important in the Democratic Party as first president of the Berkeley Grassrooters Democratic Club, Board member of the Democratic Council, a member of the Berkeley Parks and Recreation Commission, a member of the Citizens Committee Against Discrimination in Housing. He was also a successful and much loved Jungian psychiatrist. At his memorial, held in that same Maybeck building, The Town and Gown Club where we had just a few months earlier celebrated our twenty-fifth anniversary, Jack spoke, *"In appreciating Jim, it has helped me to think about him in terms of his whole life. I have wanted to know all that I could about his childhood, his family, and his main stages of growth and development as a distinct individual. I have wanted to learn how such a remarkably comprehending and warm human being was created."* Reading this again I feel a huge sob developing. It truly was the end of Camelot for us.

The '60s were in full swing. In Berkeley the new Democratic majority on the city council had the effect of opening a flood gate behind which liberals and progressives and radicals had all been held back. Jack's position seems to me to have been rather like Gorbachev's would be many years later. He had pried open the door, and then in poured the next generation of activists, pushing past him, past all of us. Yes, **THE SIXTIES,** which we didn't yet quite understand, though our own sons were acting out some of the symbolic behavior of the day. The style of politics was changing, becoming more confrontational and proactive, and a parallel movement was occurring in the planning profession. The emphasis was on social change on a worldwide scale. All well and good; Jack (and I) also deplored starvation in far-off places, the suppression of civil liberties, but these did not fall, in his view, within the bailiwick of city planning. So it was rather amazing that his book, *The Urban General Plan*, at odds with the trends of the day, was published in '64. Today it is still considered a classic text and a few years ago was reissued.

His second term as councilman ended in '65 and he was honored at a party and presented with a decorative plaque: *"The Democratic Party of the City of Berkeley through its organization for two-party Municipal Home Rule, the Berkeley Caucus, does now bestow upon one of its stalwart sons, Thomas John Kent, Jr., this token of its esteem and gratitude. Ever gracious in office, you have been heedful of small voices, faithful in the craft of building for beauty, bold in the architecture of government for the family of man, we are proud to confer on you, a true son of Thomas Jefferson, our thanks and gratitude."*

I doubt that anyone but I was aware that at those long council meetings every Tuesday night for eight years, while he was being "heedful of small voices," he was sometimes also reading a book that lay in his lap under that great curved arc of wood behind which the council members sat in dignity, raised above the people, beneath the American flag. At that time it might have been Rossiter's *The First American Revolution*, or *Thomas Jefferson on Democracy*. In '66 he took a two-year leave from the University to become San Francisco Mayor John Shelley's coordinator for development.

Chapter Seven

December 1999

*P*arallel to all this was our life in Inverness, an entirely different setting, with other activities and friends (though the Whitneys were major players in both our Berkeley and Inverness milieus.) Since that's where it all began for us, it was natural that we should find a way to continue it. But the purchase of our first house was as illogical as it was perfect. The war was on, I was pregnant with the baby that would be stillborn six months later. We had no money: $50 a month G. I. stipend plus family charity. It was in the summer of 1944. Jack was home on leave. Tommy was twenty-one months old, about the age that his twin grandsons are today (how's that for continuum?), running around in training pants (a term not heard of for decades, sort of like training bras), when Jim's mother, Dr. Elizabeth Goodrich Whitney, an awesome woman with enormous breasts, a Jungian analyst (as were her deceased husband and her son Jim) for some reason, I suppose because I was her daughter-in-law's sister, took us under her analytical wing, so to speak. She "prescribed" and loaned us her small, charming guest house, once a chicken house, therefore known as "The Roost," at Chicken Ranch Beach in Inverness (for she was also heiress by marriage of some very choice property on the shores of Tomales Bay) to spend Jack's precious furlough in. It was like a honeymoon, except that we had Tommy, who was full of mischief and so pleased to have Daddy around for a change that he kept climbing into bed with us.

Deborah and I used to compare our mothers-in-law. I rather envied her her more intellectual one, although Jack's mother, Belinda, bought me the most wonderful clothes that I would ever own. I really didn't know how to shop, and reverted to feeling like a Berkeley hick, standing in those I. Magnin dressing rooms in my J. C. Penney underwear while shrewd Belinda negotiated with the sales lady, someone she knew by name. If on my own, I would rummage around in the racks, not knowing what I really wanted, therefore unable to communicate with a sales lady. But with Belinda, who admonished me, "You must *always* ask for Mrs. So-and-So," I simply succumbed to hers and "Mrs. So-and-So's" taste, which was excellent. I still remember a beige two-piece knit dress that I wore, with an orchid pinned on my shoulder, when we sailed on the *DUIVENDYK*; three suits over the years — a blue knit, a black wool and a tweed; a silk dress with coat to match with a bold splashy design of gold and blue squares. Each one of these garments had something special about it, either in the originality of the cut or the uniqueness of the fabric. I never understood Jack's mother. I had her pegged as a simple, unsophisticated Oakland girl who had a beautiful divorced mother that she was in awe of. I don't understand to this day how she knew how to shop as she did.

Dr. Elizabeth, Deborah's mother-in-law, on the other hand, wore sensible shoes, swam in Tomales Bay, and spoke over my head in the language of symbols and myths. She was an early feminist. "Oh, woman.... " she would cant in a doleful tone to Deborah and me and all of us young war brides with too little money, too much work, and loneliness. I see now how oppressive such talk could be to a daughter-in-law, and a year or two later, Deborah, struggling with postpartum depression after her second child, Peter, was born, became only more depressed. But for us in that summer of 1944, Elizabeth was a paragon.

And then onto the scene appeared Margaret Schevill once more. She was one of those whose ego, though seeming very strong, still imposed it on others, in need of constant reaffirmation of its strength. I wonder what Carl Jung had to say about Margaret's ego. I told Jack, I'm sure, how she tried to match me up with her son Jimmy. (He hasn't been called Jimmy for years — he's James Schevill, poet and playwright, emeritus professor from Brown University — but I shall call him Jimmy here in order not to confuse him with Jim Whitney.) Well, Jimmy has always been my friend, Jack's too. But when Margaret was matchmaking, something she loved to do, I was already smitten by Jack. Jimmy's still my friend and I'm worried about him now because his daughter, Susie, told me just today that he's had a stroke. (Susie lives in that same house across the Street, #77 Tamalpais Road, where she grew up, the same one in which, decades earlier, Margaret organized a private kindergarten that Jimmy and I both attended when we were five years old. So once again I'm reminded of how "intertwingled" — there's that wonderful invented word of Jack's — five generations of our families and houses and friends have become, and how deeply my roots are embedded in this place, and in Inverness too, which helps to sustain me after the loss of Jack and Steve.

When Margaret Schevill was visiting with her fellow Jungian, Dr. Elizabeth Whitney, that summer of 1944, she casually mentioned on the beach one day that she had decided to sell her Inverness cottage. (She had become enamored with the Indian cultures of the Southwest, had built a house in Tucson where her interests now lay.) Would we possibly like to buy it? She would consider selling it to us, because of all our familial long time connections, for $2500.

Would we ever! It was a little gem of a house — another of Margaret's creative successes — a large, high-ceilinged living room with redwood walls and an enormous stone fireplace, a tiny kitchen and bathroom and two balcony sleeping areas, all nestled in banks of ferns with fine old live oaks and bay trees all about. Not only was the price possible, but she made it easy for us to pay her in small monthly amounts and our parents helped us out. We couldn't actually occupy it for two more summers as the war was on, and we still, as it turned out, had our life in Washington, D. C. ahead of us, and then after the war Jack's months in Berlin. Did we rent it out? I can't remember. Jack's kind diplomatic father took charge of all dealings with Margaret, who, I am sure, he'd had to deal with before as she was his daughter's mother-in-law.

Oh boy, planning the details of Janis and Karl's wedding — May 25, 1937, I think it was — must have been fraught with complication! Belinda Kent and Margaret Schevill were two strong women with entirely different values and lifestyles. Belinda believed that those who couldn't succeed in the "real world" taught. Margaret (as did my parents actually) believed just the opposite, even though she would soon divorce her own scholarly husband, a distinguished professor of Spanish. I'm sure that both sets of parents were not entirely happy with the union. However, when Jack and I got married four years later I think perhaps it was only his mother who was disappointed. His father was a quiet, private, nonjudgemental man; and my parents adored Jack, despite whatever intellectually snobbish thoughts I suspect they secretly harbored against his parents and sister.

Jack used to tell me how my mother overwhelmed him with friendliness when she happened to run into him at North Gate. That's where she did her errands, at Reed's Drugstore on the corner of Hearst and Euclid that also had a small post office in the rear, or at the cleaners' or the shoe repair shop, or Hagstrom's Grocery, though she ordered most of her groceries from the Lincoln Market on University Avenue and they were delivered to our kitchen door. The North Gate neighborhood — I still get my hair cut there — was where Jack too hung out, near the old Architecture building where he was studying, also near the Beta Theta Pi fraternity house on the corner of Hearst and LeRoy where he lived for those four years from 1934 to 1938.

I find it hard to imagine my mother, usually so reserved, in this role of matchmaker, just like Margaret Schevill. Thank God I didn't know it at the time. I would have been as mortified as I was when, on my way to the Anna Head School for girls one day in '37 or '38, late and disorganized, I somehow dropped my tennis shorts from the clutch of binder, tennis racket, book bag, right in front of Jack's fraternity house, which I passed every day for four years on my twenty-minute walk to school. They were seersucker, green-and-white striped. One of his fraternity brothers picked them up and handed them back to me with a sly little grin. Oh my God, how could this have happened? A Freudian slip, my father would probably have said with delight if I had told him about it. At any rate, I guess my parents recognized Jack as a real catch, someone with both charm and brains, who might elevate this rather unfocused, flighty, stubborn second daughter of theirs. His mother, on the other hand, was losing yet another child to Berkeley academia. Blame it on Inverness, where Berkeley and San Francisco progeny were bound to meet, and did.

Janis and Karl's wedding was lovely, an evening affair at the warm-hearted house in St. Francis Wood that Jack's father designed, with live music and dancing in the canvas-covered courtyard. Our Tolman family was invited because of the Schevills. We hardly knew the Kents in those days, though I had had my eyes on Jack for several years. I wore a white moiré evening dress with mauve ribbon at the waist and shoulders, and though Jack and Jimmy were both busy members of the wedding party I got to dance with each of them.

The war was over. It was the summer of '46 when Jack was twenty-nine years old, Tommy was three-and-a-half, and I was twenty-five that we finally moved into Erinveine (the Irish version of Margaret's maiden name, Erwin) and began the long succession of summers there, surrounded by the beauty and the community and family that sustained us as we lunged through life. We owned that house for nineteen years and spent most of our summers there. That first one, though, turned out to be hard and lonely for me and the days were very long. I was nostalgic, I guess, for earlier carefree Inverness summers, or even for intense bittersweet times when Jack and I were at least together.

There had been that famous camping trip with Deborah and Jim, for instance, shortly before Jack was drafted. Jim was in medical school and would soon be in the Navy. October 1943, the photo says. We farmed our babies out with various parents, and rented a rowboat. The war was on, of course, and we had to get a permit from the Coast

119

Guard even just to row down Tomales Bay. That felt weird, like so many aspects of wartime. We went to Kilkenny Beach, where we sat around our campfire singing dirty songs that Jack and Jim had learned in college. I remember the words but am too embarrassed to repeat them here. We renamed Kilkenny "Bawdy Beach."

But in '46 Jack and Jim commuted to San Francisco every day, alternating using our car and the Whitneys'. Deborah and I were stuck in our respective houses with our offspring, who seemed to be forever having colds and earaches. We didn't have telephones in Inverness then, and wouldn't have for another twenty years or so. We were cut off from the one family doctor five miles away in Point Reyes Station, we women cut off from each other. And the weather that year was foggier than usual. We went to the beach, though, no matter what, just to break the monotony. Children are always happy on beaches. It didn't matter to them about the weather. They collected polliwogs, ever hopeful that they would get to see their transformation into frogs. They slathered themselves with mud from the marsh behind the beach. Huddled in sweaters, we women, half a dozen or so regulars, helped each other through the boredom, while Jack and Jim each had stimulating jobs and cemented their friendship forever on those commutes.

Lifetime connections were formed on many levels in those early Inverness summers. I'm thinking of Steve, how when he was only three or four, decided, one nap-time afternoon, that he had to go see his cousin Nick. At some point I awoke from my own nap and became aware that Steve was missing. Fortunately I wasn't frantic for long because he soon reappeared in the wooded driveway, barefoot, in his underpants, grinning and full of garbled information about his adventure. The Whitneys lived a couple of miles away along the two-lane country highway that ran along the shore of Tomales Bay. I'm sure as I hugged him to me I gasped, visualizing the enormous hay trucks and milk trucks that careened along that road. He chattered on about a nice man he met on the road near the beach. Later we pieced it together. Mr. DeLaRosa, an old Italian fisherman who lived in a cottage on the shore, saw this barefoot child in underpants running along the highway. He apparently managed to make friends with Steve enough to get him to talk them back home to our house. Through my hugs and tears of relief I glimpsed a figure who waved, then disappeared. That was Mr. DeLaRosa, and we did get the opportunity to thank him later. That same summer (1950 I think) Steve ran off several times like that, connecting up with cousins and friends.

Jack and Jim developed a playful confrontational relationship, egging each other on. Once Jack got so outrageous that Jim shoved him into the blackberry patch rambling down below our house. I have no memory of the subject matter or the year or what political minutiae they might have been so intense about. I still see Jack's expression of astonishment, though, and then hear his uproarious laughter. Perhaps it had nothing to do with politics, but with judgment about how to construct the enormous driftwood porch, to be shaped like the prow of a ship that the two were building onto Erinveine, having hauled the silvery rounded planks for months from ocean beaches. Another time they decided to embark on a mammoth blackberry jelly-making project, but their plans kept shifting, diverging, eventually involving all our pots and pans and both of our kitchens. Deborah and I had to finish up the job.

Over the years those two helped each other with major building enterprises in both Berkeley and Inverness. I remember Jim's lists: around 100 items in his small, tidy writing, of **THINGS TO BE DONE**. Deborah once gave him a Dymo Labeling gadget and he was in seventh heaven, labeling and organizing tools, records, kitchen drawers, and shelves. Our entire families got involved in their projects. There's a photo of Deborah, looking put upon as she lugs a heavy bucket of sand for the Whitney's brick patio in Inverness, and another cute one of Steve, with Nick, also carrying a bucket between them. They were only about two and three years old but were really into the project. Jack helped Jim line the two bedrooms of that wonderful house with cedar, and after Jim died, Dave and Nick, teenagers then, built stairs leading down from the meadow to the beach far below. That was an amazing building feat, a memorial gift to Jim, who would have been pleased and very impressed.

That house with the brick terrace near the bluff above Tomales Bay has been a major environment for our extended family for over fifty years. There's a basket-ball hoop, a ping pong table. Once there was a sandbox and on the great meadow that stretches beyond there have been variously games of football, baseball, croquet, boule, horseshoes. There have been weddings, barbecues, and countless Thanksgiving, Christmas, New Year's Eve, and Fourth of July parties. And then there have been the family memorial gatherings — for my father, for Jim, and finally for Jack, summer before last. That's the very spot — on the bricks, and meadow under the Bishop pines — where, after Steve lowered his ashes into the ground next to Jim's, we all sat around and reminisced about Jack's life. People said the most amazing things, though because of my deafness, I missed a lot. I couldn't hear Rebecca or Margaret or Dave. They were too far away. Tom said being with his father when he died was the most important event of his life. Hannah talked about Jack's expressive hands and some of us laughed, remembering how, when playing **THE GAME** he used his hands to illustrate — a mountain, a sea, a house. Peggy Love talked about photographing him, how unself-conscious he was. Deborah remembered many wonderful trips we all took together. Nick remembered how strict he was when the children were all little, and how he mellowed out, so that in the "terrible '60s" he was the tolerant one. Steve, while dying himself, spoke of what a sweet man his dad was. Many people remembered his smile, his intellectual honesty, his loyalty to friends and family. I talked about the many wonderful, difficult books we read aloud together over the last twenty-five years of our fifty-seven years together. We started that in Corsica.

I wish I had been a perfect wife to him. I have found that this is a common regret that widows share, probably widowers too. Of course there's no such thing. He was not perfect either. There were times, when the children were young, that he made me feel trapped, just a useful appendage to his central life and burgeoning career. And there were times when, punishing him, and myself too, that I denied our mutual sexual needs. Oh, I wish I'd never nagged.

December 24, 1999

Christmas Eve Afternoon

On the night of the winter solstice, the moon was full and larger than it has been for 133 years due to some astronomical phenomenon I can't explain, can't understand. I sometimes think that in another life I would learn about the skies, but in this one I am simply in awe. The sunsets lately have washed the sky with deep raspberry, tinged with baby blue, pale yellow. I am alone in the house, my first Christmas without either Jack or Steve.

Tonight I'm going to Kathleen's Christmas Eve party again. It will be interesting as always with her, Deborah's oldest child, and the first grandchild in both the Tolman and Whitney families. Tom's fifty-seven, so she'll be fifty-eight in April. But she still seems like the young free spirit she was when she roamed the world in her youth, exploring Spain and Katmandu, going to the Sorbonne, serving two years with the Peace Corps in Nigeria, acting, painting. She still paints, also teaches, swims in both San Francisco and Tomales Bays, has raised one severely retarded daughter, Mimi, also a supremely normal son, Patrick. Kathleen took risks, pushed at the boundaries, explored religions and lifestyles, befriended people on the fringe while not quite going beyond the fringe herself. She has a special empathy for Steve. In a letter she wrote him near the end she said, "I don't want you to die." He never saw that letter. It arrived too late. But she was with him when he died, leading them all in song.

Patrick has been the designated driver of the four old ladies tonight, and I realize that I have now become one of those symbolic ones, like Aunts Clara, Kate, and Margaret used to be so long ago, sitting on the sofa after dinner in Jack's parents' living room, telling jokes, burping, even smoking cigarettes. They were clowning. That was their role. Now I know how brave they were. Tonight it will be me, Deborah, her ex-sister-in-law — Frances — a Whitney cousin, Sally

Davis. These symbolic old ladies are all in their eighties. I will be the youngest elder at age seventy-eight.

We did the boccle baking thing at Jack's niece Kathie's last Saturday. And again, I was the symbolic elder. Jack and Janis were not there this year to keep me company. Janis hasn't died, like Jack, but she lives in Oregon now and has no memory of boccles or much else, poor dear. This year it was Kathie and Bill, their son Brian, Tom and Deb, and old symbolic me. The reality of how time has passed hit me as, while rolling out the pastry, the conversation of that generation just below me turned to hot flashes and cholesterol counts.

I'm homesick this Christmas, just the way we all were in Austria back in 1955. There we were in a gorgeous snowy setting — ice-skating, skiing, a tree lit on Christmas Eve with candles, Midnight Mass — but so far, far from home. Now I'm homesick for Jack, his optimism, and our three little boys sitting around the living room table, cutting up bright-colored construction paper, pasting and drawing, making Christmas cards. Nothing seems familiar anymore.

━━━•━━━

For nineteen summers, except for those sabbatical summers of '54, '55, '63, we moved to Erinveine in Inverness, renting out #84 Tamalpais Road. Every year "efficient Mary" listed the house with the University Housing Office, went through closets, got rid of things. It was as easy for me as organizing a precinct, running a meeting, playing tennis. In my brain I know that was so, but I cannot recall the energy. I close my eyes and try to watch that old scene as a movie — me slim, motivated, involved, mind clicking, emotions under control because there wasn't time for the indulgence of breakdowns.

Sometimes Jack would occupy the two downstairs boys' bedrooms and bath at #84 for part of the summer and come up weekends and maybe the month of August. Sometimes he came for the whole summer. For seventeen of those years, again with the exceptions of '54, '55, '63, he attended weekly meetings of the Berkeley Planning Commission, then the Berkeley City Council, and he usually had a summer writing project, either on his book or articles for planning publications. I can't believe how hard he worked! Well, I did too, of course. We both went to lots of meetings, together and separately, juggling evening boy-sitting arrangements. In Berkeley we sometimes had live-in students working for room and board. I could write a whole novel about them.

First was sweet practical Marion Tsuda, whose father grew strawberries in Watsonville and part of whose childhood was spent in a Japanese internment camp in Utah. Then there was Darryl Lee from a Chinese farming family in the Central Valley who, I think, was genuinely afraid of us because we had books like *Red Star Over China* in our bookcase. He split after only a few weeks without a word of warning. Next was a charming French fellow named Phillipe, and finally Elie, a pre-med student whose last name I can neither pronounce nor spell. He was the only son of an Israeli family and had grown up in an urban apartment in Tel Aviv. He hated Berkeley. There were too many trees! He was homesick for the bustle of a city. We liked him and felt sorry for him, but he was totally useless to us since he'd never washed a dish or dug in a garden or cared for a child. Our own children could accomplish chores more efficiently than he. Tom knew how to rescue his younger brothers in case of fire. They all knew how to wash dishes. For us Elie was like having still one more boy in the house, but he was over six feet tall and ate like a horse. I have a cute picture of him washing windows, smiling proudly into the camera: *"Look, Ma, I learned to wash windows!"* Years later we got a letter from him, apologizing for his youthful uselessness, and informing us that he had gone on to medical school and was now practicing medicine in Tel Aviv.

The meetings we went to during the '50s and '60s were of our Democratic Club, The Berkeley Grassrooters; campaign committees for Stevenson, Sherriffs, McKibben, Williams, Harris, Cohelan, Kent, Whitney, Brown, Sweeney, May, Gordon, Dewey, Dellums, Nichols, Swingle, Grodin; Nursery School and PTA and Cub Scouts; endorsing conventions of the 18th Assembly District Precinct Organization, The Berkeley Caucus; and as delegates to statewide Democratic conventions in Fresno and Sacramento. Besides all this I was the editor, for a while, of a monthly newspaper, The Democrat, and Jack had professional and campus meetings galore. So going to Inverness for the summer was a change, if not exactly a break, for there, too, we worked with The Inverness Improvement Association and other mostly ad hoc groups in efforts to save beaches, keep farmlands, establish Tomales Bay State Park and the Point Reyes National Seashore. This was at the beginning of environmental awareness and a very exciting time, laying the groundwork for the Coastal Commission, the Environmental Action Committee, The Tomales Bay Association, Marin Agricultural Land Trust, among others.

What I sat down to write about here, though, was the demise of our Inverness house. So, in the summer or '64, our last at Erinveine, as in previous summers, I guess we spent three months in Inverness, although Tom no longer lived at home with us. He and one of his sleazier friends were sharing a cabin in Inverness Park and Tom had begun to do tree work, something he happened upon almost by accident a year or two earlier when he had a summer job with P G & E down on the peninsula clearing trees in the way of new power lines. He loved the thrill of climbing, and he has become, over the years, almost spiritual about the beauty of trees — sometimes saving the trees from his clients, the people — and also has become a licensed arborist.

My memory of those last Erinveine summers are confused. I seem to have no photos of '64, although quite a few of '62 ('63 we were in Europe) — Tom in the pale green cardigan I knit for him that he later lost on a beach, with a cast on his right hand and arm up to the elbow. Fortunately it was the right one, for he is a lefty — that's why he's always played first base. Tom with his first motorcycle. Steve with Dave and friends taking off in our little outboard, named after me, The Mary K., to go camping down the bay. They all look healthy, happy, clean-cut, yet I learned much later that Tom and Steve were already drinking and smoking by then, and a few years later they would be doing acid trips and smoking pot, growing beards and wearing their hair long.

It was just two or three years ago that Steve described to me the awe his of first acid trip in Inverness. Both Tom and he were entranced by the all-year-round locals whose families were working-class, hard-drinking, and in some cases abusive. A few years earlier Tom and two friends had been hauled off to Juvenile Hall in lower Marin for harassing a guy they didn't like. At some point, while drinking, Steve totaled Grandpa's Anglia that we had inherited and got a concussion. (That was in Berkeley.) All three boys had concussions at one time or another. It wasn't all disaster and civic obligation, though. The boys learned to swim and sail and work on boats and camp and fish and hike and play tennis and horseshoes and golf. They learned to dance and fall in love.

Over those nineteen summers we put our own stamp on Margaret's ERINVEINE, expanding the kitchen and pantry area, building a sleeping porch and enormous deck. Steve built a little open cabin off from the house. Dave, although only fifteen in '64, was already an accomplished builder. He started in nursery school, learning to hammer before he learned to tie his shoes. (I suddenly remember that in London when he was five he learned to knit.) In Berkeley he had started collecting tools, then making bird houses for relatives and neighbors when he was eight or nine and was soon being commissioned to build small tables, record cabinets, bookshelves, even to remodel a bathroom into a darkroom. Later it would be boats, houses, more furniture. At Erinveine he made us a sturdy redwood sofa/bench which, adorned with lots of pillows, faced the big stone fireplace. Dave's night life had not developed much in '64 and the three of us — Jack, me and Dave — played endless games of Parcheesi sitting around that fireplace. Did we play Pounce then too? Pounce, an expanded version of Double Solitaire, to this day is part of the extended family ritual, along with "The Game," a variation of Charades. (I think it is now Dave's sixteen-year-old Rebecca who is the Pounce champ. Or perhaps it's Nick's daughter, Dakota, in which case we will all have to play by Whitney rules, which are stricter than Kent rules.)

As that summer of '64 came to an end, Tom asked if he might move into Erinveine for the coming winter. After a good deal of agony we said no, we thought it best if he really be on his own now that he

127

was almost twenty-two. In the last days of that summer, Steve's dog, Snewy, a derivation of sinewy, a wonderful German short-haired pointer, took off with the Eastmans' Keeshond and the Plants' Red Setter after a female in heat. None of the male dogs were ever seen again, probably having strayed onto a ranch, begun chasing sheep, and been shot by the rancher. It seemed sadder than usual going home that year, leaving both Tom and Snewy behind.

On Wednesday morning, October 28, I was sitting at the kitchen table at #84 Tamalpais Road in my bathrobe drinking coffee, reading the paper when the phone rang. (The guys should have been off at work and school, but Dave says he was there and remembers the following conversation.) I got up from the table and reached for the phone on the kitchen counter.

"Mary, this is Mr. Mery from Inverness (a neighbor and owner of the general store and post office). Are you sitting down?"

I sat down. "Yes."

"Mary, your little house slid down the hill."

"Oh, thank God," I said, "I thought it was something about Tom."

I think he laughed. He too had sons, the youngest one of whom I had had a wild crush on when I was eleven. Then he went on to tell me that at about 5:30 that morning he had been awakened by what sounded like a garbage truck that had lost its breaks careening down Douglas Street, our street, directly behind his house. And all the time he was talking in his kind gentle telling of the complete destruction that he'd gone to look at, I was silently saying, Thank God, Thank God, though I didn't then believe in a God. (Now I'm not so sure, being at an age where the comfort of a God is tempting, and having witnessed Steve's astonishing epiphany.) It was only a house, a summer house, a luxury, and having been brought up to have compassion for the oppressed — starving Armenians, persecuted Jews, disenfranchised American Indians — I actually felt grateful. After a while, though, the reality of loss sunk in. I envisioned, as Mr. Mery described it, the upright piano lying on its back next to a crab net and an oar. Memories of music, crabbing, rowing over nineteen summers flooded over me. I began to cry, thanked him, called Jack at his office on the campus, and tried to break the news to him gently, as Mr. Mery had to me. "Dearie, are you sitting down?"

The newspaper account said, *"The Jack Kent residence in Inverness is now a mass of mud and toothpicks under its roof, 75 feet below the foundation site. Light showers Tuesday and yesterday may have helped push it over the ledge, but neighbors of the Kents say the leaky water pipes running along the pathway above the Kents' caused the house to be undercut"* ... *"It sounded like a lumber truck unloading a ton of boards and glass"* ... *"an employee of Citizens' Utility commented, 'I sure hope this was an Act of God.'"*

Before the day was out we had gone to look at the disaster ourselves. It was absolutely appalling and unbelievable. The scattered wreckage lay on a river of mud. There were the piano and the crab net and the oar as Mr. Mery had described them. The toilet had landed way down the road in someone else's yard. Eventually we found the kitchen drawer with all the Kent family silver-plated flatware under a bush. Tom wrote the following:

"...You would never suspect a violent break in these woods. The bay trees looked like grass from a distance, elemental and uniform, basic life on the hillside. In among them it was always an hour past sundown and when you entered the overhung house you didn't just wipe your feet, you picked forget-me-nots and cobwebs out of your socks and hair.

"But one day in October the ground turned a disgusting shade of orange and it was agony to choose between looking to the top of the huge triangular vomit where the rusted pipe still dribbled, or down past the innards of a dislocated oak to the dismembered remains, where half the roof jutted, supported by the upended piano."

We got a good lawyer, sued both our insurance company and the Citizens' Utility, got $30,000, just enough to purchase, within the year, another house in Inverness, The Shambles, which we almost lost to another watery disaster in 1982.

But before the house, we bought a sailboat, filling an instinctual need for something playful and joyous, I suppose.

———•———

In the mid '60s I started to write stuff down — anxieties, impressions, angry letters to Steve and Tom that would never be sent. It was a form of therapy. We were living, for two years, in a fantastic house on Washington Street in Presidio Heights, surrounded by the rich and famous, because Jack had been appointed as Mayor Jack Shelley's Development Tsar. The owners, more or less our age with children more or less grown, like ours, were politically liberal, collectors of modern art, and had gone to Tanzania with the Peace Corps. It was a crazy time and I wanted to embrace it. I suppose I had a fantasy of two urbane, culturally enriching years in San Francisco, surrounded by original art on the walls, a life-sized nude sculpture by Manuel Neri on the living room carpet, an esoteric wine cellar that we had open access to. There was a piano. I would take jazz lessons. We would rub elbows with San Francisco's political and cultural movers and shakers.

It didn't quite work out that way. Oh, I did get season tickets to the symphony on Thursday afternoons. I found a nice little beauty salon down on Powell Street, got my hair cut, bought some clothes, acquired a new look of sorts. I went on the pill which had a wonderful effect on our sex life. We went to the theater and all the museums, and politicked a bit with young Diane Feinstein and Willie Brown years before they became celebrities; met Art Hoppe at a neighborhood party; did some good community work — parks and open space, public transportation — with Jack's long-time planning colleagues Phoebe Brown, Julia Porter, Dorothy Erskine; and of course enjoyed the exuberant, optimistic Irish Mayor Jack Shelley.

We resumed acquaintance that developed over the years into deep friendship with Allan Jacobs whom we'd first met in London in '55 where he too was a Fulbright scholar. In '66 he became San Francisco's new director of planning, the job Jack had had in 1947.

I don't know what Jack's fantasy was — to help Mayor Shelley dramatically move the city into the new era of President Johnson's Inner

Cities Program probably. But it was slow-going. He worked with a group of angry black women, "The Big Four," he called them, who were quite rightfully flexing their political muscles. And our three sons, whom we idiotically had assumed would be launched by now, instead caused us ever-increasing anxiety. I wished, sometimes, that like our landlords, we were across the world in Africa doing "good works in time of strife" — an old-fashioned, condescending, concept perhaps, but one that was deeply ingrained in my up-bringing. Instead we were in San Francisco where a new counterculture that we neither liked nor understood was erupting.

Jack turned fifty while we were there on Washington Street. We had a champagne brunch. Tom moved in with his would-be first wife, a student nurse, leaving his old dog, Laddie, behind with us. Steve went off to Friends World College for about a year, leaving his three cats — Phoebe, Jesse, Maxine — behind, then dropped out. We didn't know where he was, maybe right near by in the Haight-Ashbury District during that "Summer of Love," turning on and tuning out, chanting, "Make love, not war," smoking pot. His cat Maxine split too.

Dave was going to Washington High with Donna Mocine whose parents had begged us to take her in. She needed to get away from the Berkeley scene and drugs. How could we say no? Dave and Donna hardly spoke to us, just moped around with gloomy faces, as they did their chores — setting the table, washing the dishes. I didn't understand girls, even though I'd been one myself. They seemed more secretive and devious than boys. Donna wore drab clothes, the fashion of the time — earth colors. Her hair was long and lank and fell in front of her eyes. She had some very peculiar friends who came to see her from Berkeley. There was a girl in a long green cape who handed me a bunch of flowers purloined from the elegant gardens of our neighbors in Presidio Heights.

Dave was growing like a weed, lethargic and lovesick because his girlfriend, Chandra, was at Berkeley High. In fact we learned years later that he sometimes took our car at night, after we had gone to bed, drove over to Berkeley, spent the night with her, and got back in time to go to school in the morning. That sneaky kid! He'd learned, from watching his older brothers mess up and get in trouble with us, to just do stuff behind our backs. How come we didn't even notice how much gas we were using? Too distracted, I guess, by the unpleasant events of the times.

Our nephew, Nick Whitney, dropped out of UCLA and landed on our doorstep while his recently widowed mother, my sister Deborah, was in Nigeria, visiting his sister, Kathleen in the Peace Corps. The Vietnam war was accelerating and so were the demonstrations in Golden Gate Park. We didn't understand the new political style. We didn't understand the music. Bob Dylan's songs were tuneless whines, obscuring the lyrics. We didn't understand the movies. Remember the movie, *Blow-Up*? I was unhappy, bewildered, homesick for the familiar, just as I am again now on the eve of the new millennium. And I began to write.

For twenty-five years I filled notebooks. I also wrote four novels, about thirty stories, some poems. Very little was published and about five years ago I destroyed all the notebooks. I still keep what I call *A Book of Lists*, books read, plays and movies seen, but it now has expanded to include events and musings. The first page of the current one, dated 3/30/98, reads: "Perhaps this is a new notebook, effort, outpouring, whatever, the notebook of aging," and then in the margin I've noted, "This written a little less than a month before Jack died."

Chapter Eight

January 2000

Between the time we went to San Francisco in 1966 and our last long sabbatical leave in Europe — 1970-71 — Tom had been married and divorced twice, Steve married and divorced once, Dave married. (His divorce came later.) We had returned to Berkeley at the end of '68. Martin Luther King, Jr. and Bobby Kennedy had been assassinated. Jack had served a term as president of the American Society of Planning Officials, and we had a great trip to New York in that connection. In Berkeley the anarchistic energy that had been released in '64 by the Free Speech Movement erupted into the occupation of Peoples' Park, and Governor Reagan's sending the National Guard into Berkeley. It was a war at home with tear gas and one death. There was some fear that other parks, including our own Codornices half a block away, might become similar battlefields. Helicopters droned overhead. We couldn't wait to get out of the country.

We sailed from Oakland on a French freighter in early July of 1970 and had another restorative month at sea. Deborah was to be in Europe too, so we arranged to spend a month together, first in London where we went to plays, then picked up the Volvo we had ordered in Berkeley and took off for Stonehenge, Salisbury, Dover, then across the English Channel to France. After Paris we roamed along the Loire Valley, visiting chateaux, visiting the farm house and studio of our dear friend Calder's famous and lovably eccentric uncle, Alexander (Sandy) Calder for whom he was named. (Actually we didn't get to go inside the studio because Sandy, who resembled a large, cuddly, absent-minded bear, couldn't find the key! So we had to be content with peering through the windows, but even that was a thrill.) We continued on, then, eating and drinking our way through Provence — Aix, Arles, Avignon — all the way south to Marseille, then all the way north to Amsterdam, where Deborah left us to go home. Some time in London, some time in Zurich, and finally eight months in St. Florent, a seaside town of eight hundred people on the island of Corsica, made us sane and whole again.

That whole year was a capricious adventure, something that had been lacking in our lives for a long, long time. The choice of Corsica itself was made on a whim. For a while we thought we might go to Yugoslavia, but the language barrier would have been enormous. The idea of an island was very appealing, also a perverse desire to go someplace no one we ever knew had been. As we toured through France in the summer with my sister, we mused, all three of us, though Deborah would be returning to Berkeley, about the perfect spot for Jack and me to spend the year. We were so enamored by everything French — the food and wine, the personality quirks, the language that I miraculously found I could speak and understand again to some degree — and one day as we sat in a farmer's field eating our "pique-nique," Deborah said, "How about Corsica? It's an island and it's French!" (Later, of course, we would learn that the Corsicans are, above all, Corsican, and though their official language is French, they have a real written and spoken language of their own, Corse, that sounds more Italian than French.)

This was unlike my usually thoughtful sister who is not prone to impulsive flights of fancy. But well, why not? In London where we had a flat for a few weeks while Jack checked out the London Greenbelt and conferred with colleagues at the London County Council, I went to bookstores and looked for information on Corsica. Other than the fact that it was Napoleon's birthplace, there was practically nothing written about the island. This seemed to make it even more intriguing. Well, we would just go there and try it out! Yes! We didn't have to stay if we didn't like it. Oh, this adventure was getting increasingly exciting. In October we drove once more across France on our way to Zurich, through vineyards buzzing with the activity of the harvest. Wagons full of grapes and pickers swayed along the country roads and everything was golden, tawny. We drank the fizzy new wine with our lunch in a small country hotel.

In Zurich Jack conferred with Swiss city planners, among them his former student, Karl Otto Schmid. June Schmid took me shopping and I bought a long burgundy-colored velveteen lounging robe, so unlike anything I'd ever owned that it must have been symbolic of some deep-seated yearning. We went to the American movie, Easy Rider, in which a close-up of Peter Fonda, riding a motorcycle, his hair blowing back, looked, to us, exactly like our son Tom. It was a shocking reminder of all that had seemed to us to be going wrong in America, aware, even as the image flashed by, that to our sons it was everything that was going right.

This is when I noticed that I was losing my hair. Great clumps gathered in my hairbrush. A typically efficient Swiss druggist connected it to recent stress, recommended Vitamin E. Stress. Perhaps that also accounted for my fainting spells. Off and on throughout my life I have had a tendency to faint, often in public places, causing me much embarrassment. I fainted at the breakfast table at boarding school, also in Switzerland, when I was twelve after running in the snow, then taking a cold shower, our morning routine. Perhaps it was the onset of puberty. I fainted on the stage in high school while singing in the Glee Club. I fainted at an engagement party that Jack's parents gave for us. And once in Washington, DC where we'd taken Steve and Dave for the Easter break to do the obligatory, educational tour of the nation's capital. (Where was Tom? Probably off on some wild Easter orgy with his fraternity brothers.) As Dave and I were eating in a cafeteria I suddenly knew I was going to faint. I told him to get a waitress, which he did. She brought ice for the back of my neck. I lay on the bench in our booth while she called a taxi, and I was escorted back to our hotel by my ten-year-old. I wonder if he remembers this.

And lately, in the fall of 1970, I had been fainting at restaurants again. Low blood pressure, poor circulation, had been the usual medical explanation in the past. Now perhaps it was the onset of the menopause. Or perhaps it was the recent years of stress. Oh, poor Jack, having to lug me up off the floor that first time at a lovely little seaside hotel in England just after we had left Deborah in Amsterdam. After that I learned to recognize the warning signs, and we could usually get out of the restaurant before I actually passed out. I sat on curbs, my head between my knees. I lay on rest room floors. I took to carrying smelling salts in my purse. (I've only fainted once or twice since, and never since I gave up smoking.)

But in spite of the fainting, we were having a wonderful time. In Zurich we went to museums — I remember an exquisite little show of Giacometti sculptures. We rode on the tidy, efficient streetcars, affirmation to Jack, my darling, that only first-rate public transit would save us from the devil automobile. He used to say, in his usual optimistic boy scout fashion, and was often quoted in campaign literature, the media, and urban planning circles, "I saw the emergence of the automobile age and I'm going to live to see its demise." One of the saddest thing for me to hear was his mutter a couple of years ago, "I guess I'm not going to see the end of the automobile after all." Did he mean that he was dying, or his optimism? Either way, it broke my heart.

In Zurich he showed me the inn on the lake where he'd had Thanksgiving dinner with Carl Jung and all those others in 1938. We ate in a restaurant, one of the places where I almost fainted, where James Joyce used to go, with photographs of famous authors on the walls. We went with the Schmids in a fantastic Alpine vehicle — a cabin hanging and swaying from a cable that transported us high up into the mountains. Still thumb tacked to the wall above this desk is a snapshot of Jack and Karl Schmid up there in the Alps.

Finally we headed for Nice from where we would sail to Corsica. We ate heavenly bouillabaisse in a small waterfront restaurant, then in early evening boarded the *Napoleon*. It was a large ferry accommodating both human passengers, providing us with bunks for the overnight trip, and cars including our Volvo, Vivienne Lamalou Kent, her name and sex chosen with the same capriciousness that seemed to determine everything that year. Lamalou was a lovely spa in Southern France. I have no longer a clue as to where Vivienne came from, just a pretty French name, I guess, that seemed to suit our nice Swedish car.

We arrived at dawn, and the sight of the island was dreamy. Dawn is something we don't experience in Berkeley, facing west as we do.

Since Jack and Steve died I've become a sunset freak, another form of therapy as I grieve. Also I gaze at the moon and the stars. Last night there was a total eclipse, and though I couldn't see the beginning when the moon was obscured by the shadow of the earth because it hadn't risen high enough behind our eastern hills, by ten o'clock it had, and I sat out on the little deck off this study and watched as the shadow gradually moved away, exposing the full bright beautiful moon. Dawn could become addictive too. Corsica is a mountain dropped into the Mediterranean Sea, and as we approached from the southwest the town of Ajaccio, Napoleon's birthplace, was a watery rosy glow. Then, as we got closer, the buildings took on outlines against the mountainous mass behind them.

But the reality of Ajaccio, a small provincial city, was less compelling. We drove on, northward along the western coast, on a road that is very like our winding, precipitous Highway One in California. We shared it with numerous fast French drivers of snappy racing cars. They'd been on the ferry the night before and we'd learned that our arrival would coincide with the annual race around the island, "La Course de Corse." The drive was hair-raising and exciting, the weather still warm from the dregs of summer, though this was November 5th.

Our plan was to have no plan, to feel our way around the island. And so we proceeded, leisurely, soon left behind by the racers, soaking up the vistas of the sea and sky and mountains, inching through the narrow medieval streets of Cargese, where we lunched on Salade Nicoise. There we met an innkeeper from the mountain town of Guagno. Oh, he told us, we had to go to the mountains to know the *real* Corsica. "Venez-vous a ma petite auberge," he urged in that slow, drawn-out Corsican way of speaking French with which we would become so familiar, nothing like the staccato high pitch French of Paris.

Months later we did go to Guagno, truly a different world up there in the chestnut groves with wild pigs snuffling through the dry leaves and snow, but for now we were drawn to the sea, on to the Gulf of Porto where the beaches are the color of brick vividly contrasted with the dark green pines and deep blue water. We spent our first night there, then to Calvi and L'Ille Rousse at the northern edge of the island, charming old cities with ramparts and citadels and watch towers and beaches where, in summer, many tourists come. On the late afternoon of our third day as we headed eastward across the Agriate Desert, we first saw the Gulf of St. Florent, and the town, all lit up by the sun descending into the western sea.

Winding down, down toward it, I had the feeling that this is where we just might stop our search. I don't to this day know why I had that feeling. There was a putrid-smelling garbage dump burning on the side of the road. Our dinner of stringy goat meat stew was mediocre. Perhaps it was the size — a town of 800 people — neither a tiny village nor a city. In the morning we decided, though both of us were attracted to something about this place, to plod on around the island before making a hasty decision. We would have done that too, had we not heard a familiar American voice call out as we were loading suitcases into the trunk, "Is that the Kents?"

It was Bill Rouverol from Berkeley and Inverness, whom we'd known a little over the years. He'd given Tom, a teenager then, a job as a carpenter's helper when he built his Inverness house. He and his wife had entertained us once or twice, and we them. We had politicked together, but had lost track of him after his divorce, after he gave up his professorship and tenure in engineering and became an artist and inventor. But here he was, in the plaid flannel shirt and khakis that is still his uniform, standing outside Milo's Bar-Cafe in St. Florent. That chance meeting has had such an effect on our lives, it's hard to believe that it was mere coincidence. Before that day was finished we had met his young, shy, beguiling second wife, Sandra, at the low stone house they'd built three years before, inspired by the peasant huts of tawny-colored stone that dot the countryside, on an acre of land a mile outside the town, surrounded by vineyards. They had fruit trees, a donkey, a dog and several cats. We ate lunch under the olive trees, then Bill took us to meet a Mme. Vermonet, who lived on the post office square in one of the handful of four-storied blocks of faded pastel houses, joined together by lines of colorful laundry waving above the narrow alleys. The sea lapped against the sea wall. The church spire thrust up from between the rooftops. It was an urban village with a bar-cafe, a charcuterie, a butcher shop, chickens, and donkeys too.

Yes, Mme. Vermonet had several rental units tucked here and there in the vicinity. In the short summer tourist season, about six weeks when cruise ships anchored in the harbor and hordes of Germans and Scandinavians occupied the town and beaches such lodgings were hard to come by, but in November she was delighted to rent us one, reached by climbing stone steps, walking through a stone archway painted blue, next to a small yard of chickens and a little dog named Jeudi, into our own front door. We settled right down in our cozy apartment — small living room looking out onto a rocky lane, a vegetable garden, a clothesline from which hung the green and white soccer uniforms of the local school team, a Citadelle such as guards every Corsican port, and an old man dressed in black corduroy who spent his days smoking his pipe and whittling in a doorway; small kitchen, large bedroom, bathroom, and a roof terrace with a staggering view across tiled roofs and past the church spire of the Gulf of St. Florent and the Agriate Desert and mountains beyond, reached by climbing a ladder from the bedroom up through a trap door. That view was very similar to the one I have from this study of Jack's — across the bay to Mt. Tamalpais. The rent, as I recall, equaled about $40 a month in francs. By the end of that day we had unpacked the car, hung our clothes in the closet, put our toothbrushes in the bathroom, and gone back for a sumptuous roast lamb dinner at Bill and Sandra's house.

It's so curious, the human need to free oneself by means of travel from the troubles of rutted lives, and then the avid response to the familiarity of fellow countrymen abroad? We and the Rouverols had both fled America, and when we met by chance in St. Florent, fell into each other's arms. We all came back to Berkeley, to the complications of our own families and ourselves. I don't see the Rouverols often. But Sandra's growth as an artist is expressed here and there around our house on the walls. Her latest obsession is working with ceramic tile and their house is now filled with little tile-topped tables, as well as many cats, and yes, another unruly dog, something else we have in common. Inspired by these memories of St. Florent, I've invited them for lunch on Sunday.

I was reading Jack's journal the other day. In St. Florent he began to sleep again. No more headaches or constipation. His instinctive connection to environment was nurtured. He drew beautiful, detailed maps of the town and diagrams of those daily meanders of ours out from the central square with the locust trees and boule games, through the little vegetable plots, past stone walls and olive trees to the Cathedral, standing all alone, punctuated by cypress trees, goats tethered nearby, donkeys, vineyards. We did watercolors. We began to read aloud — difficult books by Norman O. Brown, Gloria Steinem, Herbert Marcuse, Freud, Jung. We both were writing — Jack, articles and essays on Berkeley politics, environmental concerns about open space, governmental theory with a hope of revising the Berkeley City Charter; I, masses of introspection mixed with an intense observation of our Corsican surrounding that became the basis of my first novel, *Islands of the Mind*.

In St. Florent we soon became part of the little group of expatriates — French, English, American — who played bridge and tennis and entertained each other at small dinner parties or picnics. Jack and I didn't play bridge; we played Scrabble with each other every single night though. I still come across the scores that Jack so meticulously kept, in his beautiful architectural-delineator printing, and saved, just as he did the statistics of weight during our many dieting campaigns.

Scrabble began back in '55 aboard the *Duivendyk* and continued as an accompaniment to vacation time — in Corsica, Greece, Yugoslavia, Mexico, Inverness — until about five years ago when Jack could no longer understand the game. I found a list in his desk drawer —

"Things I have Stopped Doing: check book, laundry, wearing glasses, drinking." The printing is no longer meticulous. He doesn't mention Scrabble. He doesn't mention baking bread, planting a vegetable garden, burying the compost; nor collecting postcards, sending Christmas cards.

Our tennis games began in Inverness as kids and continued as recreation both in Inverness and Berkeley, again until about five years ago. Jack fell on the court and hit his head. He was beginning to have his breathless spells. What a surprise to find a tennis court in St. Florent, set down haphazardly, it seemed to us, in the midst of small truck gardens, an incongruous possession of the Catholic Church.

All three of Jack's sabbatical leaves had had the intended restorative value, but this was especially true in Corsica, perhaps because we were in greater need than we had ever been before. Perhaps, also, because we had finally separated ourselves from our sons. Even when a letter from the Marin County Public Health Department was forwarded to us: *"It has come to our attention that lot # (?) on Douglas Street in Inverness is apparently occupied... ."* by Steve, and there was no running water or sanitary facilities; would we please take care of this, etc., etc., we calmly forwarded the letter to him c/o General Delivery, Inverness telling him to take care of it himself. It was no longer our concern. So he rented a Porta-Potty for $20 a month. *"Shit, $20 a month to Shit! But I never used it,"* he said self-righteously.

Another momentous event that had occurred before we left home was Steve's coming out of the closet after leaving Annemarie. He left a note in our mailbox. *"... I'm sorry, I know this hurts you, but I can't fight against myself anymore. Don't try to find me."* We were too numb to worry, not surprised, but sad because of Annemarie, whom we'd grown to love very much. He showed up a few weeks later. He'd been in Inverness, staying with his friend, Joe, and the two of them were washing dishes at Manka's again. He asked if he could build a cabin on our vacant lot on Douglas Street, the one where Erinveine had been.

We all conferred. Tom and Dave didn't want that property; we didn't want it, having long since (1965) settled into "The Shambles," in First Valley; why not give the lot to Steve as an early inheritance? We had already given Dave (and Chandra, worse luck) 84 Tamalpais Road.

So that's when he got his toehold into owning land and created the first of his several fantastically original and appealing abodes. The one in Inverness was like a playhouse, tucked into the woods, with a loft, a wood stove, and lots of light from the many windows. He sold it to Joe a few years later for $7,000, and he's still there, having added his own nice touches — stonewalls, bamboo gate, plantings. That's when Steve bought a steep hill near a cluster of trees planted by some earlier settler, at a series of work-party weekends, but Steve was the architect. Recycled doors and windows and sinks and bricks from Inverness and Berkeley gave it a familiar feel. His animals were housed underneath in the way he had learned, when he and Annemarie were students in Austria with Friends World College, that the European farmers built, the animals providing heat, and the whole place shook when the pigs rubbed against the walls.

Just thinking of all Steve's houses makes me smile at the charm, and hospitality expressed in each. Never mind the lack of plumbing or electricity (although eventually there would be solar electricity, propane powered hot water heater and cooking stove), the windows were always carefully placed to bring the views inside. (He could have been an architect like his Grandfather Kent, who never even finished high school, because of the 1906 earthquake. At seventeen he began apprenticing with established architects like Willis Polk and Arthur Brown, rebuilding San Francisco.) There were some staggeringly beautiful views in Humboldt County — the circle of dark blue-green, tree-studded mountains with Steve's various flocks of sheep and horses and cows and turkeys moving across the meadows that sloped off from the house, light and shadow shifting all day long, finally ending in sunset, then lavender-sky-time over King's Peak to the west, galloping horses silhouetted against the horizon.

Montana, ten years later, was a much bigger canvas. The craggy Rockies jutting up behind Steve's land made the Humboldt mountains seem like hills and then to the west the broad Mission Valley and the Buffalo Range, a huge reserve where those amazing animals have been saved from extinction. Steve was with Tom Freeman, then, who'd lured him to this larger landscape that he could not resist. Indian country, 124 acres on the reservation compared to 40 in Humboldt County was a graduation from a little hippie play-pad to a real, grown-up ranch. And there he really learned his trade. I will never forget going down to the barn, a handsome log structure that he and Tom had built, in the evening with him when he did the chores — milking at least a half a dozen cows, giving bottles to some of the calves, pitching hay, cleaning stalls, watering the horses, all by the light of a kerosene lamp. And the whole process would be repeated the following early morning. My God, he was a worker.

The house in Montana was a trailer that had been pushed out in several directions with added-on alcoves, bay windows, verandas, again with views featured in every direction. Even the outdoor john — a toilet seat secured above a deep pit — situated in the open air behind pine trees for privacy — had a view, straight up to the top of the rockies, where once, as I was sitting there, I saw elk grazing on a craggy knoll.

At one time or another Jack and I experienced every season in Montana — snowy winter, blazing hot summer, and the gentler subtler spring and fall. The vegetable garden was superb, the orchard lush with apples. Oh, we had wonderful meals at Steve's round oak table. That table, and most of the other furniture, had traveled first from the Bay Area to Humboldt County, then to Montana. There was the Shaker chest that was my bureau growing up on La Loma Avenue, and the sideboard with the marble top that was in Jack's family's dining room in St. Francis Wood, and Auntie Margaret's rocking chair. Ten years later it all returned to Humboldt County, after Steve and Tom Freeman parted ways, after Steve's health began to fail. Now it's been distributed among his surviving relatives. Hannah has the sideboard, the table is stored in the garage, Rebecca has the Shaker chest, I have the rocking chair.

I went riding with Steve in Montana, such a thrill, taking me back to my horse crazy youth. I loved his horses: Tolman (named for Grandpa), Ferjessie, Angela, Resolute, Norma Jean, Tina, Sassy. Have I left anyone out? Oh yes, Mercy, one of the early ones. I remember a ride along the canal where the blue herons swooped along with us, and there were signs of bears having rolled stones near the creek, eaten rotten apples fallen beneath an old abandoned orchard planted by some earlier homesteader than Steve. I wrote a poem about it.

Bears

Once I was a fourteen-year-old dude
and a cowboy asked, "Y'all ever seen a bear?
So I fell in love with him for a season.
Now, decades later, I rediscover the mystique.
Once a man was street-wise in the city.
Now he's in Montana
where instead of derelict neighborhoods
occupied by the homeless
it's abandoned homesteads
become bedrooms for the bears
that he sniffs out.
Only minutes from the barn we're in wilderness.
"Bears," he says,
pointing at an apple tree.
Its un-pruned branches straggle wildly.
The ground beneath is strewn
with rotten fruit and fresh bear scat.
Our horses snort, dancing sideways
in the long shadows
and we sing cowboy songs
to let the bears know we are near.

Our first trip to Montana, Jack and I took Grayson, who was twelve, and we drove north to Portland, then east along the Columbia River, western Washington, Idaho, Montana, taking our time, spending three nights along the way. It was fun having a young boy with us again, like old times with Steve and his brothers. I have a picture of Grayson, grinning beside an enormous chrome-studded semi outside a truck stop in Pasco, his hand splayed out on the fender, another by a lake in Montana with the Rockies, both the actual ones and those reflected in the water behind him. I will never forget that first sight of the Rockies as we came down into Mission Valley from the west.

Steve was a wonderful host with lots of adventures planned for us — swimming in the canal (that was another time I almost fainted), rowing in McDonald Lake, meeting Walt, Steve's neighbor, the old Indian Chief, seeing real live buffaloes in the Buffalo Range. We ate buffalo burgers, too, in a diner and watched the Fourth of July Parade in the little town of Ronan, and later that day went to a picnic on a ranch full of lovely brood mares run by a group of lesbian women. It was fun and funny. I don't think Grayson had a clue as to the unusual mix of people. He was the only child there and amused himself chopping wood, stroking the velvety noses of the horses, playing volleyball with the women.

Deborah went with us to Montana once, and Walt, the Indian Chief, took quite a shine to her. Steve wrote that Walt always asked after his beautiful dark-eyed aunt. Perhaps she reminded him of an Indian princess with that exotic dark streak she inherited from our mother. We went to Glacier Park that trip and drove over the Rockies on the Highway to the Sun. It felt like the top of the world and we really did see bears.

Usually we flew to Montana, and rented a car in Missoula, fifty miles south of Steve. Twice we went by train, two nights, one day. It was on one of those train trips that I first sensed that something was wrong with Jack. He got lost and completely disoriented. And the whole time we were at Steve's that time — it was June, I remember, probably about 89, nine years before Jack died — he was distant and confused as we did the chores that Steve assigned us to, the things Jack usually enjoyed, like mending fences and shoveling manure and digging post holes and harvesting apples and vegetables. One night in bed he clung to me and said, "I'm so unhappy," but he couldn't tell me why. As usual, Steve had made lots of friends who became our friends too, but I'll never see those kind folk, I'll never go to Montana again.

On our final trip, in the early 90s, we had the usual three-hour layover in Salt Lake City, and then our plane to Missoula was at least an hour late. When it finally arrived, the pilot hurried out into the airport looking harassed, which made me nervous, for this was to be our pilot. Where was he rushing off to looking so strained? Maybe they'd put another pilot on to replace him. But no, a few minutes later he reappeared, still looking pressured, with a plastic cup in his hand as he hurried back into the cockpit. We passengers boarded, the plane took off, and Jack and I held hands as we always did at take-off time, a silly little superstitious habit. Suddenly an ominous clattering noise began beneath us, probably just the wheels folding up, yet it went on and on. Something was wrong with this plane. I still clutched Jack's hand, convinced that this was the end as the clattering noise continued and I looked out at the gorgeous clouds, mountains, and down at Great Salt Lake. We would crash and die. And then I felt an extraordinary surge of gratitude for the long, full life I'd had. We were together, and we would not have to endure lingering illnesses, painful deaths. What a way to go.

Tom wrote us in Corsica, telling us he was in the Seattle area fishing for salmon. He enclosed a drawing of the fishing boat he shared with a friend, then, almost as an afterthought, said that he was living with a beautiful redhead named Deborah Dee Marie Antoinette Quinn. As I recall, we were neither particularly glad nor upset, just neutral. Tom had already been married twice. We actually felt pleasantly remote from our three sons and their lives.

In the spring of 1971 there was an election in St. Florent. Our old political curiosity was reawakened, especially since everything seemed topsy-turvy to us compared to Berkeley, where, we'd recently heard, the city council was now dominated by the New Left. In St. Florent the staid incumbent communists, the establishment, were being challenged by the young, outrageous, prodevelopment capitalists, the radicals! To our surprise and delight we were invited to a political dinner by the nice old communist mayor. We couldn't vote, so it was a genuine gesture of friendship, or perhaps just good business, since he owned the little market where we sometimes shopped. On the other hand, we'd heard of all kinds of illegal shenanigans the Corsicans engage in to express their passion for independence — outbursts of bombings at a French-owned asbestos plant on the coast, mysterious fires in the mountains, and padding election returns with illegal votes by the deceased, to say nothing of paying relatives who'd long since emigrated to Marseilles, whose names were still on the rosters, to come home and vote. Perhaps there was some clever plot afoot to get our vote. We went to the dinner just the same and nobody tried to coerce us. It was a wonderful show of Corsican spirit and hospitality. We thanked the mayor, both for the dinner and his valiant fight against needless progress. Then we went home to bed, but around midnight we were awakened by a fusillade of gunshots and flashes of light through the window. Hurriedly we put on our wrappers and climbed up through the trap door to the roof and watched the fireworks. It was almost as spectacular as those fireworks we'd witnessed in Venice, back in 1955 with the boys and the Elkuses, celebrating the end of the plague in the fourteenth century. We didn't find out who the victors were until the next day. "Mais, alors, Monsieur le Maire, naturellement!" our landlady, Mme. Vermonet declared. Good! For, as Jack was well known to pronounce, "When it's not necessary to change it is necessary NOT to change!" (Once when we were having a drought in California I translated that into signs posted on all of our four toilets — two in Berkeley, two in Inverness, "When it is not necessary to flush, it is necessary NOT to flush!")

Early in June of that year, seated in the big open boat of the owners of the charcuterie who had invited us to join them, we watched the spectacle of the blessing of the fishing fleet of St. Florent. In the rosy late afternoon the boats cruised slowly about while the priest from his boat, in which the golden statue of St. Florent, brought from the Cathedral for this special event, stood in the prow, also cruised and sprinkled holy water on each sturdy craft.

A few days later I finished the green sweater I'd been knitting for our neighbor, the Corsican grandfather, who'd been sitting in that doorway across from us in his black corduroy suit and red cummerbund all winter and spring, watching us, smiling, lifting a hand in greeting as we moved through the seasons. Island weather was capricious, sometimes fierce and extreme. Heavy snow, accompanied by the sound of gunshots in the woods as the locals shot small birds (a delicacy marinated in garlic butter and eaten, bones, eyes, tiny claws and all for those who had the courage) who came too close in search of food, was gone and melting in no time. Before we knew it wild flowers were bursting out all over. We went swimming. But then the mistral came, pelting everything with sand and dust, driving us back inside to finish up the jigsaw puzzle spread across our dining table. The adage repeated over and over by shopkeepers, fish mongers, and our Corsican grandfather neighbor was, "No matter what the weather, it only lasts three days."

He had whittled a salad serving set from the local myrtle wood for us, also woven a basket from willow. The sweater was my farewell gift. "Oh, merci, merci. Vous etes en partant, alors?" he asked, the phrase, 'en partant,' a Corsican version of French, implying that leaving is more than an act, it is a process. Yes, it was, and we were. We wrapped the Quimper pottery we'd bought in Brittany the previous September in newspapers, packed it, along with the shells and stones we'd collected on Corsican beaches, into the peasant baskets from the local market. We played boule with the Rouverols, tennis with the Lenoirs and DuMauduits. We accepted, finally, an invitation from the owner of the tiny bar-cafe on the post office square to come in and have a glass of pastis. He had asked us several times over the preceding months.

Soon after we arrived in November we were aware of the curiosity the locals had about us. And this old fellow used to stand in front of his bar cafe, smoking Galloise cigarettes, watching our every move as we did our errands, parked our car, picked up our mail. By June we had become confident enough of our French to make small talk with him and the craggy men who played cards in there. Many of the natives, especially the older ones, spoke only Corse to each other, and their French was sometimes almost as halting as ours. When they did speak French it was very slowly which made it easier for us to understand. Perhaps it wasn't so much the language that had held us back, as a lack of common experience to make small talk about. At any rate, we did enjoy that one daring excursion into the smoky cave-like room to visit with those proud old Corsicans.

On one of those last days a final Corsican irony was a visit from one of the gendarmes stationed at the great round Citadel at the end of the road. Smiling, smart-looking in his blue uniform and hat with touches of red, he handed us our permits to be visitors in St. Florent. It had taken eight months to process and now we were "en partant," but we didn't tell him that.

Our Italian freighter, *Lorenzo d'Amico*, would not leave from Lisbon until the middle of August, but we had no desire to see our dear St. Florent infested with tourists. So one day in the middle of June we loaded up the car and drove slowly, for the last time, out of the post office square, past the War Memorial, through the miles of vineyards that when we first came in November had been a pattern of fierce black stems, sculpted twists and gnarls, and now were all gentle and frothy and green. We passed the tiny town of Patrimonio, and drove in second gear up over the mountain, Col de Teghime, from where the Germans were driven back into the sea by Corsican partisans near the end of the war. We were on our way to Bastia, where we would board a ferry to Marseilles, but not before we took one last look at Napoleon's statue, hidden deep in the bushes of the park. The Bastians of the north have little respect for Ajaccio, and its native son, of the south.

February 2000

That was thirty years ago, yet I've managed to put myself back into the mood of that lovely second honeymoon time of our life together. Tom and Deb seem to be at that stage now. In fact they're on a holiday in Mexico. Yes, he did marry the "beautiful redhead, Deborah Dee Marie Antoinette Quinn" after several fits and starts and fathering her two children, separations and recouplings and finally coping with his alcoholism. Their sons, Thomas Grayson and Fletcher Quinn, were seven and six when their parents got married. There's an adorable picture of them, all dressed up — blazers, white shirts, neckties — grinning from ear to ear. What a joyous affair that was on a perfect August summer day at their place in Inverness, a truly organic, homemade, heartwarming environment. By the time of the wedding it had expanded from prefab log cabin, trailer, outhouse. The trailer and outhouse were gone. There was a large kitchen with gorgeous rough hewn beams and two-foot wide polished planks for the floor, windows and decks everywhere looking into Tom's sculpted trees. There were chicken houses and greenhouses for Deb, a shop and a junkyard for old cars and trucks and automotive parts hidden in the woods for Tom. For the wedding party there was an upright piano plunked down in the grass where one of the local plumbers played jazz all afternoon. A horseshoe court had been set up for the occasion.

Grayson and Fletcher are now twenty-five and twenty-three. Tom and Deb's grandsons — twins, Fletcher's sons — Nicolas Quinn and Patrick Hatton are two years old today. As infants they lay in Jack's arms in his hospital bed. Fletcher and Kristina brought them all the way from Portland to see him because they knew he was dying. And they were Steve's final human contact last March. As usual his attitudes in relation to humanity in general and children in particular were strikingly contradictory.

Overpopulation was a big concern of his. Even as a little kid he used to shout at us, *"I never asked to be born!"* He had a bumper sticker on his truck: **"THANK YOU FOR NOT BREEDING."** But he was a sentimental patsy about specific children, especially his own nieces and nephews (and now great nephews.) He left everything he had to them. It didn't amount to a lot, but the final payment on his Montana land was $20,000. I had the great pleasure of carrying out his wishes and giving $4,000 to each of the five. That's a pretty nice windfall when you're somewhere between sixteen and twenty-six. In curious ways Steve was a role model for each of them — a nonhero rebel who lived more than most are able according to his beliefs. And as his friend Yvon said to me as we visited on my porch in Berkeley shortly before Steve died, both of us bursting with sobs, he was so completely honest, too honest sometimes.

I wasn't there, but they told me how Kristina put the twins on his chest, and then, as though he'd been waiting until they came, he died. Kristina's always had a special empathy for him, his love of horses, his rebellious spirit. His saddles and saddle blankets are now hers.

Back in 1971 we were in no hurry to meet Ms. Quinn or to reconnect with any of our three sons. It had been so therapeutic to disconnect that we lingered along the Camargue where the Rhone empties, finally, into the Mediterranean and wild horses gallivant across the endless shallows. Slowly we drove over the Pyrenees down into Andorra, and on to Spain. We had a month, more or less, depending on the freighter's demands, before we would sail from Lisbon, and neither of us had ever been to Madrid or Toledo or Granada or Cordoba or Seville. Neither of us had been to Portugal.

As I recall, we traveled in our usual fashion, without reservations, feeling our way, which in itself adds adventure to an already adventurous time. I remember the balmy warmth as we drove through the countryside toward Madrid, struck by the verdant grasses and wildflowers that grew right to the edges of the road. I remember gleaming white villages, confined to their chosen places. There was, in those days, none of the urban sprawl that had already overtaken America. When we were growing up the Santa Clara Valley was full of flowering prune trees in the spring. The losses of that and of the whole of

Contra Costa County where Jack used to go with his parents to visit the Newells on their ranch was a big part of his motivation to become a planner, I imagine. Poor Wynne Newell. He caved in and sold it all for big bucks. They named a street out there in Walnut Creek after him. There's a big green and white freeway sign, **NEWELL AVENUE,** and a ramp whizzing off to the right. I can't imagine anything more degrading, but I think he died before that freeway was built. I hope so anyway. And in Spain, then Portugal, we kept wanting to say to the natives, "Oh, don't spoil it all the way we did." Yet there we were, touring around, contributing to the perhaps inevitable problems humanity creates for itself.

It was hot in Madrid, the way we felt it was meant to be in Spanish summertime, a time for sleeveless dresses and sandals, and my bare arms and legs, tan from Corsican beaches, could still get away with such comfort. I was only fifty. I didn't yet have varicose veins and flabby upper arms. I remember a favorite cotton dress, patterned with great splashes of red-yellow-blue-orange-magenta — Matisse colors — another one of those marvelous things Jack's mother had bought for me. What did Jack wear? I don't seem to have any photos of that time in Spain. Probably short-sleeved cotton shirts. We found a fine little hotel on a big park-like square, and soon adjusted our life to the ways of the Spaniards in summer — sightseeing in the mornings before the heat of the day set in. The Prado with the Goyas and El Grecos is what I remember most. Then lunch in the quiet dark dining room of our hotel with fans whirring overhead, followed by siesta, and reading — all about Ferdinand and Isabella, Cervantes and the Moors and Llorca. I remember tapas, gazpacho, sangria, late dinners, then on to watch flamenco dancers. Late at night, after we'd gone to bed, we heard children still laughing and playing in the park outside our window.

The mood of Spain, the layers of civilizations and faiths remains with me as I look again at all those postcards Jack bought of the cathedral within a mosque in Cordoba and down the street a synagogue, the moorish Alhambra at Grenada, the tiles and filigreed iron gates of houses in Seville.

In Portugal it was mostly beaches again, our addiction to sand and salt water as strong as ever. The stocky Portuguese plunged into the waves, screaming with pleasure. They couldn't swim. It was a dangerous surf. The lifeguard kept warning them but they paid no attention. That beach north of Lisbon was covered with blue-and-white striped tents for dressing rooms.

By now it was August. Lisbon was our headquarters, but each time the freighter was delayed we went off to a beach for a few days. The last one was south of Lisbon in the Algarve region, Salena Beach, a small fishing village with a few tourist accommodations, just our style. But finally *Lorenzo d'Amico* arrived in Lisbon. Our car, Vivienne Lamalou Kent, was lifted by an enormous crane onto the deck where she spent the next three weeks wedged between storage containers. There were only five of us passengers — a nice gay man from San Francisco named Bob, a couple about our age from the University of Washington in Seattle who'd spent a year's sabbatical at the American University in Beirut. I can't remember their names. He was in psychology and knew about my father. That was nice. Things were getting pretty dicey in the Middle East and they were glad to be leaving.

Things were getting pretty dicey at home too, or perhaps we were just beginning to pay more attention now that we were heading back. All this time the Vietnam war was still going on. Just before we left Lisbon we heard that Nixon had ordered a ninety-day freeze on prices and wages trying to curb inflation. Jack and I knew zilch about economics, but this seemed ominous. And then, as we sipped our aperitifs before dinner one night, nearing the Sargasso Sea, we were informed by the captain that there was a general strike at all American ports, like the one back in the '30s when Jack was a scab on a cruise ship sailing from San Francisco to New York, recruited by the Boy Scouts of America. His father even drove him through the picket line. My God, he could have been killed! It's kind of funny in retrospect. He went with his girlfriend Margery's brother and both of them became real radicals a few years later and wouldn't have dreamed of crossing a picket line, especially Harry Bridges' picket line.

We would not be able to land in Oakland, the captain said. We could either go all the way to Vancouver or get off the ship in Mazatlan, Mexico. We opted for Mazatlan, a place we'd been to three times already — twice on freighter trips and once to Tom and Norma's wedding. Oh my, what a fiasco that was, although at the time we were full of optimistic hope that Tom's life was getting on track at last. She was a lapsed Catholic, but a wedding within the church meant a lot to her parents, even though they were separated from each other. The idea of Mexico was some kind of romantic nonsense. Mazatlan in August? Tom had been "instructed" in the faith in San Francisco. But in Mazatlan it wasn't that easy to find a priest who would perform this marriage of a Catholic to an infidel, even though instructed. I remember our trudging all over town in the humid heat, into narrow alleys and up dark stairways, following one lead after another until we finally found our guy. The wedding itself was quite nice, held in a beautiful and very ornate basilica. Tom wore Jack's pinstriped blue suit, which was much too warm; he was developing a heat rash. Norma's dress was ecru, maybe satin, mid-calf length. We liked her. Among many nice things about her, she was a nurse. Tom could do with a nurse. That night Jack and I celebrated, sat up late drinking rum and coke on the balcony of our hotel room. Ha!

His next marriage, about three years later, coincides in my memory with the time of Peoples' Park. I was trying to buy something new at a little boutique on Telegraph Avenue to wear to the wedding, Andre's I think the shop was called, right across from what was then Fraziers on the corner of Telegraph and Channing, this whole area my old high school stamping ground when, as happened frequently that spring of '69, a riot broke out. Angry people, mostly young, were dumping over newspaper racks. There were sirens and tear gas and shoppers like me hiding out in the store until it all blew over. I never did buy something new. The bride, voluptuous sixteen-year-old Becky, wore a bright red sexy dress and boots. Half of the guests were stoned, including Steve, I realize now, looking at the pictures. Her parents were so nice. They and we felt sorry for ourselves and each other, though we never said it out loud.

Again it was summer in Mazatlan, hot and humid, when *Lorenzo d'Amico* steamed into the harbor. We spent the next two days dealing with the Mexican bureaucracy. The problem was that since we had no official papers saying we had entered the country, we could receive no official papers letting us leave. We sat around in various offices until some clerk, finally realizing that we didn't catch on, weren't going to pass money under the table as was probably expected, got sick of us, and filled out the necessary forms to allow Vivienne to be lifted, by crane again, off the deck and down onto the wharf. We said farewell to Bob and the Seattle couple, who had opted to stay aboard until Vancouver, thanked the charming Italian officers and crew, got into the car whose battery had miraculously not gone dead, and drove north about five hundred and fifty miles, spending a night in Guaymas on the way, to the border town of Nogales. The inspectors, looking for drugs in our trunk, were perplexed by all those rocks and shells from Corsican beaches, but let us through.

The rest of the trip is blurred with many other trips up and down the state, except for the vivid and delightful memory of sneaking into Berkeley through the back door, so to speak, up over the East Bay hills from Orinda, winding down Shasta Road to Tamalpais and parking in front of our house as though we were just coming home from a hike up in Tilden Park instead of from fifteen months abroad that had changed our attitudes and lives.

Nobody, including ourselves, had been quite sure when we would be arriving home. Our tenants had been Phyllis and Bernard Taper. He used to write about urban affairs for *The New Yorker*, but had joined the journalism faculty at U.C. Berkeley. They had, fortunately, moved out. The house looked and felt wonderful. We were glad to be home. For an hour or two we savored the old familiarity. No rush to get in touch with everyone. But of course before that day was over we had telephoned our kids, our sisters, Jack's mother.

Chapter Nine

I wonder how it is that history seems to fit so conveniently into decades. The '20s can be defined as the age of flappers, jazz, and Prohibition, ending with the stock market crash in '29. Of course I was conveniently born in '21, so the '20s can also be defined as the decade of my childhood. The '30s were the Depression, Roosevelt, the New Deal. For me it was growing up and falling in love. The '40s was marriage, war, and children; the '50s ... well, you get the idea. Jack and Steve were born three years before the decade — 1917 and 1947 so their lives cannot quite so tidily be fit into history. And even history slops over the edges. For instance, when we came home from Corsica in the early fall of 1971, the Vietnam War continued, in fact had spread to Laos and Cambodia, despite the killing of four Kent State student protesters by the National Guard the year before. And it was the energy of the '60s that propelled Steve, somewhere in there in the early '70s, to buy the land in Humboldt County.

There was a trip he took in a small plane with some guy who knew about this big ranch that was being sold off in forty-acre plots. Dave and Chandra knew him too. In fact, I think Dave flew up there with Steve to look at it, leaving Chandra and this guy's stoned girlfriend and her dog behind with me at The Shambles in Inverness. The details are fuzzy — it's been almost thirty years. Where was Jack? At some meeting in the City, I guess. By then it would have been People For Open Space, or the Berkeley Charter Review Committee. Not in our bed though, I know, because this girl, who'd earlier been lying on the living room floor, practically having sex with her big German Shepherd while I was crowding past them, back and forth from the kitchen to the table, trying to serve dinner to whoever all these people were, came crying into our bedroom, stark naked, in the middle of the night, and crawled into bed, clinging to me. Jack definitely was not there. "Chandra," I yelled to the next bedroom, "Help!" And she came and led this poor girl who was on an acid trip, Chandra said, back to the other bedroom with her. In the morning the sun was shining on the deck, the creek gurgling over the stones below. Chandra had made coffee. The girl and her dog were serene. Had I imagined it all? I wonder if Chandra remembers this. I haven't seen her for years, although I got a sympathy note in her perfect handwriting — large, symmetrical, slanted — after Jack or Steve died, I'm not sure which.

So Steve bought that land in Humboldt County. For ten years up there and another ten in Montana, our lives were periodically deeply immersed in helping him with his projects. It was before that, though, in Corsica where we'd been writing and painting and reading, that we began observing firsthand the beautiful simplicity of peasant relationship to the land and animals. We'd begun to integrate the environmental awareness we'd acquired through our Bay Area efforts — stop burning garbage; save the Bay, open space, redwoods, fish — into an ecological philosophy. Americans in general were becoming aware of the personal fulfillment that could be derived from growing food, flowers, trees; building a table; baking bread; cooking a soul-warming meal. Alice Waters was roaming around in Provence gestating a food revolution. Our sons had been learning these things too, but we'd had to go thousands of miles away to even begin to do so. I remember, Steve saying to us some years later, "You are my children, and you're learning REAL GOOD!"

Our place in Inverness that fall of '71 more than lived up to its name, The Shambles — after that street in York that I talked about before where the medieval buildings have a dizzy, topsy-turvy look with nothing quite aligned. All of our houses over the years, often in a state of flux — unfinished projects, conflicting lifestyles of several generations, to say nothing of floods and landslides — have tended to have a shambly appearance, but none so much as The Shambles.

The first thing we saw in the driveway, when we got back from Corsica was an enormous truck with at least one flat tire, like a Dorothea Lange photograph of Okies back in the '30s, but this one was stuffed with old bedding, broken dishes, burned pots, garbage. I recognized a J. C. Penney cotton blanket (pale green with white stripes), Auntie Margaret's broken wicker chair, a beach umbrella. It was the dregs of a drugged-out commune, we later learned. After the truck, the next thing we noticed was the barren ground. Where grass and blackberry bushes and ferns had been was bare, used dirt. Thankfully nobody had informed us while in Corsica of the naked children and stoned adults that camped next to our bubbling creek and roamed around the valley. That was the era when hippies occupied empty houses as though they had a perfect right to do so. Our house wasn't empty though. We had rented it to a friend of Tom's and his wife and baby, but the guy left, and she, in order to be able to stay on, turned our acre into a campground, renting out plots. It would all grow back, we reassured ourselves. Then, through the alder trees we saw the house where the wife, Shirley, had apparently painted all the trim. A nice gesture, but what a color! Nauseous chartreuse. Oh well, we could paint it over. Tom, who had returned from Seattle, leaving Deborah Dee Marie Antoinette Quinn behind in the first of several separations, and now lived in our old garage at The Shambles, got rid of the truck full of junk. And that was that. We were definitely mellower than we used to be.

In the '70s we began to learn from our grown children and develop new relationships with them. And our Berkeley and Inverness communities we also seemed able to view more clearly, having been away for a year. The beginnings of rapprochement between the generations translated into community life as well as familial. The Inverness Improvement Association now reflected the interesting demographic changes that had been taking place. Quite a few former summer kids, like Tom and my nephew Nick, were now living there full time. And there had been an influx of artists, musicians, and hippies from all over the country who'd heard of the area by word of mouth. The president of the Inverness Improvement Association was a young physician, former English major and poet who a few years later would deliver our oldest grandson, a home birth in a home without electricity or indoor toilet. The treasurer was an acupuncturist and the business manager of the local rock band, The Youngbloods, that had gained a good deal of fame. One of the first thing this new young group did was to delete the word, improvement, from the Association's title, feeling that it was prodevelopment. It became and remains today, The Inverness Association.

There were still a few old-timers, and at some point in there I was recruited as a candidate by them, to represent the neglected interests, as these old-timers saw it, of the summer community. I was elected and soon became secretary and served with that interesting group for several years. It meant we had to go to Inverness once every month for Board meetings which were held on Friday nights, in those days, in the back room of Vladimir's Czech restaurant. We really enjoyed having a weekend a month there throughout the year. After a while, though, it became tedious, and I didn't run for reelection. Tom was nominated to take my place. Yes, the generations were having a rapprochement. And it was happening in Berkeley politics too.

The Democratic Club Movement had already begun to lose some of its influence by the mid-sixties as radical pressure from the political left heightened, due, I believe, to the continuing intensification of the Vietnam war. In 1965 The Vietnam Day Committee marched on the Oakland Army Terminal. The new leftist Community for New Politics was formed and endorsed candidates for the Berkeley City Council — Robert Scheer in 1966; and in 1967 Jerry Rubin for Mayor; Avakian, Horawitz, Neilands and Dellums for City Council. Dellums was elected, the beginning of his long and distinguished political career. Liberal Democrats became anathema to the New Left, who were doing something similar in the '60s to what we had been doing in the '50s — learning to take control of government at the local level. And I suppose we were doing what the Republicans had done back in the '50s, hanging on to power. But we were also, some of us, becoming increasingly disillusioned by the policies in Washington that kept the Vietnam War going on. Jeff Cohelan, a Berkeley friend, neighbor, and former colleague of Jack's on the Berkeley City Council, whom we'd been so proud to elect as our Congressman, seemed unresponsive to the growing restiveness in his own constituency. I remember that as early as 1966, not long before Jim Whitney died, he was drafting a letter to Jeff, a beautiful and articulate letter that I believe Deborah sent on to Jeff posthumously, urging him to listen to the voices at home.

By the '70s friction between the leftists and the liberals began to ease. We were older, mellower. They sometimes sought our advice, and Jack, of course, responded with enthusiasm, his teaching and political instincts as sharp as ever. A decade or so later at a dinner honoring him Loni Hancock, by then the mayor of Berkeley, or soon to be, described the phenomenon better than I can:

"In 1969 I met Jack Kent the politician — a leader with a group of change-agents and advocates who elected the first Stevensonian Democrats to the Berkeley City Council... .In 1969 I was running for the Berkeley City Council for the first time — representing a group of change-agents and advocates seeking to inject the ideas of the peace movement and the "new politics" into public Dialogue in our city. In that election of 1969 Jack and I were on opposite sides. We were allies within a few years. . . . During those years (the '70s) of working together, Jack Kent has helped me, and many of us political neophytes in more ways than I'm sure he knows. . . ."
and more, about the specifics of his help. She spoke about this again at a gathering in Wurster Hall after Jack died.

My first clear memory of Loni was at a small meeting at our house — some people from the New Left tentatively approaching the Liberal Democratic Establishment. She was charming, not at all strident, even a bit shy, or perhaps just well-mannered. She was almost as young as my children and I was fascinated by that generation of women's libbers. My great grandmother had been an abolitionist and suffragette. So had my mother. I felt already liberated. For me *not* getting a college degree back in the '40s was a form of liberation in a family that took great stock in such achievements. So I was a little perplexed by the new frustrations expressed so vehemently by some of these younger women and found some of their antics just plain silly, like burning their bras. And my interests were subtly shifting from activist politics to something more introspective, though at the time I could not have told you what that was. I worked for McGovern in '72, not as a precinct organizer, but as a low profile volunteer in the headquarters on Shattuck Avenue, stuffing envelopes, making coffee. I'm still pleased, flattered when I remember being begged to negotiate between the Democratic Establishment and the New Left to create a more effective campaign.

But I no longer wanted to be in a leadership role, so volunteered as an official in our neighborhood polling place which was a very satisfying job for many years. I hope technology doesn't wipe out that nice old-fashioned, human-scale arrangement where neighbors meet neighbors while participating in the democratic process. Scholars, bankers, students, a Nobel Laureate, poets and musicians, city planners and politicians, a university president, teachers, secretaries, artists; Republicans, Democrats, Communists, Socialists, Libertarians, Greens — to name a few — of three and four generations have come and gone all day long on election day for all the fifty years I have lived on Tamalpais Road. In the early days we still counted the ballots by hand and posted the results on the outside of the door of the garage at #19, our polling place still and for as long as I can remember. Now the ballots are counted electronically at City Hall or County Courthouse. One can no longer peruse the list the next morning and speculate about who voted for who, a great loss, I think, in the name of progress and efficiency. (Since I wrote this George W. Bush was not elected but became our president anyway!)

In 1972 I joined the University Section Club's Writing Section and started writing about Corsica. Jack began to garden. He planted a few tomato plants up back, also an orange tree. We already had a hedge of Meyer lemons. We still lived next door then, at #84. Plants outlive buildings, outlive their planters. Those gnarly apple orchards and old rose bushes at Steve's, both in Humboldt County and Montana, were left over from some former homesteaders' efforts long ago. We'll never know their stories. And in time Steve's grapevines, plum and peach and fig trees will have some future farmer wondering who he was, what his story was. They might wonder who laid the bricks beside the remnants of a retaining wall. (That was Jack. How he loved laying bricks!)

At the former site of Erinveine, where Steve's friend Joe still lives, those poplars we planted down by the road in the early '60s still stand. (I just saw Joe last night at a party for Fletcher at Tom and Deb's in Inverness. He said those trees are enormous now, also that he's been having dreams about Steve as the first anniversary of his death approaches. Nick's been having dreams too. So has Fletcher.) And at The Shambles the onslaught of the hippies and ten years later the flood of '82 could not keep down the blackberry bushes and alders for long.

From this study window I can see the orange tree next door, loaded with fruit. Sometimes Elizabeth, who lives there now, brings me some. And here, at #74, the garden is filled with arugula and greens, forget-me-nots and nasturtiums that have reseeded themselves from those Jack planted years and years ago. Mint, too, and chard. When did he stop gardening? Probably in the late '80s, after his hip replacement. Rebecca still remembers picking off the broccoli florets when she was small. Now she's almost seventeen. Like building fires and laying bricks, digging — garden beds, graves for family pets, holes for fence posts — seemed to be a basic instinct for Jack. There are lots of pictures of him leaning on shovels, grinning. I never tried to understand the necessity for so many different sorts of shovels. The subject bored me. Now every time I think of getting rid of some of them, I'm stymied by all their various shapes and sizes and can't decide. So there they still are, those many shovels — on the back porch, in the basement, in the garage.

I cooked some greens with garlic and olive oil and lemon for supper just the other evening. Absolutely delicious. I thought of Ora who sometimes used to cook "a mess of greens" for us on La Loma Avenue as they did down in Louisiana when she was a girl, long before we began to hear about soul food, sometime in the '60s, when white kids like Steve went down South to register voters. He just loved those old black women cooking up their greens and chitlins and corn pone. He wanted to BE black. I could have those greens every night for a year and there'd still be more. Arugula has become a very trendy salad green at gourmet restaurants, also nasturtium blossoms. Perhaps I should get into marketing my organic greens. The apple tree we planted when we first moved here has died, but the Meyer lemon thrives and yields enormous crops. And the plum tree that Tom has shaped for years is blossoming outside the window as it was last February, that bittersweet, comic-tragic time Steve and I had together then. From up here in Jack's study I look out on two bursts of flowering plums amid the dark evergreens in my neighbors' yards to the east and south. ("My" neighbors instead of "Ours"; I say that almost without thinking now.) Steve would have liked the greens I cooked, the idea of them coming from right outside the kitchen door, the smell of the garlic, but he would only have been able to take a bite or two, for his liver was closing down.

Jack's mother was another major concern of ours in the early '70s I remember our Wednesday afternoon ritual, in the years before she died in the fall of '75. Jack walked from the campus to her little house on Webster Street. (The San Francisco house had been sold many years before when Jack's father's health began to fail.) Heaven knows what they talked about. Perhaps she asked him, as she did throughout his life, "And NOW, son, what are you going to do next?" as though being a professor, a city planner, a politician could not possibly be his main occupations. I would drive over and join them around five. We'd have two Old-Fashioneds each, fixed by Jack, just the way his dad used to do — "put into an old-fashioned glass and stir 1/2 teaspoon sugar, 2 dashes angostura bitters, 1 teaspoon water; add 2 ice cubes; fill glass to within 1/2 inch of top with Bourbon; stir; garnish with a twist of lemon peel, a thin slice of orange, a maraschino cherry." His mom would always have some old photograph or letter from the past to show us. She spent a lot of time rummaging through the memorabilia of her life, just as I am doing now. I don't believe she was depressed, only confused. "Why did Flommy (her pet name for Jack's father) die? We were so happy!" More and more often she misplaced her watch, lost her glasses, locked herself out of the house. Thank goodness she had never learned to drive. She became convinced that there were drug runners using the basement as a hangout. She smelled strange odors in the night. We arranged for Meals-on-Wheels to bring her a hot lunch every noontime. At first she protested, "I NEVER eat dinner at noon!" (Well, you HAVE to eat dinner at noon, I muttered under my breath.) But after a while it was, "Oh Mary, how nice, it's a party! Get out the placemats, dear, and let's have a glass of sherry. Of course I'm doing this for charity, you know."

For the last few months of her life she lived at the retirement community, Piedmont Gardens. It was not a happy solution, I'm very sad to remember. In hindsight it was probably too late in her life to make such a big change. I think she was eighty-four. Her last birthday she spent with us in Inverness: August 18, 1975. Grayson had just turned one on August 3. He and Tom and Deb were there. Janis was there with Karl. Where were Dave and Chandra? Steve had come down from Humboldt County. It was a beautiful sunny day on our porch. I had made several hearty salads — pasta and shrimp, chunked up cold pork and apples. I'd stuffed eggs with curry seasoning. I'm good at salad, though I'm not a very enthusiastic cook. We had hot cornbread. Nana, for some reason, didn't like the food. Everybody else did. She claimed we were trying to make her choke. Poor thing. I think she was beginning to have trouble swallowing. The same thing happened to Jack, toward the end. The memory loss of old age includes forgetting how to swallow. Steve, was furious with Nana. He told her he'd made a big effort to come down for her birthday, getting his friend Allan to feed the animals, his friend Mary to ride the horses and water the vegetables because Humboldt County is "as hot as hell in August and you're just being a mean old woman!" She was tough, though. I should know. I was too. We toughed it out together over the years, and she just laughed and hugged Steve.

Steve talked to Jack that way before he died, when he kept pulling out the oxygen tubes in his nose. "Dad, you're dying! You can't breathe without oxygen!" But he stayed right with Jack as he trailed those tanks around the house, even insisting on panting up the steep stairs to this study to take care of things, poring over piles on the desk, throwing things away.

When I first noticed he was tearing up reports, destroying books, about a year before he died, I got a nice man from the Bancroft Library to help us go through everything in both this study (where I now write) and his University office, to take whatever was important for the Archives. But that didn't cover a lot of personal things that are lost forever. And for some reason Jack excised his essay from all the copies of a wonderful resource book, *Experiment and Change in Berkeley: Essays on City Politics 1950-1975,* published by the Institute of Governmental Studies, a project that was his idea. (Why, oh why, did you do that, Jack? I need it now for this project of mine!)

Steve sat with him hugged him and joked with him about that gorgeous photograph of a French nude thumb tacked on the wall. (That photograph, which irked me of course, was one of the things that mysteriously disappeared in those last days of his life.) Again Steve said, "Dad's such a sweet guy," of him whose work he had sometimes said was meaningless, removed from reality, "talking about, reading about, writing about, but not DOING!" Steve was fully aware of the irony of his lifetime swings in attitude. He laughed, and reminded me once more, "Well, of course; I'm a Gemini!" as though that excused everything. Tough love was what he dished out, to Nana, to Jack, to me last year as he was dying. I think the reason might be that he couldn't handle too much love, either given or received. Why was that, I wonder?

Deb brought her rich chocolate cake for Nana's last birthday, a regular for family parties, made with mayonnaise so it's very moist, and strawberries and whipped cream spread over the top. There's a picture of Grayson in his high chair with chocolate all over his face.

March 2000

I see the timeline of life like this in my head:

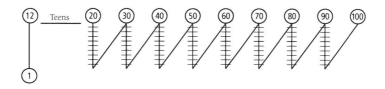

This chart helps me balance accounts, figure expenses, but most of all it helps me keep track of my life. In the '70s I was in my 50s — half a century — and now my children are too. That seems to be significant. Steve is stuck there forever, not quite fifty-two years old, his life cut off right in the middle. (People do live to be one hundred these days.) Until last year I never gave a thought to the vernal equinox. Now I will never forget it, for that is when he died.

1970-71 was our Corsica year. Also in 1970 Marxist Salvador Allende was elected in Chile. In 1971 New Leftist Loni Hancock was elected to the Berkeley City Council. 1972 Nixon was reelected, and it was the beginning of the Watergate scandal; 1973 was the end of the Vietnam War and the overthrow and probable murder by the CIA of Allende in Chile. We got two puppies that spring — litter mates Luke and Lotta — lovely little Shepherd-Collie mixes that were our loyal companions for fourteen years. They were so cute that summer, staggering around on Chicken Ranch Beach in Inverness, digging holes, playing with the constantly moving water's edge, and I have almost forgiven them their puppy mischief, though their baby tooth marks, especially Lotta's, on the rocking chair, on the edge of the hall rug remind me twenty-seven years later, long after their deaths. We still had Phoebe and Jesse then, the superannuated cats left behind by Steve and Dave when they left home. After Steve died he left three dogs, two horses, and half a dozen barn cats, but we found good homes for all of them. There might have been flocks of chickens and ducks, a small herd of sheep, a few half grown calves, for in those last years Steve flailed wildly, delusionally, back and forth between a sensible paring back of his herds and crops and household possessions, and an obsessive acquisitiveness as he clung to life with the same fury that he had exhibited the day he was born. But fortunately his live-stock had finally been cut back to the minimum.

The autumn of '73 we went with Deborah on a pilgrimage, insti-gated by Jack, to re-examine our New England heritage, Deborah's and Ted's and mine. Jack's forbears had all come to California in the 1860s and '70s from Ireland and England and Germany, some across the Isthmus of Panama, others around South America. His grandmother — Nana's beautiful mother Louise — was actually born on shipboard at Cape Horn, which seems pretty adventuresome to me, but my for-bears — Quakers and Pilgrims — had come to New England earlier, in the 1600s, at least one, Elder William Brewster, on the Mayflower, and Jack was fascinated by our history, filled with characters who had names like Lemuel, Seth, Abigail, and Ebenezer, who lived in places like Barnstable, Dedham, or Valley Falls. This was three years before Alex Haley wrote about his African roots and a new craze for genealo-gy began. But, as usual, Jack was ahead of the game.

The agenda was to visit our Grandfather Tolman's factory in Shirley, Massachusetts, from whence our unearned income was derived, and to see some of our cousins. Samson Cordage, my grand-father's company and factory, was the result of his invention of the first braided rope just when someone else had invented the double-hung window, so it was timely and assured of success. The logo was the fig-ure of Samson slaying the lion, the inspiration of my Great Aunt Harriet (my grandfather's spinster sister, the same Aunt Harriet whose bold handwriting on labels attached to all the family heirlooms explains their purchase, when, where, by whom, etc.) who had seen this statue in Italy on one of her Grand Tours and thought it most appropriate to denote the strength of the cord.

Shirley was a pretty New England factory town, typical, I imagine, of a company town, with the big house of the owner, our fraternal grandfather, graciously situated on a sloping meadow with huge shade trees that were in brilliant color that fall. Some of the workers in the factory actually remembered our grandfather, had spent their entire lives under Samson Cordage patronage, which felt rather strange and uncomfortably feudal to me. No wonder my father wanted none of that. Later, after double-hung windows went out of use, this same braided rope would be used by sailors and later still for experiments in space, but by then it had been taken over by a Texas firm, Ensearch. (Ted and I got rid of our Ensearch stock years ago. Deborah says that she unfortunately did not.)

Another theme of this trip was to see the autumn colors, so we rented a car and ventured into Vermont and Maine, gaping at those trees, whole hillsides in every shade of yellow and red. We ate lobster, and read Kurt Vonnegut novels aloud. Deborah had discovered Vonnegut and he fit perfectly into our personal history rediscovery mode. The next project was cousins. All the aunts and uncles were now dead, and of the nine cousins — Elizabeth Carter Minor, Martha Carter Hill, Esther Babbitt Howe, Edward Babbitt, Edward Allen Drew, William Sinclair Drew, Lionel Drew Jr., Henry Drew, Elizabeth Drew — we managed to visit only four. First, Martha who I remembered as a glamorous young mother back in the early '30s. In '73, then widowed and living alone in a house in West Newton she was a hospitable, perky, charming aging lady. Next was Ed Babbitt (son of the same Uncle Irving Babbitt who, on his deathbed back in the '30s, had admonished me when I was twelve to study Latin and Greek) whom we visited with his wife, Cecile, in South Hadley, where he worked in the administration on financial affairs at Mt. Holyoke College. We went to Amherst nearby and absorbed the aura of that very pretty town and college and its famous spinster poet. Then on to Long Island to see Allen and Bill Drew and their families. These were the cousins we knew best and had the most fun with.

The Southern cousins from Savannah, Georgia, I never saw after those New England summers when we were all children. There were three of them: Lionel Jr., the one shot down, but not killed, over France in the war, who I believe, became a businessman of some sort and died a few years ago. His younger brother, Henry, had been killed soon after World War II aboard an aircraft carrier that blew up in an East Coast harbor. Chita (Elizabeth) died of Lou Gehrig's Disease. I don't even know if those Drew cousins had children. I believe my mother had a falling out with her sister-in-law, Aunt Patti, who was very southern and probably had racial prejudices that my mother could not abide. Uncle Lionel, her younger brother, had in earlier years worked on a coffee plantation in Guatemala. We used to get gifts when we were children of bright-colored woven belts, dark-faced colorful dolls in native costumes. He came to visit once in Berkeley and Inverness, but visits from those eastern aunts and uncles and cousins were not frequent.

Along with the proclivity toward business, there was in my family background on my mother's side that colonialism — in China, in Guatemala. Her sister, Elsa married an English banker she met as a girl in China. He worked for the Shanghai-Hong Kong Bank and she spent most of her life in the Far East and London. Bankers, engineers, business men, teachers, academics. In my generation there was a little branching out — one pilot, my cousin Allen; and one farmer and forest service employee, my brother, Ted. And the generations of our children and grandchildren are all over the lot — a farmer, a minister; some arborists and artists; a midwife, a drummer, a tennis coach, a teacher; a Jehovah's Witness, a Catholic; surfers, fishermen, gardeners, weavers, knitters; chefs and waitresses and students. No doctors or lawyers or professors that I know of; nor architects, though there are builders. I've lost track of many of them.

When we were on Long Island with Allen and Bill, we also visited Steve's ex-wife Annemarie who was then living for a while with my cousin Bill's ex-wife, Wrennie, in Northport which was also Annemarie's hometown and where Steve and she were married on that beach with Nana's high heels sinking in the sand. And we visited Deborah's son Peter, his wife Victoria (first of three) and three young sons in Connecticut. Another wonderful trip, full of interconnections linking us together in strange ways. Perhaps, like my grandfather, I'm inventing a new kind of rope. A cross-section we saw at the factory showed the many ends of the cotton fibers and though we could not see the braid we knew it was there in the length of the rope. That trip, organized by Jack, was like one of his field trips for students. And we all fell right into our roles: Jack the Professor, Deborah and I the students.

At home in the early '70s Jack was already baking bread, growing vegetables and involved with the Berkeley Charter Review Committee, an intensive three-year project in which he hitched up with the radical minority. Joel Rubenzahl, one of his new young friends on that committee, wrote of this later: "Jack was willing to look beyond parochial political interests to formulate a system of local government which could reflect Berkeley's political diversity, and, at the same time create a system where responsibility for decisions is with the clearly identified majority of the Council ... Jack impressed me with an interest in new ideas, even ideas which challenged some of his basic political assumptions."

1974 was full of important events. In the Spring Semester I signed up for Susan Griffin's U.C. Extension writing class. It was listed in the catalogue as "Women's Voices," something like that. It cost $65. In those days that was a lot of money, but I thought, well, I sometimes spent that much on a new dress. So why not? And that turned out to be the beginning of the Writing Group that has met almost every Tuesday for more than twenty-six years. I am the only one left of the original nine or ten that grew out of that class, but we have continued to be about that size, and changes have been gradual, so there is continuity. We still have coffee and lunch snacks at each others' houses from 12:30 until 3:00 on Tuesdays. It's quite remarkable, I think, for it not only to have survived for so many years, but for its continuing vigor. Jack was enthusiastic and supportive of my involvement from the start, that same old instinct of his kicking in, just as though I were still sixteen, encouraging me to broaden intellectually, to overcome my resistant streak. He was the only one who sometimes was able to break through that armor. Perhaps I'm more like his mother than I like to admit — opinionated, stubborn and provincial, though her province was San Francisco and mine is Berkeley.

On the night of August 3, 1974, Thomas Grayson Kent was born. Early on the morning of the 4th Tom's big red truck came careening into our driveway at The Shambles. I saw it from the kitchen window through the alder trees and ran out onto the porch. "It's a boy! eight pounds, six ounces!" he yelled over the noise of the creek as it splashed on the stones. "Come on over and have breakfast." And that was the beginning of the entirely new and wonderful experience of grandparenting, which still goes on and now includes great-grandparenting. Our participation in the lives of our five grandchildren has been, for both of us, about the most satisfying adventure of our lifetimes, so completely different than being Mom and Dad, yet perhaps as important.

On August 9 Nixon resigned. Hallelujah! And Jack had already retired in June at the young age of 57 and become Professor Emeritus We moved here to #74 that fall, and Dave and Chandra moved in next door. It seemed like such a fine arrangement to us at the time. Jerry Brown ran for Governor, and in the process dismantled, by ignoring it, our efficient local precinct organization. From then on media politics reigned as the election technique. But a counter action also took place — the establishment of Berkeley Citizens Action (BCA) — which we soon joined, leaving the increasingly stodgy Democratic establishment behind. Our dear Grassrooters had fallen apart along with most of the other Democratic Clubs. Only the conservative Berkeley Democratic Club remains to this day. I still get the BCA announcements but haven't been to a meeting for years. Now I'm a member of the Green Party and tomorrow, Election Day, will vote once more for Ralph Nader.

What were Jack and I reading in those days? Biographies of Virginia Woolf, Eleanor Roosevelt, Tolstoy, Emma Goldman, Darwin. We read most of Michener's big novels aloud: *Hawaii, Iberia, Chesapeake,* and learned a lot of history that way. We read *Trinity,* about Ireland by Uris. Jack had temporarily put aside Lincoln, Jefferson, the Civil War, and was reading about Kropotkin, Bakunin, William Morris, all of Page Smith's histories. I read most of Flannery O'Connor's and Eudora Welty's works, also Dorothy Bryant's, Doris Lessing's, Iris Murdoch's, Nadine Gordimer's, Joan Didion's, Grace Paley's. I read Lawrence Durrell's *The Alexandria Quartet.* I started, I think in the '70s, John Updike's *Rabbit* novels, and for some reason quite inexplicable to me, I developed great empathy for nonhero Harry "Rabbit" Angstrom, "ex-basketball star, uneasy suburbanite, and undependable husband…" from a *Chronicle* article telling me that Updike is bringing us up to date on those Rabbits left behind after his death in a new, small piece called *"Rabbit Remembered."* I can hardly wait. I wish I liked Jane Austen more, and Shakespeare. I wish I understood poetry. We read *The Sand County Almanac, The Greening of America, The Making of a Counter Culture, Ecotopia.* I tried Faulkner, but wouldn't be able to appreciate his mythology until two decades later, last summer when my oldest grandson, Grayson, and I read *Absalom, Absalom* aloud together.

Jack read all of George Kennan, all of Wallace Stegner. We read Stegner's *Angle of Repose,* aloud, and sometime later, probably in the '80s, our friend and neighbor, Andrew Imbrie, composed an opera based on it. We went to the premiere performance at the San Francisco Opera House. I wonder what I wore, what Jack wore. Andrew also, first as a bachelor, then with his bride, had lived here in this house, #74, at one time. I used to love hearing him composing music, being privileged to absorb through sound someone else's creative process, from where we lived next door.

I was finally perfecting, in the '70s, the creation of blackberry and plum jelly and applesauce from our Inverness bounty of fruit. I had been a knitter, and sporadically a sewer. Then I tried embroidery, the funk and flash homemade art embroidery that had begun to appear emblazoned on the back of Levi jackets and on the rounded rumps of the counterculture denizens. My embroidery didn't amount to much. Writing about the counterculture was more fun for me. I kept on taking classes in U. C. Extension and had two writing groups. And Jack continued to perfect the art of baking bread, steaming up the kitchen so the yeast would rise, drinking red wine the way French bakers did. People began giving him enormous crockery bowls for mixing and loaf pans and aprons and cookbooks from Tassajara as birthday and Christmas gifts. We played tennis every week.

In '76 Jimmy Carter was elected President. Our second grandson, Fletcher Quinn Kent, was born. When Tom and Deb and Grayson, not yet two, and baby Fletcher came to stay we crammed them all into my former study (that same little room that Steve stayed in last year when he was so ill) with a double bed, a small-sized crib, and a bureau drawer for the infant. I used to worry that perhaps Grayson, in a fit of jealousy, would slam the drawer shut with his baby brother in it. He never did. Those two, now twenty-five and twenty-four, are as close as brothers can be, although as they were growing up they had fierce physical fights, reminiscent of some Steve, had with both his brothers. Dave told me not long ago how Steve banged his head on the floor of the porch at Erinveine. And Tom thought Steve might kill him throwing bricks at him. But we all wept for him over dinner the other night, on the first anniversary of his death.

In '76 we spent ten weeks in Greece. At first we were horrified and shocked by the smog and traffic, even worse than in Berkeley, our Athens of the West. Soon, though, we were entranced by the Acropolis always hovering somewhere just over our shoulders. We read Lawrence Durrell's *Bitter Lemons*, and his brother Gerald Durrell's *My Family and Other Animals,* set on the island of Corfu, which we visited. We read Henry Miller's *The Colossus of Maroussi.* In Greece we played Scrabble at cocktail time, perched on hotel balconies or on beach chairs by the sea. We experienced another midlife cultural adrenaline rush. Traveling, like reading aloud, was something we did very well together. I have lost my taste for travel since Jack died.

Dave and Chandra had gone to Greece a few years earlier and visited with her father's fascinating, eccentric friend, Kenneth Scholes, a former professor of English and now an expatriate living in Athens. Perhaps that's where they were at the time of Nana's birthday party. That's why they weren't with us all in Inverness that day. Remembering Chandra, the connections with her interesting, complicated family, is painful all over again more than twenty years later. Chandra was as beautiful as her name, which in India means "moon." The first time I saw her she was about fifteen, sitting on David's bed, looking at one of our family photograph albums. (That's something we do a lot of in this family. Not only do we take pictures and put them in albums, but we keep pictures in our heads and sometimes actually photograph people looking at these albums!) They had met across the street in Susie Schevill's kitchen when the three of them were in junior high.

Yes, those same Schevills. They're still there. Tomorrow I'm going with Susie's eighteen-year-old daughter, Vanessa, now my grand-daughter Rebecca's good friend, to visit her grandfather, Jim, my old pal from kindergarten days. His stroke has left him partly paralyzed. He will probably never walk again, but he's mentally alert and still writing poetry. When Jack was dying in that hospital bed in our living room two years ago, Jim came and sat beside him many times. He reminisced about all of our lives. In the old days, in the early '50s when we lived next door and he and his first wife, Helen, and their two little girls lived here at #74, when Dave and Susie before they knew how to walk would crawl through the hedge together, Jim would greet us on a Sunday morning, standing on the steps between our two houses, newspaper open in his hands, and read to us in that deep slow voice about the disasters of the outside world. It would have been about the McCarthy hearings or the U.C. Loyalty Oath in those days. I believe he has mellowed in his pronouncements of doom and gloom.

In Athens we looked up Kenneth Scholes and he immediately took charge of us, moving us into a small hotel in the Plaka, just around the corner from his charming flat with a view of the Acropolis, and a never-ending supply of gourmet food and drink, and most importantly, the introduction to his young Yugoslav friend, Karlo Djurovich, an artist, a homosexual, as was Kenneth, though their relationship was that of the older mentor-patron and young creative companion. They became intense additions to our lives for many years, until each of them died, Kenneth of a heart attack and Karlo of AIDS. They were, in fact, so intense in Athens that we had to escape from time to time, which turned out to be a wonderful arrangement. We enjoyed going off, traveling at our own pace, and we loved, equally, coming back to them and their incredible wit and hospitality. The hotel in the Plaka and Kenneth's flat became our urban hub, and our excursions — to the Aegean islands, the Peloponnesus, Corfu, Crete, Rhodes — like the spokes of a wheel. Kenneth had been living in Athens for some years, Karlo was a recent arrival from his native Dubrovnik. My story, "Expatriate," is based on Kenneth and Karlo.

They both, to our surprise, moved to America shortly after we returned, and Karlo became a surrogate son. We certainly didn't need another son. Twice years earlier we had thought of adopting — first, after we lost the baby in '45 and thought we could have no more children of our own; next, in the mid-50s after Russia invaded Hungary and there were said to be Hungarian refugee children in need of homes. The boys were really excited for a while about the possibility of having a little sister. Since Jack and I seemed unable to create anything but boys, this would be our chance to have a girl. What happened to that idea, I wonder? In 1977 we were already grandparents when Karlo more or less adopted us as parents.

Over the years as we got to know him well, we came to understand his neediness. An Italian Fascist soldier, billeted during World War II in a Dalmatian villa, impregnated the housemaid. These were Karlo's parents. He never saw his father. His mother gave him to the lady of the villa, and when this lady found the job of raising him too burdensome she sent him off to an orphanage in Split at five years old. When he was grown he sought out his real mother in Belgrade, but she would have nothing to do with him. (No wonder he learned to both charm and connive. *"I be's a pragmatist, mein Gott!"* he often announced in his peculiar idiom as he described the events of his life to us.) Next he sought out his adoptive mother and installed himself in the villa whenever it fit in with his needs and convenience. In the mid '80s we traveled with Karlo to his native Dubrovnik, met his "adopt mother," as he referred to her, in the beautiful villa. She reminded us of Nana — bosomy, jovial, tough, dressed in flowery prints.

Karlo did well as a tapestry artist. Quite soon after he came to America in 1977 he began to have one-man shows, in Dallas, Philadelphia, Monterey, Palo Alto and San Francisco, among other places. He was also a printmaker and painter. He had an enormous ego and charm, generosity and poor judgment, and got into various scrapes, mostly to do with money or stepping, figuratively speaking, on peoples' toes as he pushed himself ahead in the world of art. When things from time to time got desperate he came crying to us for help, pulling out all the emotional stops. And we usually helped him, though not always.

Reading over some old notes about Karlo, I came upon these comments of mine:

"Karlo's reception (in honor of the publication of my writers' group's book, *My Neckline and the Collapse of Western Civilization*) at his gallery in Sacramento was a charming fizzle. Hardly anyone came! I think that's what my instinct told me would happen, but Karlo, the great dreamer/promoter, promoted me into dragging myself and my whole writers' group (and their mates) into this charming fiasco. Enough of that! ... Karlo has been arrested for embezzlement!... But I am not Karlo's mother, though I suspect one reason I put up with him is because I think of him as a surrogate son. Perhaps it's because he's gay, like Steve; outrageous too, like Steve and Tom; creative and innovative like all three; and stumbled upon, by chance, in Athens, just as my children no longer needed me ... Karlo called this evening. Now everything is 'hunky dory. Fuck it Mein Gott, this is a small town!'" (referring to Sacramento where he then lived.)

It's strange that Steve and Karlo never met. Of course Steve lived away. Still, it's amazing that we never made a point of getting them together. Perhaps, subconsciously, we were afraid to have them meet. It would surely have been an explosive encounter, considering their equally tumultuous personalities. Of Karlo's last days I wrote, "He's a cadaver. Eye sockets, teeth, bones. Like a Holocaust victim. Yet his personality is intact — dramatic, egocentric, humorous. He's kept his illness from us. We haven't seen him for two years. And we couldn't speak about Steve's HIV status because he doesn't want to know of others' troubles... Karlo Djurovich died of AIDS on Halloween morning, 1991." He was forty-six years old.

Chapter
Ten

*I*t was toward the end of the '70s that signs of homeless people began to be evident in Cordonices Park right in our neighborhood, the same park our children had played in and where we walked our dogs every day. These seemed to be disoriented Vietnam veterans. It was upsetting and sad and even a little scary to come across one sprawled under the Dawn redwood trees, or another half hidden under a clump of Scotch broom. I have never known how to cope with my emotions about the homeless (now a constant presence in Berkeley), an irrational mix of fear, pity, disgust. My response to their pleas is accordingly inconsistent.

In November of '77 Dave and Chandra told us, acting so cool and civilized and modern, that they would be separating after Christmas. They didn't meet each other's needs anymore. I almost choked on the chocolate decadence cake, left over from Dave's twenty-eighth birthday party. We knew of course that their generation looked at marriage differently than we had. They had books like *Open Marriage* and *The Joy of Sex* lying around as well as *The Green Revolution*. No exchange of gifts this year, please. They were going to Disneyland for Christmas. *Disneyland?* We would have supper together one night before they left, at a new little trattoria down on Telegraph Avenue. (Another meal I almost choked on.) In the meantime would we please not be so neighborly. They needed to distance themselves from us. That's when Jack transplanted all the tomato plants from our communal garden and single-handedly built a fence to separate our two back yards in one afternoon.

I kept remembering the trip to New Mexico we'd taken them on, not so long before, to Santa Fe where we stayed at the La Fonda Hotel on the plaza, drank margaritas, ate spicy southwestern food, swam in the hotel pool, and went to all the wonderful museums; and to Acoma, St. Ildefonso, and the Taos Pueblo to watch the ceremonial Corn Dance. We went to Bandolier Park, climbed into Indian caves and down into the lush canyon. Again, there are pictures — of Chandra, looking like an Indian princess with her dark eyes and glossy hair, smiling out from one of those cliff dwellings; another of her and Dave from the back, holding hands, he towering over her, as they climbed up to Acoma. She was very shapely, very photogenic. I suddenly remember another photo of her, years earlier — she was about nineteen — on an Inverness beach, looking poignantly sad. It was at a crabbing expedition, a farewell party before Steve, and Annemarie took off on their eastward move in the late '60s. She and Dave weren't married yet. Soon after that she went to New York to study modern dance. Dave just followed right after her with his carpenter's tools and began remodeling lofts for artists in Manhattan. Perhaps he shouldn't have.

By the time of our New Mexico trip, David was a partner in the new firm, Abrams, Milliken & Kent, that was building gorgeous houses and developing the Fourth Street complex in West Berkeley. Chandra had gotten her degree in physical therapy and had begun her pre-med studies. (What had happened to modern dance?) They had put their own attractive stamp on the house and garden next door. Everything seemed hunky-dory, as Karlo might have said.

After Dave and Chandra's pronouncement, I kept remembering family events with Geigers and Kents enjoying each other's company. They were intellectual, interesting people — Chandra's family — from the midwest, with a different and fascinating American saga for us to absorb. And we felt real empathy for their troubles. Chandra's father, Don Geiger, had multiple sclerosis and by the time we knew him had to use a wheel chair.

Chandra's mother, Carolyn, was an attractive, intelligent, resourceful saint of a woman, as far as we were concerned, although Janis muttered to us once disapprovingly, "She's full of herself!" Well, it's true, she was, but I thought perhaps she had reason to be. And so we were stunned when Carolyn and Don separated, perhaps a year before Dave and Chandra. Also around this time Chandra's younger brother, Geoff, attempted suicide. The decade seemed to be unraveling, even though we still had a couple of years to go.

In the first months of '78 there was the divisive, nasty divorce with the high-powered feminist lawyer, Faye Stender (yes, the same Faye Stender who defended Huey Newton) taking advantage of Chandra's youth and sex, pushing her to a greed that I refuse to believe was true to her character. The aggressive, confrontational approach of lawyers, at least that lawyer, was terribly offensive to us, perhaps especially to Jack who was a master of compromise and consensus and a kind of Boy Scout gamesmanship. Perhaps if Dave and Chandra had gone, as we suggested, to Henry Elson, our lawyer and friend whose interest was specifically in helping couples execute decent (if not friendly) divorce, things wouldn't have been so painful. But apparently that wasn't possible because very quickly Dave's whole firm — (Abrams, Milliken and Kent) — was financially threatened by Faye Stender's tactics. The situation immediately became adversarial. Some years later Faye Stender was shot and crippled by another adversary, and eventually committed suicide. Amen. A few years ago Chandra returned some family jewels I had given her with a very sweet note suggesting that they belonged to our granddaughters (David's daughters) now. Maybe that's just ordinary etiquette for divorcees — how would I know? — like Norma returning the family silver, and Annemarie the silver teapot. (Becky wasn't married to Tom long enough to acquire heirlooms.) Still, in each case I appreciated the gesture and admonish myself when I start feeling mean, remind myself that I loved each of these women once.

Dave moved out of #84, which, sadly, would have to be sold as part of the divorce settlement, and rented a room on Stuart Street from Margaret Love, a single mother of a four-year old daughter, Hannah.

In February of '78 Jack, in the midst of all this emotional turmoil for which none of us had any guidelines as to how to bear it, went to

Washington, D. C. to drum up interest and money for People for Open Space, something he really did know how to do. I quit smoking while he was on that trip to Washington, finally, after forty-four years, not because of the Surgeon General's pronouncements years earlier, but basically because smoking was no longer socially acceptable, or perhaps I needed to do something brave, definitive to offset the dissolving of Dave and Chandra's marriage. Who knows? At any rate, my first thoughts, wherever I went, had become "Where are the ashtrays? Am I the only smoker?" The amount of energy I expended every day on such mundane concerns was appalling.

The day I quit went like this. At the old co-op on Shattuck Avenue I bought a carton of Carletons — at least I'd downgraded from Phillip Morris, Kents, Players (in England), Gauloise (in France) to this innocuous filtered brand. Halfway home I stopped the car and threw the entire carton of cigarettes into a garbage can. Later that day I went back to retrieve them, but the can had been emptied of everything, including my carton of Carletons. That was it. Fury, humiliation, then pride were the emotions that followed one right after the other until by the time Jack came home from Washington I felt almost saintly. He'd quit smoking years before, first his pipe, then cigars, obeying doctors' orders without question or fuss. I knew he wanted me to do so too, though he never pressured me. In practically every snapshot for the past forty years, through pregnancies, child rearing, politics I had a cigarette between the index and middle fingers of my right hand. My fingers were stained, I know I must have smelled (my hair, my breath, my clothes) as did our house (curtains, bedding). Didn't he notice anything different about me, I finally asked after a couple of days?

He looked me over. "A new haircut?"

"No, come on, Jack. Something really basic. Smell me!" Finally I had to tell him.

In March he had that scary internal bleeding incident, probably brought on by stress of which there had been plenty. Days in and out of intensive care. Blood transfusions and the threat of colostomy. Margaret Love, whom we had never met, brought a bouquet of iris to the hospital from Dave, who was very ill himself with the flu. She found us walking around in the hospital hallways, Jack attached to an IV machine, looking scrawny in a hospital gown. I'll never forget how up-front, open, and friendly she was. She looked directly at us with those blue, blue eyes. "I'm Margaret Love. These flowers are from Dave," though knowing her as I now do so well, I'm pretty sure it was her idea. She often brings flowers. Her own house and garden are always filled with blooms. (Just yesterday for my seventy-ninth birthday she brought an exotic arrangement of mock orange, pink dogwood, and iris.) Later she told us how scared she was. She tried to leave the bouquet at the nurses' station, but one of them said, "Oh, there's Mr. Kent, right there!" and she was more or less compelled to face us head on. By then she and Dave were really living together. In fact later she told me that she and Dave "got together" on February 22, the same day I quit smoking.

On November 18th over nine hundred of James Jones' disciples committed suicide in Jonestown, Guyana. And in San Francisco a few days later another horror resulting from mental derangement occurred. Both Mayor Moscone and Supervisor Harvey Milk were shot and killed.

November 18th was also Hannah's fifth birthday and we were invited to her party in that spacious sunny apartment in a big old house on Stuart Street. We met Margaret's mother, Peggy, and her brother, Douglas, and his girlfriend, Coral, who would later become his wife and mother of their three daughters. We liked all of them, but were naturally cautious about involvement with another clan and all its inevitable complications. I thought of course of Chandra's family, the Geigers, but also of Annemarie's — all prematurely dead, except for her, from accident or cancer — and of Becky's, the Dixons, related to the painter Maynard Dixon. We had been compatible Inverness neighbors, but never developed a real friendship because of the briefness of that marriage.

That year we spent another Thanksgiving with Steve up in Humboldt County, plucking turkey feathers, manicuring marijuana, walking over the hillsides to visit with all those friends of his, before the days of electricity, indoor plumbing, telephones. When I reread the stories and poems and the novel I wrote at that time I remember the relentless culture shock — seeing those Weiss manicure scissors in the supermarket in Redway, on display along with the candy bars at the checkout stand, tempting the impulse shoppers. I couldn't figure it out, until later when we were all sitting at the round table at Fritz and Simon's, as though it were a tea party or a quilting bee, snipping off the precious buds of the cannabis plants with those same Weiss scissors. My God, how blatant! Steve laughed and said the girl at the checkout stand knew the score; she probably had her own little stash of weed to manicure. Thanksgiving in Humboldt County was, as with the Pilgrims at the first Thanksgiving in Massachusetts, a time of celebration for a bountiful harvest.

Making pleasant conversation in some sunny field with bare-breasted women we'd only just been introduced to, or watching little children stoned on pot, or collapsing in bewildered fatigue at the end of the day as Jack and I did in our funky motel, or sometimes under the stars in sleeping bags, protected from wandering horses and sheep by the corral fence, often sleepless, questions of morality, legality churned in our hearts and minds.

MARIJUANA HARVEST

Chores all done and
it's lavender sky time again
with horses presenting their silhouettes
and the sheep like hummocks
on the hills.
Ellen's in the garden
picking greens for supper.
Joe's inside the cabin changing his shirt
when the roar crashes into the quiet —
a neighbor on his motorcycle come to get the gun.

The Closing Circle: A Memoir

"Some guys are snooping about," he says
and my throat feels tight.
this must be a play
and myself a character in it:
old woman sitting on the step
looking up from her crossword puzzle.

Just as one does not literally remember pain, one does not remember fear. In retrospect I loved the way it was then, stretching my vision, informing me of Steve's world. I tried to call Allan this last Thanksgiving. And Mary. And Joe and Maggie. Now they all have answering machines. I left messages. They have computers and make fine wine that wins prizes at the County Fair. The growing of marijuana is a sophisticated mini-agribusiness. Locked gates, greenhouses, camouflage. They're on the internet. (I'm waiting for somebody's baby to be named WWW Dot Com Org.) Even Steve had a phone at the end, though never an indoor toilet! I feel sad, left behind in those old hippie days.

In 1979 the Shah of Iran was ousted and nearly one hundred U.S. Embassy staff and Marines were taken hostage.

A near-disaster occurred at the Three Mile Island nuclear power plant.

Bernard Malamud wrote *Dubin's Lives*, Kurt Vonnegut wrote *Jailbird*, both of which I read.

In Nicaragua Somosa was overthrown by the Sandanistas and a Marxist government installed.

Margaret Thatcher became prime minister of Britain.

In June Steve asked us to come to the Gay Parade in San Francisco. It seemed an obligation, like attending one of Tom's swimming meets or Dave's Little League games or Steve's graduation from Berkeley High, only this time we were filled with trepidation and doubt. What should I wear to a gay parade? How would we find him in the crowd? We'd meet at the grandstand at four o'clock at the end, he said. Oh, then per-

185

haps we could just skip the parade and … no, he wanted us to bear witness. He never said so, but we got the message. And so we bore witness all day long standing in front of Woolworth's on Market Street, me in my new plum-colored corduroy pant suit with a Liberty silk scarf at the neck, Jack in his gray flannel suit and regimental tie, his uniform for weddings and funerals, watching the floats and banners — **"DOCTORS FOR GAYS," "I LOVE MY GAY SISTER," "I LOVE MY GAY AUNT," "GAY MEN'S CHORUS," "I'M PROUD OF MY GAY FATHER."**

"HUMBOLDT LESBIAN COALITION" floated by in a mass of balloons, and next to me one man was telling another of the trauma caused by his circumcision. The sidewalk was a parade in itself. Sequined Drag Queens perched on light poles. Young men with arms around each other drinking from brown paper bags. Jehovah's Witnesses passing out copies of Awake. Jack of course loved it. A San Francisco kid, he'd been raised on parades. I imagine him — skinny little red-headed guy with freckles sitting on the Market Street curb, safe between his dad's wing-tipped shoes. St. Patrick's Day, Armistice Day, Labor Day. He and I had been on Peace marches together, and some years later we would get arrested outside Las Vegas in protest against nuclear testing in the desert. (Mellow and I were arrested last week at our neighborhood park — unleashed, unlicensed dog!) But this Gay Parade was so personal for us. Finally, making our way to the bandstand in front of City Hall (where Jack, an establishment guy, used to have his office), pushing past huggers, weepers, drinkers, women strolling with women, their arms around each other, men in tight black leather and chains, hair dyed pink, chartreuse and dusted with confetti, through the thickening acrid smell of marijuana, we found Steve. We hugged and cried and laughed and then went to dinner in Chinatown, just like the night before he was born. Except for his summer country toes, callused and jutting from his huaraches, we looked pretty urban San Francisco. I remember thinking, as we stood on the corner of Post and Sacramento waiting for the white-gloved policeman to wave us across, that even Jack's mother, Belinda Stanton Kent, who considered herself the arbiter of San Francisco manners and fashion, might not have disapproved of us.

On August 24 Marlowe Kent was born at home on Stuart Street to Margaret Love and David Kent.

In October Jack and I had a wonderful trip to Mexico with our friends the Cardwells.

I can't remember what we did for Thanksgiving and Christmas that last year of the 1970s.

April 2000

The 1980s was the decade of Reagan, the Iran-Contra scandal, Central American wars. It was the decade of AIDS.

In '81 Jack's brother-in-law, Janis' husband, Karl Schevill, quite suddenly became ill with leukemia and, only sixty-six, died just before Thanksgiving. Long years of depression began for Janis that persist today. She lives in a shadow world. At least in losing Jack I did not lose my own identity.

There were fierce rains that winter of 1981-82 , causing disastrous floods and landslides here and there throughout Northern California. On the night of January 3rd two storms met in a twelve-hour standoff above the Inverness Ridge. We had just been there for New Year's Eve with a group of old Inverness friends, a tradition going back many years. We had planned to stay on a couple of days, cozy by our fire, reading books, walking in the rain, but our two dogs, Luke and Lotta, were freaked by the weather. They whined, hid in corners, and refused to walk with us up the valley along the creek. So we came home on Sunday, January third, our forty-first wedding anniversary, and celebrated by going to the great movie, *Reds,* with Warren Beatty and Diane Keaton.

It poured all night. The dogs continued to be edgy. We called Tom and Deb in the morning to see if everything was all right, but the phone lines were down. Finally Tom called us. "It's not quite as bad as last time," he said, referring to the demise of Erinveine. But our house was almost destroyed, assaulted by landslides from the bank behind it, by a fallen oak stabbing through the bedroom roof, and huge tree trunks, carried by the raging creek down from Mount Vision, cata-pulting through the walls and floor, tearing off the entire deck. Once more it had earned its name, The Shambles, as it had ten years earlier when the hippie commune moved in.

For years I had had a recurring dream in which I knew that the ocean might overflow and spill over the ridge. It was imperative that I scoot up the sides of the valley to save myself. Sometimes it was a good dream, an adventure, a picnic when we were all young. We laughed and scrambled our way to the top, making it just in time, and there was the beautiful Pacific spread out before us and we dove into the waves. Other times it was a nightmare.

It was another nightmare version of my dream, but this time it was real. Oh, poor house. We saw it a few days later, as we slogged up the valley in rubber boots, having been escorted by convoy along the still flooded road into the village. We just gaped at the battered landscape and the littered belongings: a bicycle wheel, a toilet seat, a red car, a roof — our garage roof which we'd only just had repaired and paid $5,000 for! — crashed against the tennis court fence, and finally saw our bedroom tilting toward the creek. That's when I began to cry. Windows were blown out. Furniture had fallen through the floor. The beautiful dining table that Dave had made when he was only sixteen lay upside down beside the chimney. I was ready to throw in the towel, just give up. Not Jack, though. The whole ghastly sight seemed to challenge his imagination. Was it his architectural background? Or perhaps this is a male trait. All four of those guys were gung-ho to repair and rebuild. And so we did.

There was lots of damage in the area — trees down, roads washed out. One house in Second Valley was blown up by an exploding propane tank. Our house was one of the few others that was almost destroyed. Schools were closed and the National Guard cruised around in big Army trucks. Out on our road strangers gawked and took photographs TV cameras and reporters with mikes appeared. The Red Cross brought sandwiches and coffee as we cleared debris and carried out furniture. Perhaps our being targeted was part of some grand plan, for the miraculous part of this saga was that the storm was the final shocking event that motivated Tom, at thirty-nine, to quit drinking. The storm was both a family and community disaster. Men were expected to pitch in. And that's what he wanted to do. He was a tree man, an expert woodsman who could go up there in the hills, and clear the logs that were crashing through the rain forest causing havoc, diverting the natural flow of streams and slamming into homes. But he got drunk instead and wrecked the family car. On one of our early trips up there to clean up the mess of broken dishes, move out the furniture, rescue bedding from ruination, I found a fifth of Jack Daniels and a moldy Deli sandwich in the bathroom cupboard. But by then, Tom had committed himself to a six-week rehabilitation program in San Rafael. That was eighteen years ago and he hasn't had a drink since.

By summer The Shambles, though reduced in size — the deck was gone and also one bedroom and bathroom — was mended and livable. We had a big barbecue to celebrate and thank all the workmen and neighbors and family who had helped and supported us in so many ways. It was a terrific party — salmon, chicken, salads, watermelon — and I have almost never worked so hard in my life, carrying dishes, chairs, tables across the creek to our little meadow where the party took place. People gave us trees to plant. We reminisced about the storm. Those who were in Inverness at the time said they would never forget the sound, no matter which of the five valleys they were near. Beyond the rain and the rough bay waters slapping against the shore, there was what sounded like a squadron of planes and beyond this roaring a snapping, cracking, crashing, as though the whole mountain ridge was giving way. But on this June evening it was quiet as we watched the sky gradually darken behind Mt. Vision. Tom thanked us for putting everything back together, a poignant message with several meanings.

It was a strange and wonderful summer. The landscape had been altered from a wooded creek environment to a windswept, barren, sandy, muddy, exposed wasteland devoid of our former quiet privacy. The noise of backhoes, chain saws, road scrapers made it feel like a frontier town. Neighbors were more neighborly, families were more loving. And in August Tom and Deb got married.

It was in 1981, two years after we'd been to the Gay Parade with Steve, that scientists identified Acquired Immune Deficiency Syndrome, but as with the Nazi concentration camps back in the '30s and '40s, we didn't grasp the enormity of the disaster until some time later. There were newspaper stories describing symptoms — purplish skin eruptions, weight loss, susceptibility to all sorts of infection — appearing in gay men in San Francisco's Castro district. I can't remember exactly the sequence of our concern or understanding. Lots of other things were happening also in our lives.

Rebecca was born in March of '83. ANOTHER GIRL at last! Jack and I went to Yugoslavia and Italy later that spring with Karlo. We went with Steve to New Orleans. In '84 we had ten perfect urban days in New York City, staying at the Algonquin, going to plays, having a Seder dinner with our friends the Cohens, seeing my Long Island cousins, Allen and Bill. But I remember watching a TV show in our hotel room at the Algonquin, about a child who had contracted AIDS from a blood transfusion. By then we knew that the virus had probably come from Africa, that it was transmitted through "bodily fluids": blood, semen, maybe even saliva. I remember feeling uncomfortable with the notion that a vulnerable child was somehow more deserving of sympathy than a gay man. In San Francisco there was much concern about bathhouses. What were these bathhouses? Tom and Dave seemed to know all about them and that Steve had been a part of that whole promiscuous scene. Really? When? But it wouldn't be until we read Randy Shilts' book, *And The Band Plays On,* that we grasped the worldwide implications of AIDS, that we began to seriously fear for Steve.

In the meantime there were other things to fear. In '85, after years of chronic pain which affected his general mood to the point that I sometimes wondered what was going wrong with our marriage to make him so uncharacteristically crabby, Jack had a hip replacement

190

operation. It was a success, even though one leg was shorter than the other. For the rest of his life he had to have a lift in one shoe. After the fact we figured out he'd been crabby because his endorphins were all screwed up by the pain.

In Humboldt County paranoia was growing as spring planting time approached. The cultivation of marijuana had become an increasingly dangerous occupation. As in any war each side became more devious. The authorities — CAMP (Campaign Against Marijuana Planting) — used helicopters to discover hidden crops; the growers learned to plant cover crops — sunflowers were a favorite. In one of Steve's typically sardonic letters he wrote: *"CAMP has thirty rooms reserved in Garberville starting April 1st. I hope a few of them die this Spring or Summer or Fall."* Years later he told me he could have been the Uni-Bomber. I believe it. And I have always been eternally grateful that he found a way to live outside the confrontation and violence so prevalent in the mainstream of society. Humboldt County was getting too dicey, so he moved to Montana with Tom Freeman in '85 (Oh, my, do I have to write about him, what Steve and he did or didn't mean to each other, how they used each other?)

All during those years I was writing, taking courses, going to workshops. In the summer of '85 I went to a two-week women's writing conference at U.C. Santa Cruz. Everybody, including me, seemed to think it was a very daring thing to do. I'd never gone off on my own like this, leaving Jack to fend for himself. We were a pretty old-fashioned couple, after all, with division of labor. He went to work and brought home the money. I did the cooking, he did the dishes, although since Corsica we'd switched roles a little. He'd started baking bread, I did the income tax. I still made the bed, but he did the laundry down at the laundromat at Shattuck and Vine, hanging out at The French Hotel drinking cappuccino and reading the papers. It was summertime when I went to Santa Cruz, so he drove me from Inverness to the Greyhound bus station in San Francisco, and off I went with my portable Olivetti and a knapsack, even foregoing our traditional Inverness Fourth of July.

It was absolutely fascinating. At sixty-four I was the oldest person there. Of the fifty-one participants (five of these were staff) only nineteen were over forty, about half were lesbians, two were severely handicapped, lots of divorcees, lots of victims of various sorts of abuse including incest, several extreme obesity cases, a few blacks, a few Asians. From my notes I quote: "...pillows on the floor. Like puppies — a hand touches an ankle, another hair, or neck — a chain of touching. This is a lesbian thing I guess....most of the women are writing from their need as oppressed, validating themselves as their families or society have not. But there are a few like myself who, on the other hand, come from such ease and normalcy that we need to write in order to understand this other world of pain and struggle."

I lived in an apartment in Oakes Hall with four other women. My room had a view looking over rolling brown fields to the town of Santa Cruz and the bay and ocean beyond. It was lovely, like being back at Scripps College, thinking about Jack and all I had to tell him.

At the time I was working on my second novel, then titled *Journey With Jonathan*, later to become *What Will Be,* based on my experience as a mother of a gay son — Steve. And though the teacher, poet and novelist Diana O'Hehir, a contemporary of mine, whom I'd actually known in grammar school and high school, was enthusiastic, there was some fierce criticism, mostly from the lesbians — *What right did I, a straight woman, have to write about the subject?* — and blacks because I had a black character based on Ora, the maid I knew from my childhood into adulthood until she died. Again, *what right did I, as a white woman, have to write about a black?* It caused a small revolution and I quote from my notes — "J. with J." has set off a major upsetment. No one slept last night. New rules for critiquing were arrived at today. I was shaky-weepy for twenty-four hours or so. Others too. Incredible. This reminds me of little girls' cliques, big girls' nastiness. The other side of all-male games. For sure I prefer heterosexual worlds, though I still need this all-woman support for my writing — bitchy-whiney as it may be... I think I have recovered from being a point woman." (It occurs to me now that perhaps I represented a mother figure they resented.) "We shall see what tomorrow brings. I must call Jack in the morning. No more fear of tears. Grace Paley tomorrow." She was one of my heroines at the time and it was wonderful to meet her, to see her sitting across the room like a plump aunty in someone's kitchen in the Bronx. She chewed gum furiously. Some of her wise advice was, "Write what you don't know about what you know ... If you're not willing to be risky, to be a jerk, you're in the wrong business ... we're usually writing two stories; one leads to the other, then moves parallel, then perpendicular, criss-cross, etc."

I remember being so glad to get home to Jack, to my so-called "normal" life, also how exhausted I was, as though I'd been on a long journey, which, in a way, I had, of course, and suffering from jet lag. I slept and slept and slept!

Jack was still active in the Greenbelt Alliance, which had steadily grown into an influential environmental force from those early beginnings as People for Open Space in Dorothy Erskine's Telegraph Hill apartment decades earlier. And in 1985 he tried once more, with Glenn Schneider and some of his students, to interest the community, this time the Council of Neighborhood Associations, in the plan he and Joel Rubinzahl had recommended to the Charter Review Committee, of which they were both members and in the radical minority, back in 1972. Their plan called for district elections and a large 60 member council modeled after the City of Bologna's parliamentary system. The Committee in '72 chose to maintain the status quo. But thirteen years later Jack was still as deeply interested and committed to this plan. Reading an article in the *Express*, December 1985, I am impressed with his sharpness still. I quote: "As a professor and student of local government, I developed an interest in large councils, and partisan politics, and no manager, and no mayor. That's the way we began our American tradition before the Revolution, in New England. Town meetings and large government by committee was the tradition. . . . My sense of democratic governing gives heavy weight to the concept of representation by different political points of view. . . . In Berkeley several minority groups — Republicans, people on the far left, neighborhood based independents among others — have been effectively disenfranchised. My argument is that to get these people into government simply makes you a stronger community. . . ." We did finally get District Representation in Berkeley, though the number of councilpersons (now the Mayor and all but one are women.) remains at nine.

Jack and I were still reading aloud every morning at breakfast as we'd been doing since the Corsican days. It's one of the things I miss the most since he died. *July's People* by Nadine Gordimer, *The White Hotel* by D.M. Thomas, biographies of Frida Kahlo and John Muir and William Blake, *A Soldier's Legacy* by Heinrich Bol, *The Unbearable Lightness of Being* by Milan Kundera, *The House of the Spirits* by Isabel Allende, *The Confessions of Madame Psyche* by Dorothy Bryant, *A Room of One's Own* by Virginia Woolf.

In the summer of '87 we had our first wonderful trip to Montana, bringing twelve-year-old Grayson with us.

We went to Las Vegas twice, in those years, to protest nuclear testing in the desert, even getting handcuffed and hauled off in separate buses, segregated by sex, two hundred miles to the county seat of Tonapah to be scolded, then abandoned, to find our own way back in the middle of the night. (I have to concede that this was an even longer bus ride than the one in my London story, *Davie's American Mum*.) But we had our support group with a van who'd followed us all the way and drove us to Las Vegas again. Finally, dead on our feet, we were crammed in the elevator at four in the morning with gamblers at the casino hotel where we were staying, almost hysterical at the dichotomy of our very different reasons for being there. Some of these people were just getting up for breakfast and another gambling session, still others were in evening clothes on their way to bed.

We had another trip to Mexico with the Cardwells, and several more to Montana in the ten years that Steve was there. At one time, after we first learned that he was HIV positive, I fantasized about our moving there, getting a little house on one of those pretty streets in Ronan with the looming Rockies as our spiritual support as we watched him weaken.

Steve and Tom Freeman had a friend, Kenny, the first person I witnessed dying of AIDS. (Karlo would be the second, and Alex Bratenahl whom Steve had grown up with and shared the land with in Humboldt County, would be the third.) Kenny got thinner and thinner and became an old man. When that happened to Steve, I thought, we would tend him and ease his dying days. It was a romantic fantasy. The reality a decade later was not at all as I had imagined it would be.

In '87 Dorothy Stroup from my writers' group sold her novel, *In The Autumn Wind*, to Scribner's, a tremendous thrill to every one of us in the group. That year also, after several years of work, encouraged and expertly guided by Jack through the steps (deciding to do it, then finding an editor, and making all the decisions about design, finance, distribution) we published a collection of our stories and poems, *My Neckline and the Collapse of Western Civilization*. Jack got motivated, I think, because he was sick of hearing me moan around about not getting published. Although he always supported me in my writing endeavors, he was not particularly interested in *what* I was writing. He wanted me to write *The Berkeley Story*, as he called it (and perhaps that's what I'm finally doing here). In response to my whining he probably said in his typically practical voice, *"So, let's **do** something about it,"* I can hear it still. I just spent the afternoon looking over the voluminous files on that project. I can't believe how I shared him with all those other women. He made us all write letters to him, expressing our feelings about the importance of the group. They are like love letters, yet I don't remember feeling jealous. At one point it was even suggested that the book be titled, *Letters to Jack*. He really was a genius at helping people work together to accomplish things. I found a letter my mother wrote to one of her sisters way back in the '40s in the early days of the war, when our lives were chaotic. She said, "People keep offering Jack jobs, of course… ." Of course, and at the beginning of his political life people kept trying to push him upward: "Run for State Senate, run for Congress." No, for him it was always grassroots, home-rule, participatory democracy.

We had our dear old dogs, Luke and Lotta, put to sleep at the end of the decade and I gave Jack a parrot for his birthday, Prince Peter Kropotkin, named for that anarchist hero of his, but he never really connected with Peter, nor he with Jack. (It was me that Peter was in love with, giving me affectionate nips on the ear and chattering sweetly.) In retrospect I see that he was polite but reserved with, or perhaps perplexed by, new pets, new people, from then on until the end. We had many wonderful adventures during the last decade of his life: trips to Ireland, to Midland School near Santa Barbara which Grayson and Fletcher attended. Our grandchildren were a continuing joy as we watched with amazement their characters take shape, each one unique. There were several journeys to Santa Fe while Dave and Margaret lived there, by train and plane and automobile. The last one was four years ago with Steve, driving in our car, the three of us plus Steve's two little Pomeranians, Big Deal and Otis. Sacramento Freeway madness, lunch in Lodi, Sonora Pass, Mono Lake, miles of empty two-lane roads through gorgeous Nevada desert and the red earth and rock outcroppings of Utah, to Zion and Bryce and Mesa Verde; and on the way back a more northerly route by way of Pyramid Lake, Susanville, Mt. Lassen — a round-trip through lifestyles and scenery; tensions, connections, revelations. And we had a final trip with the Cardwells less than a year before Jack died, when we saw the sunset and the sunrise at Grand Canyon and went to Canyon de Chelly.

We read some memorable books: James Joyce's *Ulysses*, Gabriel Garcia Marquez's *One Hundred Years of Solitude*, Gunter Grass' *The Tin Drum*, Herman Melville's *Moby Dick*, Howard Zinn's *A Peoples' History of the United States* especially come to mind. Our children put on a tremendous and joyous fiftieth wedding anniversary party for us at the Inverness Yacht Club. Five years later I put on a nice but more subdued eightieth birthday party for Jack at The Women's Faculty Club on the U. C. campus. In that last decade of his and the century's we became great grandparents three times, had an earthquake, two fires, and a war. But we didn't play chess or Scrabble anymore, and without a word of warning one day Jack shaved off his beard.

Chapter
Eleven

Memory triggers more memory, and in the process the pain of loss gives way to the pleasure of recollection that has been hidden for decades. It's almost a year since I began this project and I fear it's coming near the end. All spring as I have watched the hummingbirds from this window, Jack's window, and the magical progression of this crazy garden of ours — blossoming sprays of lacy white arugula and yellow mustard, reseeded and blown by the wind far and wide from the little patches he planted years ago; the pink flowers of Margaret's tea rose covering the back fence; clumps of purple daisies, blue borge and forget-me-nots; nasturtiums in every shade of yellow, orange, red; ferns; spiky lavender Mexican sage; jasmine and trumpet vines climbing into the hedge and trees next door, I felt the distance of time gently removing him from me. It seems so long ago, though it was only about a year before he died when my knees went bad and I could no longer squat in the garden, that he would tap at this very window where he then sat at this desk to get my attention, smile down at me where I then sat in the mass of nasturtiums and forget-me-nots, weeding. The tug of love and need and habit was powerful between us.

All last week I was aware that the second anniversary of his death was approaching, yet when the 27th arrived, I forgot until in the evening, having dinner before Aurora Theater with the Cardwells at a new Greek restaurant on Shattuck. It was Mary C. who reminded us. I imagine that she remembered him in her prayers at Mass that morning. We drank a toast to him and enjoyed the thought of how much he would have liked the food and atmosphere and each other's company, as we had so often on our travels together over the years. The play was a beautifully acted production of Pinter's *Homecoming,* an unpleasant story of unpleasant people. I had a restless night, full of dreams and anxieties that I cannot remember. But then the next day the garden was beautiful again. I love its wild independence of any orderly plans I once had for it. Tom says that people who hate forget-me-nots can't stand not being in control. I like to feel that I have given up on controlling things.

———•———

The progression of Alzheimer's Disease is gradual, and much of my understanding of what was happening to Jack was in retrospect. I didn't, for instance, pay much attention when he got lost on the train to Montana, sometime in the late '80s, on our way to visit Steve. Since trains change course, it's easy to get confused about where the sun or moon are coming from, to lose one's sense of direction. It's part of the wonderful mystique of train travel. I was perhaps as turned around as he was by the time I'd roamed up and down several cars searching for him. When we found each other we hugged and laughed, and looked out at the Columbia River, reminding ourselves that we were now heading east. No, my concern in those days was not for Jack's memory but for Steve's HIV status, and my own hearing loss.

A few years later when Jack began to fumble noticeably over facts and names, I thought, well, we all do that as we get on, don't we? There are just too many years of stuff crammed into our old brains. We joked among our aging contemporaries about these lapses we had in common. But then one day — a beautiful summer day on Chicken Ranch Beach — our friend, James Russell, a few years our senior, paced back and forth along the shore, as had become his agitated habit. And as usual his wife, Leonore, tried to tempt him to sit down next to her with a *National Geographic* or *New Yorker* and a bottle of nonalcoholic beer. No, he apparently could no longer relax with the rest of us as we'd all been doing together since we'd had toddlers digging in the sand around our feet. Now, of course, instead of sprawled on beach towels, we sat in our geriatric chairs, displaying our swollen arthritic knees and varicose veins, gazing out at the beauty of the dear familiar scene. But James, on that day, was obsessed by the minutiae of broken shells, seagull feathers, dried-out jelly fish that he trod through on his bunioned feet. Then he would suddenly look up into the ancient eucalyptus tree that had hung over the fence for as long as any of us remembered, as though he'd seen a vision, as though everything observed had become unbelievably intense. Yet it was a restless sort of awe, and I saw Jack anxiously watching him. Again in retrospect, I believe he was anxious on some level for the self he would himself become a few years hence, when he did in fact stare across our canyon in Berkeley with that same epiphanic expression at a blossoming fruit tree two days before he died.

Next James announced that he was going home. Jack hoisted himself out of his chair and started to walk with James. He would walk home with him, he told Leonore, since that's where James seemed determined to go. I was a little apprehensive. But off they went, two old men, Jack's arm across James's shoulder, up the path to the county road and on to the village, a route they'd both known for decades. Yet they got lost for an hour or so. Leonore, was not surprised. By then James wore a bracelet with his name and telephone number. He'd often gotten lost. She'd often gotten phone calls from kind strangers. But it was on that day that I first remembered and attached some significance to Jack's getting lost on the train.

From then on the decade of the '90s for me was a jumble of conflicting emotions: resentment and compassion, loneliness and anger, fatigue and guilt. I resented the increasing interruptions to my writing life. I grieved my loss of the man I had married and lived with for more than fifty years, for that's how it felt sometimes, like a loss, years before he actually died. I was lonely for his companionship, angry at his abandonment of me, exhausted by the increase in my responsibilities, both emotional and physical, then full of pity and remorse. One night, in bed, curled against him, I said, Wouldn't it be wonderful if we could just quietly die together in the night. He was horrified.

During the 90s I destroyed all my old journals, revolted by the great long whine of them. I managed to finish my fourth novel, but my agent didn't like it. I started another, but dropped it about two years before Jack died, understanding at last that I must focus completely on him. "Until death do us part." And it was a huge relief to let go of all that resentment. I was still lonely and tired and sad beyond belief at small incidents in the progression of his condition — forgetting how to make a cup of tea, losing a load of laundry — and more serious lapses that occurred when he took on impossible tasks such as accepting invitations to participate in a panel discussion for Greenbelt Alliance, or agreeing to become the secretary of the Arts Club, or giving a talk at the Senior Center on the Future of the Bay Area. Sometimes he recognized the impossibility of these commitments and allowed, or even asked me to intervene. Other times he bumbled through, breaking my heart as I watched him put himself into such humiliating situations. I believe, now, that publishing *My Neckline and the Collapse of Civilization* in '87 was the last sustained intellectual endeavor he was able to accomplish.

When we were first together I was the child, he the sometimes impatient teacher. (I suddenly remember how he subscribed to *The Peoples' World* for me at Scripps College, reflecting his own youthful radicalism, and I smile as I recall the raised eyebrows of some of my fellow students, and how avidly I watched my mail slot in the dorm for those papers and the blue envelopes of his letters from Germany.) Now our positions were reversed and I kept praying that I might do this part of my life with some grace. But it sure brought out the bossy mother side of my nature. And of course there was humor as well as pathos in our situation. In the summer of '95, for instance, desperate, I suppose, for some rest and solitude, I used the excuse of Steve's need for assistance in his final roundtrip to and from Montana to get rid of Jack for a few days. Steve's project was to go and get the last of his furniture and several big half-grown calves and bring them back to Humboldt County. He required both company and brawn, neither of which Jack was much good at anymore. Nevertheless, I put him on a Greyhound bus in San Rafael and sent him off on the seven-hour trip to Garberville to hitch up with Steve. Totally irresponsible! He might have gotten off the bus almost anywhere along the way. He would be no help to Steve; instead Steve would be taking care of him for a few days, along with all his other burdens — making the final break from a place he loved, and an awkward break from a man he perhaps had never loved.

Well, it all worked out. I did have a restorative respite from the stress I didn't even know I was feeling. Steve told me later that Jack provided a comforting lap for his dogs in the truck those several days, and also some comic relief that eased the unpleasant departure from Tom Freeman in Montana. The only hitch in that long trip was that Jack, on the way back, reading a sign "TO CRATER LAKE" insisted they go see it. He had never been to Crater Lake. This was a great opportunity. So, hauling a trailer full of calves, Steve reluctantly agreed. "I almost lost it that time," Steve said. The possibility of "losing it" often hovered in his life.

Another funny happening occurred in the Powell Street BART station when Jack in his characteristic helpfulness was suddenly pushing a handicapped homeless man to the elevator. Before I or Mary and Kenneth Cardwell, with whom we were on an excursion to the new San Francisco Museum of Modern Art, could catch up, the elevator door closed behind them. Kenneth raced up the stairs to meet them at the top and soon reappeared with smiling Jack, who in that brief time had given the handicapped guy $30, all the money he had on him.

And then there was the time we went to emergency early in the morning because Jack woke with a pain in his ribs and I overreacted, sure that it was a heart attack. He cheerily went along with every little bureaucratic glitch at the hospital, flirted with the nurses, enjoyed the medical procedures. I, on the other hand, was worrying about making a pre-arranged meeting with our financial advisor down at the bank. I hated having to deal with money matters, but I had to. On assurance that Jack would be there for quite a long time yet, having more tests, maybe even hospitalized, I left him for exactly forty-five minutes, but when I returned to the hospital I was told that he had gone home.

"What? It's pouring rain. He has no hat, no umbrella, or money. He'll catch pneumonia!" I said, or something like it.

"Oh, he's already got pneumonia — walking pneumonia — and he's got a prescription."

I could have killed that woman, but instead drove back and forth in the rain on all the routes he might have taken on the three-mile trek from Alta Bates Hospital to Tamalpais Road. (He'd told the woman he lived just around the corner!) As usual he'd apparently found a new way to go, so I just went home to wait it out, and when he straggled in, grinning, a couple of hours later, I felt like the mother of Tom, or Steve, or Dave in their teens, having listened for what seemed like hours in the middle of the night or wee hours of the morning for the sound of the car driving over the manhole cover down the street, a sign that he was home. And just as then, I was ready to kill, but instead I ordered Jack into a hot bath. Then he told me the reason he had to get out of that hospital: two enormous black men who'd been arrested for fighting with knives were brought, bleeding, into the emergency room. He lay on a gurney between them as they drunkenly cursed and threatened each other across his body. He was scared, so he just got up and found his clothes and talked his way out of there. Pretty resourceful for someone who couldn't remember the days of the week, and of course I couldn't stay mad. In fact the incident became one of my favorite stories to illustrate that time in our lives. Our trip to Ireland back in '93 had perhaps been prophetic, returning to the land of Jack's forbears, steeping us in the great mix of tragedy and comedy that permeates Irish history, literature, drama, art, and even the landscape, all of it so fitting for the years to come.

About two years before his death he had a CATSCAN and went to a neurologist who put him through a series of word and picture games to test his memory and comprehension. He loved all the procedures and thanked me for arranging them. They seemed to give him comfort. Our last summer in Inverness together was full of black humor. The move up there each summer had always been a lot of work. But this year I felt that perhaps I wasn't going to be able to manage the move, and when we had finally made it I was so exhausted that the simple chore of making breakfast for the two of us each morning seemed almost more than I could handle. I lost a lot of weight, and it turned out that I had developed a serious thyroid condition, which took months of medical attention to stabilize. And we got a puppy, a lifelong habit of ours in times of stress. She was a great comfort — still is — albeit more work for me. Jack tolerated her spending half the night nuzzled into his neck, licking his armpit, and chewing his ear. But he never connected with her emotionally as he had with every one of the previous eight dogs that had lived with us over the span of fifty-seven years.

A few months before his death he turned eighty-one.

He had developed a lot of breathlessness due to a weakened heart, but he still walked to the campus a couple of times a week, though taking many rests along the way, he told me, had lunch with kind younger friends and colleagues to whom I will always be grateful for treating him with respect and love. At home he still stuck maps and snapshots and mementos up on the walls of this study. And with a twinkle in his eye, he began singing his new refrain, to the tune of an old Beta Theta Pi fraternity song, "I'm eighty-one, and the fun has just begun."

May 2000

Fun? I don't know. Fanciful, perhaps, imaginative, the way he managed death. I'm sure I will do it in a more plodding fashion, trying not to inconvenience anyone. Not Jack, though. He turned it into a world premiere, a Shakespearean comedy. All those years of doing charades at Christmas and New Years, of acting in the U. C. Drama Section where in the early years he often played the romantic lead, of going to the theater in New York and London and Dublin and San Francisco and Berkeley and Point Reyes Station seemed to have resulted in this amazing grace. Or perhaps instead of a play it was a group therapy session that lasted exactly seventeen days, involving every one of us, having us on tenterhooks as to how we would fare.

Steve wasn't there at the end, but had been for a week until just a few days before Jack died, and was an essential element in the dynamics of this process. For in that week I think Steve and Jack resolved, without putting it into words, every difference that had ever lain between them, Steve trailing after him with the oxygen tank up and down the stairs, to and from this study where Jack wanted to be more than anywhere else, tying up loose ends. Steve seemed to simply throw away all the old resentments, put Gemini, his astrological sign, on back burner for a while, for this time of the death of his father, despite his own tenuous health, in an incredible expression of love. After Steve left Jack never came up here again.

I remember all the great food we had while Jack was dying. Hannah brought jasmine-honey ice cream from Chez Panisse, where she was then waitressing. Yes, jasmine. One night we had take-out Chinese food ordered by Charlie, who has lived in China and is a chef (also at Chez Panisse) as well as a brain. Steve and Charlie had fun pushing each other's ego buttons. My seventy-seventh birthday occurred during this time and somebody brought a rich chocolate cake. (Symbolic, perhaps, like that Chocolate Decadence that Dave and Chandra served Jack and me when they announced their separation. This was another sort of separation.) A couple of days after Steve went back to Humboldt, our neighbors, the Cateses, brought the last dinner that Jack and I, just the two of us at the dining room table, would eat together. I remember every detail of that meal — tender succulent chicken, pasta with a delicate creamy sauce, steamed broccoli with lemon and butter, a tart for dessert. Simple and delicious.

Tom and Deb rearranged their entire lives, sometimes spelling each other, sometimes coming together with their feisty little border terrier, Clyde, whom Mellow adores, all the way down from Inverness so that someone was usually here with me at night. Deb cooked tasty soups and stews to have on hand for all the company. In the evenings Jack was propped up in his hospital bed by the west windows, a fire glowed in the fireplace, and the rest of us, an ever-changing multigenerational collection of relatives and friends eating, telling stories, reminiscing. There were always several dogs. The house was full of flowers. It was a beautiful spring and Jack seemed amazed and ecstatic at every blossom, bird call, sunset as though these were brand new experiences for him. Perhaps he was, in fact, watching his whole life of aesthetic response replay itself before his eyes.

A hospice nurse came every day to check on him, and another aide came to bathe him and change the bed every third day. Susie from across the street loaned us her house cleaner. Steve's friend Adrian came several times all the way from San Francisco to walk the dog. Various people, including me, did laundry and shopping. A stream of guests dropped in and sat around Jack's bed, telling him old anecdotes from the past, holding his hand, massaging his feet. (Sometimes I retreated to the bedroom for naps or simply solitude.) He drifted in and out of sleep, but that didn't matter. Old friends visited with each other, caught up on each other's lives. Looking at my calendar for April 1998 reminds me of the intensely busy time it was. These items stand out:

Tuesday, 7th — JK feeling ill; canceled dinner at Lalimes with Adele.

Friday, 10th (Good Friday) — Canceled my appointment with acupuncturist; JK can't swallow; admitted to Alta Bates Hospital. Call the boys!

Saturday and Sunday (Easter) Tom, Hannah, Deborah, Adele visit JK in hospital. Margaret, Dave, Rebecca, Marlowe from Santa Fe.

Monday, 13th — Steve from Humboldt; Fletcher, Kristina, twins from Portland; Tom, Deb, Grayson; Family conference with Dr. Arlan Cohn. End of life?

Tuesday, 14th — (my father's birthday); blood work; writers' group at Renata's — cancel. Dave, Margaret, Rebecca, Marlowe back to Santa Fe.

Wednesday, 15th — Laundry, taxes, JK home. Hospice, hospital bed, oxygen.

Thursday, 16th — Steve. Hospice nurses.

Friday, 17th — MK birthday; Steve. Hospice.

Saturday, 18th — Steve. Dog training Mellow — cancel. Hospice.

Sunday, 19th — Tom, Deb, Steve. Hospice. Dakota massaged JK's feet. Allan and Elizabeth.

Monday, 20th — Steve left; Adrian/Mellow. Deb spent night.

Tuesday, 21st — JK fell in bathroom; cut over eye. Hospice nurse — butterfly bandage.

Wednesday, 22nd — laundry, house cleaner. Hospice, Jim Schevill, Larry Orman. Deb spent night.

Thursday, 23rd — Janis, Kathie, Bill for lunch. Deb's good soup. Hospice, bath. Adrian/Mellow. Hannah and Eli. David Cates brought dinner. Tom and Deb spent night.

Friday, 24th — JK and MK alone together. Nice. (Last time we shared our bed.)

Saturday, 25th — 6 A.M. JK fell. Heart attack? Clenched teeth.

"Don't touch me!" Hospice nurse helped me get him onto hospital bed. Stopped eating and taking fluids. Morphine by dropper inside his lower lip.

MK slept on living room couch near him. Diapers.

Sunday, 26th — (Jonas Barish Memorial — cancel.) Adrian/Mellow. Tom and Deb.

Monday, 27th — Mellow — flea treatment. 1 A.M. JK died.

"I'm here, Mom. Dad's gone." It was David, waking me out of a deep sleep. He and Margaret had arrived again from Santa Fe after I'd gone to bed. I got up and went back to the living room where Jack lay, dead now, looking peaceful and sweet. I kissed him. The head of the bed had been lowered. Debbie had tucked her crocheted afghan up under his chin. Margaret had taken off his wedding ring and now gave it to me. And so we sat around for another hour or so, unwinding, at peace, and first thing in the morning the undertakers came and took him away.

When I phoned to tell Steve, he said, "Thank God he died before me." But he didn't just give up, now that Jack was gone, even though his liver was shot, and he had to have all his teeth pulled, and a cancerous growth on his nose removed, and even though he once told us that he would never die of AIDS — he had a gun! No, he struggled on mightily for almost another year — such a strange year — when he and I became peculiarly linked, as though of the same generation, deaf and crotchety and missing connections, each dying in a sense, each living alone and celibate, our dogs with their warm bodies and unconditional love our greatest comfort. One of Steve's fantasies in those months was a trip that he and I would take together in his new truck to visit Fletcher, Kristina, and the twins in Portland, camping along the coast to and from. I even marked it on my calendar. I knew it couldn't happen, but I marked on my calendar anyway.

I was off kilter without Jack, lopsided without his optimism and good cheer. I wonder if Steve, too, remembered how his father whooped with pleasure as he plunged into Tomales Bay, and his special welcoming whistle from the Inverness porch when guests arrived? For a while after his death we were sustained by several gatherings: the first at Wurster Hall where University colleagues, former students, civic and political friends, family, neighbors shared wonderful memories; next at the Greek Theater on graduation day, when Jack was honored posthumously by the College of Environmental Design as one of four Alumni of the Year representing the four departments — Architecture, Planning, Landscape Architecture, and Design. Jack's was for architecture from which department he graduated in 1938. There have been many honors bestowed on him over the years including the prestigious Berkeley Citation. There are framed awards on the walls of our house and scrolls of parchment honors of recognition rolled up in drawers, but the experience of sitting on the stage of the Greek Theatre, along with the other three honorees, one of them Garrett Eckbo, Jack's old friend and colleague in Bay Area environmental activism, accepting the medal for him was a very great privilege. Then in July at the San Francisco Commonwealth Club a Greenbelt Alliance Memorial event was held with another whole set of environmental colleagues exchanging anecdotes (Jack's propensity to

Xerox many copies of important statements, pages from books, newspaper articles, etc.; his grin; his expressive hands; his love of mass transportation from the MUNI to BART to ferry boats). And finally in August our own family gathering on my sister Deborah's Inverness meadow brought closure to his life and death.

This was the only one of the events that Steve was able to attend, and his appearance was a shocking reminder of the deterioration of his health, plunging us into another year of sadness as we witnessed the narrowing down of his physical world. This is also when he began to explore the idea of a God. He told me that he heard an old woman on the radio say, "Don't be afraid to ask for God's forgiveness." So he did, and he had the first good night's sleep in a long time. I had several trips to Humboldt that year, with Tom, Deb, Grayson, Mellow, Margaret, and Dave; with Steve's cousin Kathleen; with his old girlfriend Judy. Our last sad Christmas together here and in Inverness tested us both. He drove himself down, bringing an enormous turkey that Kathleen cooked on Christmas Eve. He was cold all the time and wore a wool watch cap right through dinner. On Christmas morning we had planned to go to Mass, but he just wasn't up to it. Still he drove us all the way to Inverness, by way of Novato to visit his friend Elizabeth. With Tom and Deb we had a lovely Christmas dinner at Nick and Elan's, little of which he ate. That was a long, long and very trying day. But during that holiday visit we managed to go to the movies and do some shopping. He bought antique silver, a teapot, Japanese fabrics, real fountain pens, and pads of vellum paper. I'm reminded of a day years earlier when Jack and I came home from a walk to discover our living room adorned with serapes and rugs and pottery and baskets. Steve and his friend Allan had just returned from Mexico and turned our house into an arts and crafts museum. Yes, he always did love to shop, another example of the Gemini trait, considering the Spartan lifestyle he had chosen for himself. Along with religion he seemed to have rediscovered this acquisitive pleasure, reminiscent of his little boy delight in Europe of collecting souvenirs. He'd liked the Bible then too, and visiting the great cathedrals. Perhaps he was reinterpreting his childhood yearnings, adapting them to this time of impending death.

Early in the New Year there was a hospital stay in Garberville, and then that three-week experiment in February when we tried to live together. And finally, in March to the hospital in Eureka from where he called me. His voice sounded faint and sweet. "It's okay, Mom, it's been ten years," he said when he heard me crying. I wanted to say to him then, "It's okay, Steve, it's okay to let go." I finally did say it to him, less than a week later, when he was in that rented apartment in Arcata in a facility for the handicapped that was his strange final home for five days. This was another of his fanciful experiments with handling his death, to live near the sea, and by now he was in a system of medical and social services, very like hospice, which saw us through at the time of Jack's death. Tom and Deb and I had flown north to help him move from the hospital to Arcata, and once again Tom and Deb were simply remarkable. Deb organized us all, assigning duties, cooking soups and stews. Tom spent a day on a 100-mile round trip to transport his furniture — a wood stove, the sofa made by Dave, the round oak table, the lounger chair. We all knew, though no one said it out loud, that he couldn't last for more than a week or two at the most. But the apartment was full of his favorite possessions as well as flowers, helpers, family, and friends.

He had called from the hospital on Thursday, March 11th, Tom, Deb and I flew to Arcata Monday, March 15th. His friend Mary Darby met us and settled us into our motel. On Tuesday we moved him into the apartment, and on one of those evening after supper I had a few moments alone with him. That's when I said it was all right to let go of all the guilt that seemed to be weighing him down. Like that old woman on the radio said, ask for forgiveness if he needed to, but there was nothing to forgive as far as I was concerned. I told him I loved him, that he had stretched my consciousness, enriched my life. I told him it was all right to let go, to die. And after that he entered a new and final phase of life, hovering in an in-between place, but finally seeming to be at peace. The last time I saw him he was hugging the down quilt I had brought him. *"I love my quilt,"* he whispered.

On Thursday, March, 18, Tom, Deb and I flew home. I knew I would never see him again, but I knew also that his cousin Nick was coming with Elan, also his cousin Kathleen, and his old friend Joe from Inverness, and Dave and Margaret, and Donna, and Allan, and Grayson, and Fletcher and Kristina and the twins. He would not face death alone. A grieving old woman would only complicate the process. I had done what I had to do.

This time it was Tom who woke me, coming all the way down from Inverness that Saturday night, March 20, because he wanted to break the news in person. "I'm here, Mom; Steve's gone."

———

On board ship back in 1955 as I was watching, with Jack and Steve, the amazing New York sky line emerge from the infirmary cabin porthole, I suddenly felt anxious about the other two. Were they all right? Tom was then twelve, Dave, five. But I was able to reassure myself, knowing they would be taking care of each other. That's the way they always were. Yet as Steve was dying last year in that lingering daunting drama, both seemed to turn to him in a way they never had before. To witness my three middle-aged sons grow close as the death of one of them approached was my great privilege, one that a parent rarely has. Less than two months later I began this memoir, for just as I had apparently given Steve permission to die, he in dying had had given me permission to write again.

She will be an Eskimo woman
when she can no longer find food.

But you might get caught
in your weakness
be driven on a freeway
that is not free
into the valley that's lost
forever the trees of walnut and fruit.
You could of course look out at the cow on the hill,
they say.

No. She will be an Eskimo woman
closing her eyes
lying down
in the ice blue snow.

Jack

Steve

Kathleen Tolman   Edward Tolman

Mary's Parents

Tolman Children

Courting Days

Marriage

Young Professional

The Kents in Venice, 1955

Near the End

Photo by Peggy Love

The Author, 2001